AF574154

DAUGHTER OF EVIL

DAUGHTER OF EVIL

The True Story

Yolande McShane

W. H. ALLEN · LONDON
A Howard & Wyndham Company
1980

Printed and bound in Great Britain by
Billing & Sons Ltd, Guildford, London & Worcester
for the publishers W. H. Allen & Co. Ltd,
44 Hill Street, London W1X 8LB

ISBN 0 491 02126 7

To my loyal, faithful family, my daughter, my son, but most of all my wonderful husband. Without his love and support this book would not have happened.

Contents

Bow down to the earth, and salute her as your Mother.
Bend low to a mouse, and salute him as your brother.
Make an obeisance to a blade of grass, and love it as your sister.
Remove a stone from the path of a burdened ant,
and bless it as your Father.
Embrace the tree that gives you shade, and see in it your lover.
Give water to a thirsty plant, it is your thirsty self.
Succour a tortured animal, and say, 'My God, my God.'

St Francis

Prologue

10 February 1977

The canteen at the back of Lewes famous Crown Court is small. Today it is crowded – reporters, people waiting for cases to be heard, and unmistakably a small group of CID men talking in a corner. I pick up my cup of coffee just as a court usher hurries in.

'The jury are returning,' he tells me. They have been locked in an hotel for the past thirty-six hours.

We make our way to the now familiar court room, scene of so many famous trials, where several murderers were sent to the gallows, Judge Jeffreys' happy hunting ground. I feel sick, but at the same time quite calm. I'm glad I packed my suitcase this morning in the small hotel where I spent the past two and a half weeks. Tonight I will surely be on my way home to Cornwall, and this nightmare over. As I go into the dock yet again, I make plans to see Mother as soon as the verdict is given. I'll get a taxi to St George's, I think, and this time the nuns cannot keep Mother from seeing me.

I sit down in the dock. The barristers and counsels troop in. The court is packed with spectators again as it has been every day – this is an unusual trial, worked into a national sensation by the reporters, who now pack the press box getting their note books ready. As soon as the court rises they will make a dash for the phone boxes outside, and I see the headlines in my mind: 'Suicide woman not guilty.' It has to be that, because that is the truth, and in spite of all that I have listened to for so many days now, I still believe that the jury must surely have seen my innocence.

'The court will rise.' In comes the fat little judge in his red robe, and I laugh to myself; the day my trial started an usher, seeing me standing in the corridor said, 'Would you like a chair, Lady Purchas?' I told him that I am not the judge's wife, just the accused on trial. I would not want to be the wife of any judge especially after what is happening to me now.

His Lordship sits down, we all sit down, and in come the jury. I look at them to smile. Several of them have smiled at me during the trial, but now they avoid my eyes and look straight ahead. The judge asks for their verdict and the foreman steps forward. I feel sure *he* likes me. I hold tightly to my little wooden cross that I have held all through the past days of uncertainty, given to me years ago by my sister, who has been the chief witness for the prosecution. The foreman of the jury reads from the paper in his hand. The court is hushed as he says, 'We find the accused guilty.' Someone at the back cries out, 'No, no!' and I am stunned.

'The accused will rise,' says the little man in the red robe, and I stand up and hold the edge of the dock. I look across at the jury in disbelief and horror. Haven't they heard *anything* I've said? Don't they know that I love Mother more than life itself? But the judge is speaking.

'You will go to prison for two years.'

Surely that cannot be what he is really saying to me, at sixty-one years old? People behind me are crying out, and the judge raps his desk.

'Silence,' he says. 'The Court will rise.'

And in shock and disbelief, I realize that he was indeed saying those terrible words.

Unobtrusively, two women prison officers appear, one at each side, and I turn to walk down the steps from the dock to the cells below, seeing a sea of faces. Some women spectators are crying; I wish I could speak to them. Down below the court the whitewashed cells are old and small, and one of the women officers takes everything away from me, even my little wooden cross.

'Sorry love, we have to do this, it's the law,' she says. I can see the compassion in her eyes. She is about five years younger than I am.

The other woman says, 'I'll get your dinner now dear, it's half past twelve,' but I can hardly hear her.

I keep thinking of Mother. What will happen to her now that I am not there to love her and help her? She is already as much a prisoner as I am to be.

My solicitor walks in, in his black leather coat, and shakes my hand.

'Sorry about my suntan,' he says, 'I've been in Jamaica.'

This is the first time I have seen him since before my trial. I ask him to phone my husband and son in Cornwall. Will the shock kill my husband? I know how bad his heart is and how worried he has been.

Then they all go away, and I sit alone, looking at the small heavily barred windows which are below ground level. There is no daylight – only a bright naked light in the ceiling. I cannot cry, cannot feel anything, except a terrible sadness that because I loved Mother so much all my life I am going to prison, and perhaps will never see her alive again, my wonderful courageous mother, with her unbreakable spirit. She is very frail and old, and so helpless now.

Part One

In 1937, when I was twenty, my grandmother started phoning my mother every day to tell her of her progress in killing my grandfather. My grandparents had retired from medical practice in a suburb of Liverpool to a quiet road in St Annes-on-Sea. My grandfather was now over seventy and still suffering from the near-fatal attacks of asthma which he had had for many years. My grandmother was now convinced that he was about to change his will and leave her penniless. As he was seriously ill in bed, she decided to give him an overdose of his medicine. She was a qualified nurse, at one time she had been Matron of Paddington Hospital, and knew exactly what was needed. Each day she would phone Mother.

'He still isn't gone. I shall have to increase the dose still more,' she would report. Then one day she phoned to say it was all over and the poor old man was dead. He was to be cremated so there was no danger that she would be found out. All this was told to me by my mother. Who knows if it is fact or fantasy?

Before I was married my immediate family was a small one. I had only two living grandparents, Father was an only child, and Mother had one sister with whom we had no contact. For a long way back, I think they were all rather eccentric; I hope that I am following the family tradition. I loved them all dearly, and, with the sad exception of my sister, I think they loved me dearly too.

Chapter 1

My earliest and happiest memories of my mother's parents were when I was five or six years old, and used to stay in their large, comfortable house, with the big garden, where my grandfather had his medical practice. He dispensed his own prescriptions. I loved to copy Grandpa. He showed me how to make powders in little squares of white paper. I would make some up and, following Grandma all over the house, powder in one hand, glass of water in the other, insist that she should take them. It was fortunate that I could only reach the jar of Bicarbonate of Soda; it could just as easily have been Gregory Powder, much used in those days, with dramatic effect on the bowels. One day I was going out into the garden, when a working man appeared at the door and asked me for his bottle of medicine from the doctor. I cheerfully handed him a bottle of pale liquid standing on the hall table – in fact it was a urine sample handed in by another patient. Just in time my grandmother rushed down to the gate and retrieved the bottle. From then I was banned from talking to patients or going into the dispensary, much to my sorrow, for I was determined to be a doctor like Grandfather.

Grandfather was a great man for practical jokes. When their golden wedding anniversary was due, he kept telling Grandma of the truly magnificent gift he was buying, and she (who was very acquisitive) thought it would be a ruby ring she had seen in a jeweller's window. When the day came, he got her to wait in the dining room for the 'surprise', and then called her upstairs. In the sewing room stood the old 'Polyphone' from the pub on the corner; it played large round discs when a penny was put in the slot, tunes like 'Linger Longer Lucy' and 'The Bluebells of Scotland'. He roared with laughter, but Gran was furious and broke a dining chair over his head. The wound had to be stitched.

Grandfather owned one of the first motor cars in the neighbourhood, but being used to a pony and trap, he had no idea how to behave on the road. When he wanted to make a turn, he would put his head out of the window and shout, 'I'm turning right, I'm turning right! Get out of the way, you fool!' He did not know how to use the horn at all.

We lived in West Kirby in a tall, old Victorian house, with a long garden backing on to the park, with a narrow path running down past the side of the house and garden. My sister Pam and I used to climb on the dustbins inside the gate and spit on the people walking by. But Pam told Mother, so I was in disgrace. Pam usually told in the end because she said her conscience made her; I was always the one who got into trouble because I hadn't confessed.

The times when Pam and I were closest, and Mother was forgotten, were when we lay in bed in the room we shared when Father was home and talked about 'our worlds'. We each had a separate world, inhabited by the people and creatures we chose. Pam had the Brontosaurus and I had the Pterodactyl; we had seen them in the silent film *The Lost World*. There was often heated argument as to the people or animals we took, but mine were mostly romantic and Pam's more factual. We would have discussions about the children we should have. Pam would upset me very much by insisting on calling hers things like 'Pot' and 'Pan', and sending them to school in their dressing gowns. Just before I was twelve, I told Pam (who was two years younger than me) that I was now too grown up to have a a world and so mine was ended. She begged me not to destroy my world and cried bitterly. But I was adamant.

Christmas was always a very special time. When I was ill – I had several illnesses as a child – I would lie flat on my back on the sofa in the sitting room with a pillow under my head, and Pam, Ida (our maid), and I would make paper chains for decorations. We had bought rolls of different coloured paper – blue, green, yellow and red – about an inch wide. Ida would cut it into small lengths and Pam and I would stick the ends together with glue to make a ring, looping one end into another ring first, to make a long chain. We got very sticky in the process. These, holly and ivy were the only decorations available for Christmas in those days. There were no glass balls, and no tinsel. We could have had a tree but somehow Mother never seemed to think of it. The first tree I ever had was many years later, when I bought and decorated it myself.

Father was a sea captain with the Cunard Line. He went to and from New York and sometimes on world cruises. He always came home loaded with gifts for us all. He brought silk kimonos from Japan, turkish delight from Turkey – every kind of treasure to a small girl. He once brought two strange, long, narrow, wicker-work tubes which fitted over a finger. The harder he pulled the tube, the firmer the hold on the hand. He said they were called 'wife leaders', much used in the Middle East.

When Father was home on leave we sometimes went on the train to Caldy beach and took a picnic. Father scorned a thermos flask. Instead, we took along a kettle and all the makings for 'real tea'. He and I would gather driftwood and make a fire, which usually smoked heavily, upsetting Mother and Pam, as their eyes watered and they were blackened with smoke. But Father and I loved it, especially when the kettle actually boiled. We would pretend we were castaways on a desert island.

Father had many wealthy friends in America. One was the owner of Brocks, a national sweet company, and Father sometimes brought home huge tins of boiled sweets, which I hate. One kind was lemon drops, and our spaniel, Terry, became addicted to them. On picnics we always took a bag of Terry's lemon drops.

Father had always wanted a son, but all he had was me. He called me Dick and treated me like a boy. I had trains, and bows and arrows, instead of dolls; even a carpentry set one year. Father always told me that when he was away, I was the 'man of the family'. 'Always look after your mother,' he would say, and that, added to my intense love for her, made me far too conscious of my responsibilities for a young child. When I was twelve, I was allowed to stay up and see the new year in for the first time as Father was home. I remember writing my list of new year resolutions at the big dining table. The first one was 'To keep Mummy alive for another year', as I was convinced of her frailty and need of care.

I loved Father very much. When he went away to sea I would creep upstairs to his work room in one of the attics, bury my face in his old coat hanging behind the door, and cry away my loneliness. In the next attic a dried crocodile skin hung on a nail and rattled in the wind, and I was terrified.

When Father was away, I slept in a little bed beside Mother's big double one with the feather mattress. Pam slept in the room we sometimes shared across the landing. Mother was really quite young, but every night about nine o'clock she would come to bed and Ida would bring up a supper tray of Dutch cheese, crusty bread, pickled onions and a glass of Guinness. Mother would sit up in bed reading, and cut off little bits of cheese to pass down to me. Mother and I loved these little intimacies, but my poor sister was never included. I was Mother's darling, we were very close, and although Pam and I played together, somehow Mother was always there in our minds, between us.

When I was about nine, Mother – whom I literally worshipped – took me on her knee.

'I'm going to tell you something because I don't want anyone else to tell you. Gran would just love to.' (She hated her mother as much as I loved mine.) Tears were pouring down Mummy's cheeks and I felt very scared. Then she told me that my father had forced her to 'let him make love to me up against a wall', and that afterwards she was going to have a baby, me, and was not married. I did not understand at all. All I knew was that my father, my wonderful father, had done something terrible to

Mummy, and for a time I hated him. It was over a year before I even spoke to him again and he could not think what was wrong.

When I was ten years old, Mother was reading a letter (it turned out to be a demand for the rates) and she shouted, 'Your father ought to be *shot*.' I thought she really meant to shoot him.

I had many irrational fears as a child. I was terrified of big moths, which Mother called 'Dabby-Devils', and also of the wind. Mother taught me a little poem to help change my feelings about the wind:

> I hear the wind among the trees
> Playing celestial symphonies.
> I see their branches downward bent
> Like keys of some great instrument.

But nothing seemed to help very much and I remained nervous of a great many things.

When I was seven years old, I had a burst appendix and then peritonitis and was confined to a spinal carriage. I had to lie flat on my back, that being the medical treatment in those days. Mother never left me. She pushed me out every day in the park at the back of our house. A tall, middle-aged German called Mr Brauer used to walk there daily. My mother called him 'Sweetie Brauer' and she imagined that he fancied her. She would push me in and out of the bushes in a kind of mad hide-and-seek. As far as I know, he never even spoke to her.

While I had the peritonitis I had to see a specialist in Liverpool once a month. Instead of going straight there and back, Mother made these visits a day's outing. We would see the specialist in the morning, have lunch in the Kardomah restaurant, and then go to a film – they were still silent then, of course. We saw Rudolph Valentino in *Blood and Sand*, *Scaramouche* with Lewis Stone, Greta Garbo in *Camille*, and perhaps most exciting of all, Lon Chaney in the *Hunchback of Notre Dame*. My sister never came with us on these outings; she stayed at home with Ida.

I had been out of my spinal carriage for about four months when my father, who was home on a few days' leave, and mother went for a walk one evening. Ida was left in charge of Pam and me. We were in bed and supposed to be asleep. Pam was in her room across the landing, but I was still in my little bed beside Mother's. (She and Father had separate rooms as Mother said his snoring kept her awake.) They were returning from their walk, and as they turned into the road where we lived, Mother heard piercing screams, scream after scream. Somehow she knew it was me, and she ran home. I had woken up to find that she was out and just could not stop my hysterical outburst. After a while I calmed down, Mother got into bed beside me and I slept. But for many weeks after that I would not let her out of my sight for an instant, even sitting on the floor outside the lavatory when she was inside.

About six months later, we were out shopping together when I suddenly fainted. My legs just gave way and I could not walk. Mother got me home in a taxi, but she and Ida had to carry me into the house. I was perfectly normal indoors, but as soon as I tried to step outside, my legs simply buckled. So Mother hired a bath chair and once more pushed me everywhere, just like the lovely times when she had pushed my spinal carriage for nearly two years. It is obvious now that I had hysterical paralysis of my legs induced by my intense desire to return to being Mother's 'baby'. This lasted for about two months.

One day, when I was eleven, my grandfather noticed that I seemed to be dragging my left leg when I ran. He suspected I had a tubercular hip. He arranged for me to see a friend and colleague who was an orthopaedic surgeon in Liverpool. I was duly X-rayed and examined by this famous man. He could find nothing wrong with my hip, but while I was lying on the examination couch, a visiting surgeon asked if he might take a look. He ran his hand down my left shin where there was a slight lump and I screamed in pain. The consultant thought it so serious that I went into a Liverpool nursing home that same afternoon and he operated on my leg next morning. A sample of bone shaved away was sent to London for analysis as he thought it was cancer. I suffered a great deal of pain. My poor mother waited a whole, endless week for the result. (Father was in New York.) She spent all day, every day, with me. Poor Pam could not really grasp how serious things were and only saw that she was left at home again with Ida.

Mother never noticed how unfairly she was treating Pam all these years. My sister was very often ignored. She was always a figure in the background, with a passion for horses, and often quarrelling with Mother.

'What would happen if Mummy died? We would have to die too,' I once said to her. Although we were quite young she replied in a matter-of-fact way, 'Nonsense. Daddy would take care of us.'

When we were much younger and Grandfather used to visit the house, he would catch hold of her and hold her down while I pulled the hairs out of her legs – a painful business, I see now, but he thought it a great joke. So on his visits, Pam would cower behind Mother's skirts, but when she tried to explain, no one believed her. Sadly I was the darling of my grandparents as well as my mother and father.

It was Mother who taught me all the good things I know and believe in – honesty, loyalty and duty. One of her favourite quotations was 'Stern duty, daughter of the voice of God.' She showed me how to love good books, music and poetry, and instilled in me a love of animals and birds, flowers and trees. As Father gave me my love of the sea, so Mother gave me my love of the country.

My sister went to the local high school when she was eight (up to now Mother had taught us both) and after she had been there a term I went too. I was very tall and thin, and as my peritonitis was supposed to be hovering about, I wore a plaster of cod liver oil and iodoform bandaged on my stomach. It smelt utterly revolting. I fainted in prayers one day, after weeks of misery and rejection by the other children, and when I was put to lie down in the sick room, I got my hat and blazer from the cloakroom and ran all the way home. I never went to school again.

I was once more alone with my beloved mother all the time. To keep things that way, she engaged a series of governesses and tutors, but none of them stayed very long. Nevertheless, by the time I was twelve, I had read most of Dickens, Scott, Thackeray and Dumas to name just a few, yet did not know how to do long division.

Mother now became concerned about my general education, or rather lack of it. So she decided to teach me herself and we began lessons in arithmetic, history and geography. I still could not do even simple sums. For some reason of her own my mother started teaching me about fractions. We struggled and struggled, Mother became more and more angry, and I became more and more confused, until I dreaded getting up each day to yet another baffling session. I wanted so badly to please Mother, but after about a week, she threw down her pen and said, 'You are *stupid.* You are never going to learn any arithmetic at all.' The effect on me was so profound that for the rest of my life I have had a complete mental block against any kind of figures. Someone only has to say something like, 'What is 48 times 60?' and a shutter comes down and I am unable to answer at all. We got on a little better with history and geography, but my mother was not really good at teaching. She would share with me the excellence of English in Shaw, Shakespeare and the poets, as literature and English language were her real loves, so these were the things that I absorbed like a sponge.

Once I decided to try my hand at sewing, another thing about which I knew nothing. My father had given me a love of making things, but things that boys made with carpentry sets, and until now I had scorned anything as 'girlish' as sewing. So I bought a pattern with the help of a shop assistant, and some material, and set out to make a pair of knickers for myself. I laid the material out on the table, the pattern on top of it, and cut out the knickers. Mother refused to help – she said I must learn to do it on my own. Alas, the marks to indicate darts I thought were meant to be cut out, and when I had done so the whole project was a mess. Mother laughed heartily, and told me that I was as stupid at sewing as I was at sums, and because I loved her so much I believed this was true. Never again in my life have I tried to do any serious sewing. I dislike it so much that even sewing on a button is an unpleasant chore.

After Terry, the lemon-drop eater, died, we had another dog whom we called Wolly. He was a small black and tan Manchester terrier. I had seen him in a Liverpool pet shop and his sad little face seemed to cry out for a good home. So Mother bought him and she, Pam and I took him for walks in the park. A railway line ran along one side of the park, bounded by a rather thin hedge and a steep embankment. As Wolly grew up, Pam and I encouraged him to slip through the hedge and chase the trains. This made Mother very angry; she said it was stupid and dangerous. One day we were out for a walk, Wolly heard a train coming and ran through the hedge and down the embankment. We heard the train, then a fearful scream and silence as the train faded into the distance. Mother and I scrambled on to the railway track and found Wolly lying unconscious and bleeding badly. Mother picked him up carefully and I picked up his two little front legs lying a few feet away. We rushed home and phoned the vet, but by the time he arrived Wolly was dead. Thankfully he never regained consciousness. I was badly shocked and Mother got a sedative to try to stop the dreadful nightmares which haunted me for weeks afterwards.

In 1928, Father was captain of the *Samaria*, going to and from Liverpool and New York. The doctor on board was about the same age as Father, tall, good looking, Mickey O'Brien, and of course at twelve years old I fell in love. He was charming to a too-tall, too-thin little girl. He called me his 'little sweetheart', and gave me *The Valley of the Moon* by Jack London. Inside he wrote 'To my little sweetheart Yolande, from her big sweetheart Mickey'. I have it still. Unfortunately, I was extremely shy about my growing breasts and, to my horror, Mother insisted that Dr O'Brien should listen to my chest as I had a slight cough. Father and my big sweetheart had been staying in our house for a few days, while the *Samaria* was being made ready for the next voyage to New York. On the morning they left, Mother kept me in bed, and called Mickey O'Brien to bring his stethoscope. In vain I begged and pleaded with her – she didn't understand at all. He knew nothing of my shame and misery in what to him was just a routine examination, but I felt as though my life was ruined and I just wanted to die. When he had reassured Mother as to my cough, and he and Father were just leaving, I refused to wave from the window, but buried my face in the pillow and cried bitter tears.

Three years later, my father introduced me to a young man, Bill Wilcox, the son of a Mersey pilot, and at twenty-one, just starting the same job. We fell in love, at least he did, and I thought I did. He asked Mother if we could be married as soon as I was sixteen. But one day he kissed me, and I felt a hard lump in his trousers pressing against me. I thought with dismay, 'Oh dear, he's got one of *those* things'. (I had been told the 'facts of life' by my mother some time earlier.) From then on, I was 'off' poor Bill, and he did not get to kiss me again.

When I was sixteen, Mother met and became friendly with a woman who lived nearby. She had a so-called paying guest, Peter, whose hobby was falconry. He was handsome, with a little military moustache, and carried a goshawk on his wrist most of the time. I (being saturated with Tennyson) thought he was Sir Galahad and Lancelot rolled into one. Two days after my sixteenth birthday, he took me out in his sports car, with the hawk, 'to do some rabbiting'. He parked the car by a wood, led me to a bed of damp leaves, and seduced me. He explained to me that this (to me) horrible performance would 'make him very, very happy', but I found it very painful, and I bled. In fact, I was going to a Girl Guide meeting later that day, and had to wear a sanitary towel – I was still suffering from Peter's 'happiness'.

My father had a distant cousin called Lionel, known to me and my sister as Uncle Lio, who was married to a dreary little woman called Etta. They lived in Birkenhead, and a Scottie bitch substituted for the children they didn't have. About this time, Mother told me that Uncle Lio was madly in love with her, and that when he visited our house and Father was in the room, Lio had arranged with Mother that he would jangle his keys in his trousers pocket to let her know when he was crazy to make love to her. I never knew if this were true, or another fantasy like Sweetie Brauer, but my obsessive love for my mother was such that even though I adored my father, anything my mother did, literally anything, was right and perfect in my mind.

When I was seventeen Peter had left the neighbourhood – perhaps there were too many irate mothers – and I met and fell in love with Brayley, the son of the chauffeur of one of my father's friends. Father was very angry. He had a definite sense of social fitness, and although he was what I suppose could be called a snob, it was quite unconscious – he just liked people in what he saw as their right place. He was now captain of the *Aquatania* and completely at home with all the rich and famous people who made up his life. Yet he was always gentle and courteous to our various domestic helpers. The kindest and most generous of men, he still did not want his much-loved daughter in love with anyone at seventeen, let alone a boy from a different social background. However, I was in love and very headstrong. I used to climb out of the window of the room I now shared with Pam, and slide down the sloping roof of the scullery, to meet Brayley in the park. We had done some pretty heavy petting and I had begun to really enjoy sex, and to want the real thing. (The misery of Peter's efforts had vanished.) One day when Mother was in Liverpool visiting my grandparents, and Pam out riding the pony she had managed to talk Father into buying, I seduced Brayley on the sofa in the sitting room. After that we began to enjoy a pretty full and normal sex life. Then I missed a period, and oh joy, we thought we would have to get married – no unmarried mothers in my circle in those days. I went along to Woolworths, where in 1933 no article cost more than sixpence, and bought a brass wedding ring. Alas for my hopes of the excitement of eloping with Brayley, my period arrived and it was all over. He faded rapidly from my life. I think he was thoroughly scared by a narrow escape.

In 1935, I heard of Oswald Mosley's Blackshirts; it seemed that his ideals and aims were what I had always wanted to find. My family were staunch Conservatives. It is astonishing that

I did not know Socialism existed, only what my father called 'Those damned Communists'. It was one of the few times I heard him swear, and then never anything stronger. I found Mosley's ideas attractive – they seemed to promise a better life for the very poor. Since I was twelve I had been sending half my weekly pocket money to an organization called the East End Mission, run by the Reverend Percy Ineson. The Mission took children from the East End of London for a day trip to the country or sea, if enough people sent donations. It cost one shilling for each child, and I could not bear the knowledge that these children had never seen a green field or a sandy beach. Joining the Blackshirts seemed to bring nearer the day when all children would have enough to eat, and also be able to enjoy the country and sea that I loved so much myself. I was a very idealistic eighteen-year-old. So Mother and I joined (she wanted to come too, of course) and wore our black shirts and grey skirts, marched with Mosley in Liverpool, and gave the Fascist salute when they played the national anthem in our local cinemas, to the fury and disgust of Pam and my father, who were united in disliking what they called a 'public spectacle'.

One night Mosley held a big rally in the Liverpool Stadium, and the police were called out in force to protect the Blackshirts from the Communists, who tried to force their way into the meeting, armed with razor-studded potatoes, knuckledusters and bicycle chains. All the women Blackshirts were taken out of a rear entrance into police vans, driven to safety and then the vans returned to the fray. There was fierce fighting as Mosley's followers tried to leave the stadium. Several policemen and a lot of our friends were injured. Mosley's policies were not racist; he was anti-Jew, but as I knew no Jews and Mosley only seemed to object to their apparent monopoly of British money and business, it did not seem to me very important, compared with his promise of 'Equal opportunity for all'.

While Mother and I were engaged in these exciting events, Pam was studying Design at Birkenhead School of Art. She sometimes used to bring home several students for tea, including one or two boys, but mostly her own crowd of giggling girls. Unfortunately, the boys gravitated to me. One of the boys was George, who much later was to be my husband, but at first we disliked each other, and argued fiercely about everything. A group of four or five boys now became regular visitors. They came every Saturday afternoon, and we would go for long walks with the dogs. When the weather was wet, we sat around on cushions on the floor and played games like 'Truth or Dare'.

I remember one day when Mother chose a dare. She was wearing black and scarlet silk lounging pyjamas, and to carry out her dare, she stood outside in the road with an umbrella over her head to keep off the heavy rain, and sang 'Lover come back to me'.

Then we started having paper chases, but instead of paper, the 'hares' used chalk marks to avoid leaving litter all over the lanes and fields. Mother always came too. In fact I think she really felt a part of the gang and our contemporary. She often said that we were like sisters, and she also told me that I was very beautiful. Sometimes the boys joined us for a whole day's picnic on a Sunday, and we would walk to a nearby beach, and Mother (who did not like the sea) would mind our clothes while we all went swimming. I only wore a pair of brief swimming shorts, as I was totally without shyness about my body – it seemed perfectly natural to swim topless as the boys did. But Mother was angry and said I only did it to show off, which was untrue and hurt me very much. I think the boys were rather surprised that we never went anywhere without Mother, but she could not bear to be left out of anything, and I could not have hurt her feelings by trying to leave her at home.

It was now decided that I should go to London, stay with a family friend, and train as a fashion model, or mannequin as it was then. I was tall, blonde, attractive, and wildly excited to be going to London, even though it meant separation from Mother for the first time in my life. Until now I had not spent even one night away from her. So off I went on the train, and it was wonderful, and glamorous; but after two weeks away, I phoned Mother, and told her that I loved her so much and missed her so much, and that 'life is too short to be away from you, even for two weeks'. I caught the next train home.

But London for two weeks had given me the idea that I was very sophisticated. I had my eyebrows drawn like Marlene Dietrich's, lots of make-up (too much) and wore a saucy little straw boater on my newly permed hair. Our old family doctor was on the platform, meeting some of his family. He walked right past and didn't recognize me at all! I settled down once more to a life inseparable from Mummy, taking care of her as the 'man of the family' while my father was at sea.

Not far from the quiet, tree-lined road where we lived was a row of small old-fashioned shops, and in front of one of these lived an old German couple, called Riefenschtall. They were refugees in 1915 I think. He had been a tailor, but now they lived in abject poverty and squalor. Old Mrs Riefenschtall was bed-ridden with dropsy, and her husband nursed her as devotedly as he was able with little or no money. They still spoke English very badly, and were too proud to ask for 'parish relief'. The district nurse came in twice a week to bath the old lady, and when she was not there I helped Mr Riefenschtall to lift his wife (she was like an enormous bag of water) and change her ragged bed clothes – she had only one blanket. The stench of the room was appalling. Each day Mother cooked extra hot food and I took it along for them. The smell was so bad that I used to go home and vomit, and was not able to eat my own food. But Mother's dishes of stew, rice pudding and tripe and onions (the old lady's favourite) were not able to cure dropsy, and Mrs Riefenschtall died.

She and her husband were spiritualists, and the funeral was held in the same sordid front room, with Mrs Riefenschtall in the open coffin, on two chairs. I went because I knew that Mr Riefenschtall was now alone in the world, and he looked upon me as a friend although I was only eighteen. During the time I was trying to help the Riefenschtalls, I met our rector one day, and asked him if he could do anything to help them. He lived in a beautiful old rectory, with a housekeeper and maid (the living was a wealthy one) but all he said was, 'Ah, yes, I will send them some black grapes from my hothouse.' But the old lady died, and they had not arrived.

Religion was something that simply had not entered my life at all. Because I did not go to school I had never seen a Bible. I remember when I was about thirteen asking my mother what church was like, and she offered to take me to an evening service. I asked her if I could take an orange to eat, so unknown was the whole procedure. We never went again.

I once asked Mother who Jesus was – I had read his name somewhere – and she said, 'Oh, he was just a good man, who went about helping people.' Then I asked what miracles were, and was told that 'They are just fairy stories'. I think that in a normal way I would have found in Christianity the means that I was wanting for helping others. Suffering of any sort was unbearable even when I was quite small. But of course Christianity was not known in our house, and perhaps that is why I flung myself into working for Mosley, and in fact became Women's Organizer for Merseyside a year after Mother and I first joined.

It was now January 1936. The third week in that month, Father came home on leave. He was Captain of the *Aquatania*, and was to take out the *Queen Mary* on her maiden voyage, on 27 May, my birthday. His picture was on the brochures describing the great ship. But Father was never to sail in the *Queen*. He had only two weeks to live.

Father was fifty years old, six feet tall, fifteen stone in weight and had never been ill in his life. However, just before his last voyage, he had had a rather troublesome cough, and my mother called in our doctor. After listening to Father's chest, he prescribed cough linctus, and told Mother in private that it was 'just a nervous cough'. Perhaps it was caused by the sixty cigarettes my father had smoked every day for over thirty years. He smoked a particular brand that gave coupons. My mother got some quite nice things for the house with the coupons, including a pewter tea set, so she was always urging him to smoke more.

On the day he came home for the last time, my mother heard

him ring the door bell (he refused to carry a key) and, as the maid opened the door, Father collapsed on the threshold, blood oozing from his mouth and then coming in a rush. Somehow we got him inside, and Mother phoned the doctor, who came in a matter of minutes. He arranged for Father to go at once into a nursing home near by, and sent for an ambulance. The next morning, he told us that my father was full of cancer, especially his lungs, and could not live very long. So began my mother's vigil at his bedside, and when I saw my father each day I could hardly recognize the grey, gaunt face on the pillow, and could not really grasp that my beloved father, close companion all my life, was dying.

Two weeks later Mother walked into the house one night, and simply said, 'Daddy is dead.' Later she told me that the doctor, who was also a friend, had given Father 'something to ease him out', so that he would not suffer. I have never known if this were true, or yet another fantasy.

The day after he died, Mother had Father brought home in his coffin. It stood open on two chairs in the small library. She went in and sat by the coffin hour after hour, with the door locked, and this gave me an icy cold feeling of dread. I was terrified of that room now, and the waxen face in the coffin in no way even faintly resembled the laughing father I knew so well, his skin ruddy and tanned by sea winds, his blue eyes keen from looking at far horizons for so many years, watching for the dreaded icebergs in the Atlantic on the New York run. No radar those days, just the keen sight of the man on the bridge.

Besides the terrible grief of losing my father, two things worried me. One was that our rector, who had been at school with Father, had wanted to see him in the nursing home, and Mother had flatly refused. The second thing was that Father had sometimes said jokingly, 'Don't ever have me cremated, Bid' (he called her Biddy) 'I hate the idea, I want to be buried when I go.' Although he was joking, I knew he meant it. And yet he was cremated and his ashes scattered.

Father was cremated in Birkenhead, and there were a great many people at the funeral, for he had been a very well-known and popular man. All I could think of on that bitter February day was that my mother must be protected, and so I must not in any way give in to my own desperate grief. I supported my mother, and did not shed a tear, not then. Well, Father was gone, and now I was indeed the 'man of the family', and conscious all the time of my great responsibility for my mother and that I must in some way comfort and distract her from her grief.

Mother was a great believer in getting in touch with the 'spirits'. We had often had sessions of table rapping, 'once for yes, twice for no' sort of thing, and wineglass writing, with letters of the alphabet put round in a circle. Now Mother desperately wanted to get in touch with Father, and so every evening for weeks, she took me into the small room where Father's coffin had stood, set up a table with a wineglass and the alphabet on small squares of paper, and I was supposed to make the contact. I would put my forefinger lightly on the rim of the glass, close my eyes, and then open them again, and the glass would spell out messages of love and comfort from Father to dear Mother. I was secretly ashamed to fake things this way, but loving Mother as I did, anything that helped her was justified in my mind.

Then I had a bright idea. Mother had always thought that men admired her greatly, and now there wasn't even Father to tell her how she was desired. So every two weeks, I bought a lovely box of chocolates or candies out of the housekeeping money (Mother had given up running the house), put in a little note in carefully disguised handwriting, saying things like, 'From one who admires you' or 'One who admires in secret' and so on. I posted these parcels to Mother. When they began to arrive, the effect was magical, Mother came to life again, and was full of excitement and curiosity about the identity of this new admirer. She spent hours puzzling over it all and saying, 'Who on earth *can* it be? Do you think it's someone I know, or even a neighbour perhaps?' Mother never did learn the truth. After a year, she seemed to have recovered completely, and so the parcels stopped. Also we were about to move to Chester, and to have the admirer posting from there would have been too much of a coincidence.

The new house in Chester was modern, detached, and I hated

it. I was so homesick for our dear old-fashioned house, the lilac trees, the big red hawthorn by the front gate, and the huge old pear tree, which still bore masses of hard but juicy fruit. When we were small Pam 'owned' the old apple tree, a delight of pink blossom each spring, and I 'owned' the huge pear. I would climb right to the top, and sit there, looking over all the other gardens, and calling out to Joey, the parrot, who was put out in the sun next door, and was reputed to be over a hundred years old. We had lived in the old house since I was five, all my roots were there, all my happy memories of Father. There I had grown, and learnt, and suffered the pains of adolescence, and it was full of the forming of the person I had become at twenty years old.

Chapter 2

We moved to Chester in 1937, taking with us an assortment of pets. There was Pam's horse, Johnny, and my horse, Lightning, who was half-brother to a Derby winner and, like Pam's horse, so wild as to be almost unrideable. Then there was Mother's Irish terrier, Simon, who had a very uncertain temper, and my Alsatian, Wendy. I had always longed for a dog of my own and an elderly friend of Mother's had given her to me while we lived in West Kirby. She had spent most of her life chained to a table leg as her owner was crippled and unable to take her out. We had decided to let her have one litter in the hope that it would calm her nervous and excitable temperament. When the puppies were about three months old, Mother woke up early one morning and heard a noise like running water. She woke me and we dashed downstairs. There was a terrible smell of gas and Mother opened the kitchen door (the dogs slept in the kitchen) to find the room full of gas – the taps on the cooker were on, and Wendy was lying unconscious in a mess of vomit. Mother turned off the gas and we quickly opened all the windows and the door and dragged Wendy outside. The puppies had crawled under a heavy curtain hanging over the larder door and had survived in the only source of fresh air filtering in beneath the door. Wendy had apparently turned on the gas taps in trying to reach a piece of meat. Wendy was unconscious for a week; when she eventually came round she was stone deaf.

I had also acquired a poor, sad little monkey, Adam. I had been doing some part-time work in a local pet shop before we moved to Chester when one day a man brought in this monkey whose jaw had been broken by a blow from his previous owner. As soon as Adam had seen me, he had leapt into my arms and snuggled against my shoulder. So, of course, I bought him, took him home, coaxed Mother into accepting yet another pet and installed him in a warm cupboard by the kitchen fire. Whenever I let him off his lead, he would dash round the kitchen and up on to the top of the kitchen dresser where three large Victorian meat dishes stood. He once threw one down on Pam and she narrowly escaped serious injury. After that we removed the plates.

I had boarded Adam at a local zoo while we actually moved house, but he had fretted for me so dreadfully that he had refused to eat anything. It was a very sick little monkey who returned home with me. He contracted pneumonia. I sat all day in the bathroom, the warmest room in the house, and held him in my arms. He was sleepy and contented all the time I held him close, but cried like a baby if I put him down even for a few minutes. Two days later he died in my arms. I had lost one of the sweetest animals I had ever known.

Once we were settled in Chester, Pam began to long for a pet goat. She asked me to help her buy one and to persuade Mother to allow yet another animal to be added to our collection. I agreed and we set off in my little Ford car (a birthday gift from Mother) and returned with Sammy on the back seat. He was a tiny black and white kid, with little black hooves that always looked as if he had just had a shoe shine. Poor, long-suffering Mother was no match for Pam and me together, so Sammy came to live in a small shed in the back garden. But Pam often brought him into the house to play. He would rush upstairs, jump on to the beds and dig in the eiderdowns. His favourite game was to fight with himself in the long mirror on the front of Mother's wardrobe.

He had a tragic end to his life, like so many of our much-loved pets. When his horns began to grow, Pam asked a local farmer to remove them – an operation known as 'de-budding'. We kept Sammy in his shed for a few days to allow the scars to heal, but it was very hot summer weather, and all day Sammy bleated without stopping. His cries were really heart-rending. We thought that he was just asking to come out, but poor, unhappy little goat – he had tetanus, or lock-jaw, as a result of an infection in the wound where his horns had been removed. His suffering was now so obvious that the vet gave him an injection to end his life.

The horses, too, came to untimely ends. Pam's horse developed a disease called 'strangles' and had to be destroyed. My horse, Lightning, had become so wild that I refused to ride him. He spent his time in a nearby field where a flock of sheep also grazed. One day Lightning seized a sheep and tore it to pieces. The furious farmer insisted that the horse should be put down, and I suppose that that was the only thing to be done. But all I felt at the time was a great sadness.

Having disposed of Grandfather (so Mother said), Grandmother had moved to West Kirby, and she was a frequent visitor to the new house in Chester. The day before my twenty-first birthday (my birthday falls four days before Pam's), Grandmother came to lunch, bringing me a magnificent silver fox fur as my birthday gift. I was thrilled with her present – animal conservation was as yet unheard of. Just as Grandmother was leaving, she turned to Pam and said, 'And here is a shilling for your birthday next Tuesday.'

The feelings between my grandmother and sister were already very hostile and this hardly improved matters. On another occasion, Grandmother came to lunch and Mother had made her favourite dish, steak and kidney pudding. I was eating brown bread and honey as I was on what I thought was a health diet. We were sitting round the dining table when Grandmother suddenly shrieked at Pam, 'You greedy little chocolate grabber! Look at your pale thin sister eating nothing!' and she threw her full plate across the table into Pam's face. Grandmother then seized her coat and hat, and the umbrella with which she had once hit Pam over the head, and departed in a great rage. It was quite a time before we saw her again.

My mother's family were all possessed of this terrible temper, Mother herself could get into a fine rage if roused. In fact we all could. My great-grandmother was a Romany, a wild gipsy girl married unhappily to the squire of a village in Kent. My grandmother used to tell me how she remembered her mother taking her out into the woods on many a moonlit night to meet her Romany brothers and sisters, who were forbidden to contact her, both by her husband and by her own parents. Her family had strange names: one sister was called Eicet, one brother Anglo Saxon and another Auger.

When Grandmother was about six years old, her mother could bear her closed-in life no longer, and begged her husband to allow her to return to her free life outdoors. He refused, there was a terrible row, and during the cold spring night Great-Grandmother went into the orchard in her nightgown and lay for hours in the soaking wet grass. She died of pneumonia a week later and Great-Grandfather lost no time in marrying again, this time a young woman from his own social circle. She bore him eleven sons, and as they grew up, both they and Grandmother (the only girl) became more and more wild and unmanageable. They were the terror of the countryside, riding their equally wild horses everywhere. Grandmother was treated as one of the boys, and rode astride – a thing unheard of for young ladies in those days. One day they lost a cricket ball, and the boys got scythes and cut down an entire field of standing corn in their search for the ball.

When she was sixteen years old, Grandmother married a penniless young man of good family and education, but most impractical in matters of keeping a wife and family. He was an artist and inventor, and spent his time mooning about the lanes, or shut up in his study in the little house his parents had provided. Grandmother's father had cast her off entirely as she had married against his wishes. By the time she was nineteen, Grandmother had two little girls, and one day her young husband walked out of the house and was never seen again. It was rumoured later that he had emigrated. So Grandmother went to his parents for help, and they installed an elderly and trusted servant to look after my mother and her sister, and Grandmother went to London to train as a nurse. Teaching and nursing were the only occupations open to a well-born woman in those days. And that is how she became Matron of Paddington Hospital at a very early age, and met and married a young doctor, my step-grandfather, with whom she had dealt so finally in St Annes-on-Sea, if my mother was recounting fact and not fantasy.

My father's grandmother also had a very definite will of her own. Her name was Jane Tregenna, and she eloped from Tregenna Castle in St Ives in Cornwall when she was sixteen years old to marry a young midshipman in the Royal Navy only a year older than herself. They got to Gretna Green with the help of friends, and after their marriage there, returned to face Jane's parents at the castle. But her parents, unlike my other great-grandmother's, were most reasonable and helpful. The young man, Richard Rundle, had been dismissed from the Navy because of his hasty marriage, so the Tregennas took the young couple up to Liverpool. There they had friends in the Mercantile Marine. Young Richard was found work in a shipping office and a house was bought for them in Birkenhead. Later Great-Grandfather Rundle became an important figure in local politics, and the President of the Board of Trade.

Their only daughter, my grandmother, Rebecca, married Andrew Mott, the ninth Andrew Mott in direct line, who was an artist. He was the first to break the family tradition, all his ancestors having served in the Royal Navy. One in fact was Lieutenant in the ship *Belerephon* which took Napoleon to exile on St Helena. Andrew Mott had inherited enough money from his mother to allow him to live as an artist, and although he married Rebecca, this did not interfere with his painting.

Shortly after the birth of their twin sons, Andrew Tregenna and Charles Tregenna (the family name has been kept up to this present day, and my own children have it), the nurse was bathing the babies and accidentally dropped Charles on his head. He died in a few hours. Grandfather had now decided to go alone to Italy to paint, and this he did, leaving my Grandmother Rebecca with her surviving son, Andrew, who was my father. Poor Grandfather only lived four years in Italy. He died of consumption and was buried there.

Now Grandmother Rebecca had only one thing in life that mattered to her – her only son. She became extremely possessive, and also began to drink rather too much whisky. When Father was thirteen years old, he too developed consumption. The doctors ordered a year's sea voyage, away from the mollycoddling of his mother, and so my father went as a boy cadet round the world under sail. He loved the sea so much that he stayed on, and at sixteen went to HMS *Weymouth* – a training ship for officers in the Merchant Service. When the First World War started, he was in the Royal Naval Reserve.

On one occasion his ship came into Liverpool, and his doting mother went on board to see her darling boy. By now she was drinking heavily, her excuse being that she suffered from gout and her doctor had ordered oysters and whisky daily as a cure. She talked her way on board and went to Father's cabin, where he and his young fellow officers were having a drink. Grandmother Rebecca sat on his bunk – he could see she was the worse for whisky – and told his friends that when he first went to school she had sewn his name in his clothes, and he had said to her, 'I've got Doggy Mott on my Dockings.' Her name for him was Troggy, and he could not pronounce his words properly. Poor Father, it took a long time for him to live down 'Doggy Mott on my Dockings', but he made sure that his mother was never allowed on board again.

My mother hated Grandmother Rebecca, because of her hold over Father, and it was a relief to her when the old lady died. She had only been allowed to see Pam and me once, and she died when we were about four and six years old.

From her family Mother had inherited the latent temper, the will of iron and the strength of character that had so totally enslaved me. When troubles came along she would quote, 'My head is bloody but unbowed', and she taught me that duty and courage are two of the most important things in life. Of course, in my young life, love for her was the most important thing, but I needed no teaching there!

Just before we moved to Chester, I had fallen deeply in love with one of the boys in the group who came to tea at our house on Saturdays, and took part in all our picnics and 'chalk-chases'. He was a very quiet, shy boy called Richard, whose love for me was as deep and strong as mine for him, but on a much higher level, although I was too inexperienced to realize this at the time. I loved him with all the passion of my very emotional nature, and of course wanted us to make love, but Richard (Dick as he was to me) would have none of it. He was keenly interested in the study of Yoga, and meditation, and to his way of thinking sex would have had an adverse effect on what he called his 'mind control'. Dick was truly single-minded in his study and practise of Yoga, and had already reached the stage where he could suspend his breathing for a full minute and felt no pain when a lighted cigarette was stubbed out on the back of his hand. Sometimes when we were out together he would go into a state of trance, and I was frightened that he would not come out of it safely. So although we loved each other, we never did any more than just kiss.

Quite a few other boys from our old home town still came to see us in Chester, to eat cream doughnuts on Saturdays, and go for long walks with the dogs. That was how I met Jack. He was twenty-one and his sister had been at school with Pam. They also lived in Chester. He joined the other boys at our house on Saturdays, but soon became attached to me. I quite enjoyed his passionate kisses, so unlike my adored and gentle Dick. Jack had lost all his teeth in a car accident and now had dentures; when he kissed me hard my top lip used to swell up. One day I noticed that after Dick and I had been for a long walk and returned to find Jack alone in the house with Mother, *her* top lip had swelled up! I was very angry, not with Mother, but with Jack for daring to touch my beloved mother in this way. A few days later I saw him alone, and challenged him about this. He told me that he and Mother were now lovers, and that Mother was able to enjoy sex for the first time in her life. He said that Mother had never liked sex with Father, but that now at last she was 'fulfilled'. 'Being fulfilled' had only just become a subject for discussion, and even now only for the middle and upper classes; working people were supposed to find fulfilment in the drudgery of factories or domestic service.

A few weeks after my talk with Jack, Pam must have noticed something different about Mother. She came storming into the kitchen one evening after feeding her horse and started shouting at Mother. Mother burst into tears and rushed sobbing upstairs. I was so enraged I literally did see red. I seized Pam by the throat (I was normally a most peace-loving creature).

'If you ever upset Mother like that again I will beat you to a pulp,' I said and I meant every word. Mother's love affair was never again mentioned by anyone, although I knew that it continued until the outbreak of war, two years later.

After we had lived in Chester for about six months, I decided to join the Red Cross. Nursing had a great attraction for me, but of course having no schooling had made any kind of career impossible, even if Mother had agreed to my being away from home. So I started Red Cross nursing, and went to do part of my practical training at the Chester City Hospital, for a few hours each day. I worked on what was called the 'sticky maternity' ward, where all the difficult and complicated cases were sent, and also on the ward for babies born blind, or abnormal in some other way, due to congenital syphilis. These poor helpless little ones – their eyes oozing yellow pus, crying fretfully, and with no apparent hope of any normal future – tore at my heart. They seemed the innocent victims of their parents' folly, or, in stronger terms, their wickedness. Within twelve months I had all my advanced Red Cross Certificates in first aid, home nursing and anti-gas, but oh how I longed to be a proper nurse!

In 1938 there was much talk of war against Germany. Hitler was making menacing moves in Europe. I felt very confused because of my former Blackshirt connections, which had stopped completely when we moved to the new house. Hitler seemed to have done so much for his people, and yet his present activities appeared so wrong. To add to my confusion, on my twenty-first birthday, Dick had given me the trilogy *A Flax of Dream* by Henry Williamson, whose other books on animals I had read and loved. Now in the foreword to *A Flax of Dream* he had written 'I salute the great little man across the Rhine, whose life symbol is a happy child.'

Another distressing event was Dick's joining the RAF Reserve. He was learning to fly most weekends now, and yet he was a believer in Buddhism, and would not even let me kill a wasp. It was a time of upsets, of inner conflicts for so many people, including me, and for the first time in my life Mother did not give me any firm guidance. She seemed to be so engrossed in her love affair, and refused to even consider the possibility of war.

All through the lovely hot summer of 1939 the war clouds gathered, but every weekend when Dick was not flying we took a whole day's picnic and drove my little Ford into North Wales, finding remote and beautiful places in Snowdonia. We would spread our rug on the grass and talk about the problems that seemed to be facing us all. Mother did not come on these excursions; she went out herself with Jack a lot of the time. Then came a calm sunny Sunday, 3 September. Dick and I were on our way to a favourite place in Wales, and I stopped in Chester to buy a newspaper. Great black headlines proclaimed, 'England Declares War on Germany'. Dick glanced at it, then threw it on the back seat. Somehow it seemed so unreal, so impossible on that lovely serene autumn day. But it was real.

The next morning I was called to report to Red Cross Headquarters in Chester. I had been assigned to daily duty at Chester County Mental Hospital. It was expected that this would be made ready to receive service casualties. In the meantime, we worked on the wards. I was on the male GPI ward, which meant General Paralysis of the Insane, for men who had become paralysed and insane through venereal disease, which seemed to follow me in my work! Many of the patients had been in the hospital since they were young boys, and were now old and grey. All were incontinent and soiled their beds; the ward stank. But worst of all was the attitude of the so-called nurses, who were without exception callous, sometimes brutal, and almost illiterate. The medical superintendent was an old man of seventy, who was ruled by the matron, a big, coarse woman who had nothing but contempt for all her helpless charges, and a kind of slap-happy comradeship with the staff. In my ward old men lay in soaking beds, their limbs had become fixed, and they had to be moved every inch by hand. Only their eyes moved, and although the nurses said they did not understand anything, I was not sure that that was true. One of the nurses had a particular dislike for a white haired old man. She used to call him 'a stinking old donkey' when we were changing his bed linen, and the expression in his eyes was unforgettable. All the patients had to be fed, as they were unable to move their hands, and I took under my special care a boy of seventeen, who had been in that same bed since he was ten years old, and was now a twisted deformed bag of bones. He had soft brown eyes, and as I fed him I spoke gently to him, and I felt sure that he knew the compassion I felt for him.

I worked all day, six days a week in that ward for three months. Then I broke down and could neither eat nor sleep. The terrible, hopeless suffering haunted my every thought, and I could take no more. So as there did not seem to be any sign of war wounded coming in, I resigned, and stayed at home to help Mother look after two little boys who had been evacuated from Liverpool docks in case of air raids and billeted on us. I tried several times to visit the young boy in the ward where I had worked, taking fruit and sweets, but always the matron refused to allow me to see him. I felt so helpless, her authority was supreme. I can only hope that after the war conditions in that mental hospital changed; perhaps even kindness and pity crept in, and dispelled some of the misery.

Dick had been called up as I had on the first day of the war, and was now at the end of his training at an RAF bomber station near Oxford. As he expected to be moved soon to an unknown destination, I went to Oxford for a week-end. We wandered round the lovely old town, and spent hours sitting on the river bank, talking always of when the war was over. We made plans to marry and have a little place in the country somewhere, and keep bees. Dick was full of the idea of bee-keeping on a large scale, and I had been reading books about bees for months. Then we talked too of the children we wanted, but Dick only wanted one, a little girl who was to look just like me. He had always called me 'Leo', as he said I had tawny hair like a lion, and the fierce protectiveness of a lioness.

'All I want is another little Leo, with a mane of tawny hair,' he said. We loved each other so much that our hearts and minds were in complete unison, and because of this I knew how much he was dreading becoming actually operational in a bomber squadron. His whole gentle nature rebelled against killing any living thing, friend or foe, and yet he was utterly determined that bullies like Hitler must be stopped. Lying on the warm grass, with the river murmuring against the willow on the bank, I knew that this inner conflict was tearing Dick apart, and I had a dreadful feeling that something must happen before he did actually drop any bombs. We said good-bye on the Sunday evening, and I returned to Mother in Chester early the next morning.

It was October, an unusually mild and lovely month, and two weeks after I had left Dick in Oxford, the telephone rang. It was Dick's Aunt Mary. He had been killed in a flying accident the day before, 11 October. Three days later I was standing by his open grave in Birkenhead Cemetery, opposite his widowed mother and two younger brothers, his aunts and uncles. Only Mother's arm around me held me from falling, while tears flowed silently down my face. My world had ended and I wanted to die too. My intense love for Dick had grown almost to equal what I felt for Mother; without her love and understanding I could not have got through the next few weeks.

It was now 1940 and although the air-raid sirens often wailed, no bombs had as yet been dropped. When the sirens went, Mother and I would take the dogs and crouch under the dining table which was supposed to be some protection. We would crawl out when the all-clear sounded. Pam was in the Land Army, training somewhere near Nantwich. She had had her horse destroyed as there was not enough feed now, and Mother and I made the sad decision that we would have our beloved dogs put to sleep too. We were so afraid that in an air raid we might be injured and the dogs would have no one to care for them. We took them to our kindly local vet and later buried them in the garden.

Many years earlier, Grandfather had given Mother a large bottle of strong sleeping tablets called 'Medinal'.

'If Hitler uses gas, or tries to invade, we will take these tablets and die together,' Mother now said frequently. I felt sure she did not really mean it – it was just another of her fantasies. She always had a great sense of drama.

Everyone thought that when the air raids really started, Liverpool would be a main target because of the docks, and Chester was too near Liverpool for Mother's liking. She put the house up for sale. I was anxious to do some war work, so I applied for and got a job on a big farm in Shropshire. I was to look after three hundred hens, two large greenhouses, fifty-six rabbits, and a large kitchen garden. I settled down in my new life, and in a few weeks Mother had sold our house and came to stay at the farm as a paying guest. Once more we shared a bedroom, and I was as happy as I could be with the loss of Dick like a stone in my heart. We were remote from any of the real effects of war, and I was glad to see Mother so happy and well cared for. We had home-cured bacon, plenty of milk and eggs, plenty of fresh killed meat, and even jugs of thick cream at every meal.

So life went on in this lovely peaceful place, but after some months, I began to be very restless and to feel guilty that I was living so well, and not really doing very much to defeat Hitler. His atrocities against the countries he occupied and against the Jews had sickened me, and I realized too that in joining the Blackshirts I had been totally misled; they were after all linked with Hitler's policies. So I wrote off to the WRNS and also to the Liverpool Police Force, both of which were wanting drivers badly. I was pretty good on the roads by now.

Two weeks later, on the same morning, I was asked by both to go for an interview. I had decided to turn down the WRNS, as I would have had to agree to go wherever I was sent, and I could not be too far away from Mother. So I chose the police and went for an interview. I passed a very severe driving test, and became a uniformed member of the Women's Police Force, to drive ambulances and replace the male drivers who had been called into the Forces. There were only six girls taken on; we were very carefully chosen and had expensive uniforms made specially for each of us. I left Mother on the farm, knowing that she was safe and well cared for, and that I could see her often, and I went to Liverpool, to share a flat with one of the other girls.

The six of us worked in eight-hour shifts, two on duty, two on standby, and two off duty. We were attached to the big police garage in Seel Street, Liverpool, where the remaining male members of the force also worked, all of us ruled by a big hearty Sergeant Clark. The local CID worked from offices there as well, and the detectives often came and talked to us and told us of their raids and successes. They had an endless supply of expensive cigarettes, and, as these were now unobtainable in the shops, I presumed they were the proofs of success.

We had two big ambulances, each two tons in weight. They were very heavy to drive. We also did our own maintenance, and the cleaning, both inside and out. This was no joke after we had transported a party of drunks to the cells and they had been sick just about everywhere inside the ambulance. We also had two Black Marias. These were usually used for drunks, unless they were unconscious, or semi-conscious, in which case they were loaded into one of our clean, shiny ambulances. Our work was hard, unpleasant and really quite unfit for young women. We drove the ambulances with a uniformed cop in the passenger seat, and our job was to attend all road accidents, suicides and so on. During my five months service, I helped fish a man out of Liverpool docks, cut down a hanged suicide, and worst of all scoop up a tiny boy of about four years old, who had been run over by a huge brewery lorry.

There were very strict rules for the ambulance drivers. We had log books which we always carried, and when a call came for an ambulance the sergeant noted the exact time it was received in his book and ours, and off one of us went. We had to be on the scene of the accident in the shortest possible time, without breaking any laws. We then collected the victim or victims on to our stretchers, and then dashed to Liverpool Royal Infirmary. On arrival, hospital attendants removed our passengers, and we went inside to have the casualty sister initial the time of arrival that we had entered in our logs. Then back to Seel Street, where the sergeant examined our books and gave us hell if we had been even a minute or two too slow. 'That minute can be someone's life,' he would say. We became very fast, yet very safe drivers.

The girls on duty who were not on the ambulances drove the Black Marias, small black vans, with heavily barred windows, and a rear door that only opened from the outside. Sometimes I went with the CID on a raid to Chinatown's opium dens on the docks. I would wait outside by the van, scared stiff of being knifed by one of the pig-tailed figures hurrying about the ill-lit street. The Chinese hated the police intensely. Then the CID men would drag out their victims; they looked so small and pathetic, I was very often on their side.

Once I drove a Black Maria from Walton Jail to Strangeways in Manchester, with a policeman beside me, and two inside, as our passenger was a 'lifer'. We drove through the huge prison gates into a courtyard, and while the two policemen took their prisoner inside, the other one took me round the side of the prison and showed me the small barred window of the condemned cell, where men had waited to be hanged. Then he pointed to a corner, and said, 'And the bodies are put there in quick-lime.' Even then, totally ignorant of the agony of imprisonment, I felt sick and was glad to drive back to Liverpool.

When I had a week-end off duty, I always spent my time on the farm with Mother, and also talked to her on the telephone several times a week. When I only had a few hours free I sometimes went to a film with one or two of our old boyfriends from before the war. They were all in uniform now, of course, and they had known Dick well too, so meeting some of them was a relief from the grey monotony of my work and the cold emptiness I still felt without Dick.

It was 1941 and there were frequent air raids, quite heavy ones. We drove our ambulances through the blacked-out streets, past bombed buildings where air-raid wardens searched for bodies of the dead or living. Going off duty during an air raid was very frightening, having to walk back to the flat in the dark before dawn, seeing the searchlights probing the sky with their long fingers of light, and hearing the anti-aircraft guns banging away in the distance.

At the beginning of November, I had a week-end leave due, but Mother had flu, and, unselfish as always, had made me promise to keep away in case I caught it. I had never been very strong, and was already suffering with heavy colds and bronchitis. Liverpool in November was cold and damp, with fog rising from the river almost all the time, and of course with rationing so strict, none of us had enough food to keep really well. So I had a week-end free and a few days before I had run into an old friend, George, who parents lived near Liverpool, and who was in army barracks in Chester. We stopped and talked – about Dick's death, and all the happy times in the past. He told me that his regiment was going overseas shortly and that he too had next week-end off duty. Suddenly he asked me to spend it with him. Since Dick's death, I had not really cared what happened to me, and I thought, 'Why not at least help George to go off with a happy memory?' On the Friday night I met him in Chester and we spent the week-end at a little old pub just on the border of North Wales. Of course, we slept together. He told me that he had loved me for a long time, but knew that being so engrossed with Dick, I had just regarded him as one of the boys. Now there was no real love left in my heart for anyone except Mother. Early on Monday morning he returned to the army barracks and I to Liverpool. I was not to see him again until 1946, when the war was over.

Six weeks later, I thought I was pregnant and a test by a doctor proved this to be true. I had shocking morning sickness, and had to drag myself on duty for each morning shift. I was very, very frightened. I phoned the barracks in Chester, but was told that the regiment had moved to a transit camp three weeks earlier. Later I learnt that they had sailed to India just before Christmas. I was now very unwell indeed. As well as my pregnancy, I had bronchitis badly, and I asked for a private interview with the chief inspector, and told him my troubles. He was very kind and fatherly, and said that he would invalid me out on medical grounds, using my chronic bronchitis, and not mentioning my coming baby. I wrote to Mother, told her that I was now out of the Police Force because of ill health, and going to join her in Shropshire.

Pam had taken my place as a land girl on the farm, and she and Mother met me at the railway station. While Mother went to see about my trunk, I told Pam the truth, and she said, 'The shock will kill Mother.' She offered to take me away somewhere, so that Mother would not know, and I shall always remember that act of kindness.

Mother and I had single beds on opposite sides of our room. One morning I woke at dawn and lay watching a red winter sunrise. Suddenly Mother said, 'You are going to have a baby, aren't you?'

I turned my head and looked at her for a long minute, then replied, 'Yes, Mummy, I am.'

It was as simple as that. Mother and I were still so close that she knew without any doubt, and there were no angry scenes, no recriminations.

But Mother wanted to know who was the baby's father. For the first time in my life I resisted her and refused to answer. I knew that George was not able to marry me anyway, he had gone, yet I felt that Mother would move mountains (she had done for me in the past) to get me safely married. I had very strong feelings about marrying without any real love on either side. Now Mother wanted me to get rid of my baby; she gave me all sorts of revolting mixtures to bring that about. One was nutmeg grated thickly on a glass of Guinness, *horrible*, then massive doses of quinine, but they only made me more sick than I already was.

After Christmas I became very ill, vomiting all the time, and I was taken into hospital. There I was heavily sedated to try to stop the sickness; I could not even keep water down. One day the doctors told me that unless the sickness stopped in a few days they would have to remove the baby. Miraculously, I was sick no more. It was partly due to the sedation – but also I wanted this baby very much, and that was perhaps the real reason for my recovery.

I returned to the farm. It was now February 1942, and Mother and I began to make plans. The baby was due in August, and as I had always had a romantic longing to go to Cornwall, county of my father's people (my middle name was after all Tregenna) we decided to rent a cottage there. We bought the weekly magazine, the *Lady*, and found just what we were needing – a furnished bungalow in a little village called Gorran Haven, for rent for one year. We packed all our possessions (Mother had stored all the furniture from Chester – 'for the duration,' she said) and off we went to Cornwall. Pam stayed behind to work on the farm.

I shall never forget my first sight of Cornwall as the train crossed the Tamar bridge. There were primroses blooming all along the banks beside the railway track. Apart from North Wales (and that seemed a lifetime ago), I had never seen so many wild flowers. I felt somehow that I was coming home to where my baby belonged. I loved the soft Cornish accent. One day, when I was talking to an old man on the beach, he gazed out to sea and said, 'Don't see no sense in it at all. Us fights they and they fights we,' and he drew hard on his empty pipe.

Rationing was very strict and we were strangers – 'foreigners' as the Cornish say. There were no extra eggs, milk, or anything else, but one or two of the old men (all the young men had gone to the war) went out fishing daily and we were able to buy fish straight from the boats. We could buy enough for a big meal for the two of us for one shilling. Mother's gardening skill was soon providing us with spinach, peas, beans and salads. We were both making baby clothes. I knitted (no sewing for me) and Mother sewed little nightdresses and all the pretty things a baby needs, even one without a father.

I was often lonely, though, and became friendly with another mother-to-be, who was also living with her mother. But she was married and her husband was in the army. One day I asked her if I could go with her to the meeting of the Mothers' Union attached to the local church. She told me that an unmarried mother would not be accepted. This seemed strange to me – unmarried I might be, but surely I qualified as an expectant mother.

The summer was long and very hot and I grew very large indeed. The doctor talked vaguely about twins, but I hoped most definitely not. He was rather worried about my having a first baby at home, with my past medical history, but all the local nursing homes and the hospital were fully booked for August. All I would have when the time came would be the district nurse.

Mother and I (in spite of my size) were great walkers. We were walking along a cliff path one day when we found a little rabbit, half-dead, its leg crushed in a steel trap. We managed to set it free, but it died of shock. Mother and I searched for more traps. We found a total of 250 during thet next two days and every one of them was thrown over the cliffs to the rocks and the tide below. There would be no more suffering rabbits if we could help it. A few days later the local policeman called, a farmer by his side, and asked very respectfully if on our walks we had seen anybody tampering with rabbit traps.

'My whole lot, not one left!' grumbled the farmer. We looked so innocent, the bobby told him to be quiet.

'Can't you see these ladies got naught to do with it?' he said, and off they went.

A few weeks before the arrival of my baby, the weather was extremely hot and airless. I could not sleep and my patient mother suggested a walk on the beach. It was nearly midnight, with an almost full moon, and we strolled across the cool, wet sand. As we turned back, a shout rang out from the cliff.

'Who goes there? Stop or I'll shoot.'

It was the Home Guard on patrol. We called back and when we reached him Mother explained why we were out so late at night.

'You might have been shot,' he said. 'Nobody is allowed on the beach at night now, in case of invasion. See?'

About noon on 17 August my labour started. Mother went down to the phone box and called the district nurse. She said she would tell Dr Palmer, and she would be along as soon as there was a bus! She was over seventy and had come back into nursing to replace the young district nurse who had been called away to the services. She had no transport other than the bus, a lift in the doctor's car, or her own two feet. She also had no idea about modern hygiene, as we shall see. At about 6.30 she duly arrived on the bus. By now I was having regular and pretty bad pains and poor Mother was frantic with worry. The old nurse peered shortsightedly at my suffering rear end and pronounced that she could 'see the head' and all was well. Mother gave a cry of rage, and said, '*My* daughter is not having this baby without the doctor present.' My subconscious mind obeyed at once – all pains and contractions ceased. Well, Dr Palmer came when his surgery was over, examined me, and was not at all happy. He gave me an injection to get things going again, told Mother to phone at once if the baby seemed about to arrive (it was fortunate that she was a doctor's daughter), and both he and the nurse departed.

My daughter was not born until 5 p.m. on 19 August, forty-eight hours later, and then only with the help of the doctor, the nurse, our next-door neighbour (Mother could not bear my suffering), the skilful use of forceps, and a big dose of ether to put me out while the baby was delivered. Our neighbour said the room looked like a slaughter house, and even the doctor was exhausted. I woke up to see Mother holding out the most beautiful little bundle, big blue eyes wide open, and not a red wrinkle in sight! She laid my daughter in my arms, and all the agony was forgotten. *This* was the most important thing in the whole world.

So Andrea Tregenna came into our lives. We had decided before she was born that if I had a boy we would call him Andrew after Father, but as a girl arrived instead, we felt that Andrea, shortened to Andy, was just as good.

I was kept in bed after the birth, and every day the old

nurse came on the morning bus to attend to me. But she came, without gloves, having handled money and bus tickets, straight into my room without washing her hands. On the tenth day I developed puerperal fever. I was too ill to be moved, even by ambulance, and for days I hovered between life and death, while Mother cared for Andrea and gave me the medicines from the doctor – twenty-nine doses every twenty-four hours.

One late afternoon, I lay looking out of the window. Everything seemed bathed in a pale yellow light and I knew I was dying. Mother and our neighbour came in and began quietly to remove the baby's cot from beside my bed. I managed to raise my hand and our neighbour said, 'Poor thing, I think she wants us to leave it here.' I knew without any doubt that that cot was my only hold on life – my baby who needed me. Dr Palmer came in during the evening and told Mother that it was unlikely that I could live through the night. Mother kept her lonely vigil, only leaving me to feed and change our precious baby. By morning I was asleep and when Dr Palmer called in early he said to Mother, 'She's gone, of course.' Mother told him that I was sleeping peacefully. My darling mother, plus my own will to live, had won, and I was on the way to recovery.

Without Mother's love, her overpowering love, and her extremely strong will, I would have died when Andy was born. For the rest of my life I never forgot the great debt that I owed to her.

Chapter 3

When Andy was about three weeks old, our old friend Jack (Mother's former lover) came for a week's leave from the army. Both he and Mother urged me to accept his offer of marriage to give my baby a father, but I absolutely refused. He was really a very kind boy but I did not love him. Also I had no intention of sharing a husband – if I ever had one – with Mother. One day she and Jack took a picnic to a nearby beach. It was a roasting hot day – September can be like that in Cornwall – and when they came home Mother's eyelids were very badly burnt. She had fallen asleep in the sun. (She had to wear dark glasses for weeks to protect them.) But I knew she had had a lovely outing – her top lip was swollen up.

Christmas came, a very quiet one. Mother and I had a tiny tree for our baby and decorated it with little bows of coloured baby ribbons. We had nothing else. Although she was only four months old, Andy held out her hands to the pretty tree and gurgled with delight. She was such a good baby, sleeping out in the garden in her pram, no matter how bad the weather. We never had to get her up at night. But sometimes the German planes passed over in the night, on their way to bomb Plymouth, fifty miles away, and we heard the anti-aircraft guns and the far-off wail of the sirens.

In March 1943 our lease of the bungalow was over and we

had to move. Once more through the *Lady* we took a cottage in Dorset. But we only stayed there six weeks. We discovered that just through a wood nearby was a great flat plain, and there were aeroplanes and gliders by the score, being made ready for something. Mother and I used to gather wood for cooking and heating water, and we had come across this secret place by accident. Also, close to the cottage there was a searchlight battery, and almost every night enemy planes dropped silver foil to try to knock out the big lights. This was what the soldiers told us then, but after the war we realized that in reality it was an effort to upset the newly-discovered radar. At the time we could not really understand how the long strips of silver foil we found lying around in the morning could possibly affect the searchlights. Mother and I took Andy under the stout kitchen table when we heard the planes, but Mother was very uneasy and we decided to move once more. Once again we found a house through the *Lady*, this time in New Quay, South Wales. Months later we heard that a bomb had been dropped right on to our cottage which burnt to the ground.

In Dorset I had been given an Alsatian bitch by one of the soldiers stationed nearby – we called her Flicka. Moving with a baby, an Alsatian and twenty-one pieces of luggage is a terrifying experience in wartime with no names on the stations, the trains totally blacked out at night and packed with troops coming and going on leave. We travelled nearly twenty-four hours to Wales via London. Andy eventually slept on the knee of a naval officer in a first-class carriage, while Mother and I sat on our cases in the corridor. We arrived at New Quay in the early morning and managed to hire a taxi to our new home. The house was called Pleasant View, but to our horror it was anything but pleasant. It was a solitary house two miles from the nearest shop. The only means of cooking was two old oil stoves, one with an oven just placed on the top.

By now Andy was eating Mother's weekly egg and mine, our butter rations and the occasional little bit of bacon. She was a very strong and healthy child. In spite of this a month after our arrival, she developed a bad dose of chickenpox. This would not have been so terrible had not Mother also become ill with a very bad quinsy in her throat. I had to blow crushed M and B tablets down her throat with a paper funnel every four hours day and night.

Leaving Andy scratching and crying in my room and Mother dangerously ill in hers, I had to walk two miles to buy even a loaf of bread. This part of Wales was quite hostile to the English. They spoke Welsh all the time. When I went into the shop all conversation ceased and dark secret faces watched silently; as soon as I opened the door to leave a babble of Welsh broke out again. As I walked to and from the little shop, I prayed with all my strength, 'Please God don't let Mother die, do anything to me, but I can't live without Mother.' I knew that I had done a terrible wrong in having a baby before marriage, and because of that I felt that God could not bother with anyone like me. Be that as it may, Mother recovered slowly, Andy's spots disappeared, and my heart sang in the warm sunshine.

But there was cruelty and suffering in this beautiful Welsh countryside. Sometimes at night I would hear an agonized screaming across the fields, a rabbit in a steel trap, but there was nothing I could do. The Welsh farmers were dour and harsh, and all went in black to chapel on Sundays. Once or twice I found a little rabbit in a trap, its eyes pecked out by crows, and one I found was still alive, with bleeding eye sockets. I got it out of the steel jaws of the trap as gently as I could and took it home to Mother. Together we killed it. Somehow we managed to cut its head off with the axe in the tool shed, but I thought of the Welsh farmer who set the traps and left the trapped creatures from Saturday to Monday because it would be wrong to see to the traps on a Sunday – the Lord's Day they called it.

We moved two more times that year – first to Devon and then to Polperro in Cornwall. I think it must have been the Romany blood in us both that made all this moving seem quite normal. In fact Mother and I enjoyed our rather nomadic existence and always found many things to interest and amuse us. However, we settled happily in our new resting place – a guest-house right on the edge of Talland Bay – and I thought that we should probably stay there until the war was over. There was an ancient wireless in the sitting room and Mother and I listened happily to Tommy Handley in 'Itma' and to the nostalgic singing of Vera Lynn, the 'Forces' Sweetheart'. Not having seen her, I imagined a lovely young blonde with a soft, sad face.

Pam was now married. On her honeymoon she and her new husband had visited us in Devon for a couple of days. I liked John, a quiet, self-contained Yorkshireman. He was a test pilot in the RAF and he and Pam had met at an aerodrome in Shropshire where Pam was now working as a driver. They seemed an unromantic couple – no holding hands or endearments on their visit. I put it down to John's Yorkshire reticence. Or perhaps Pam was shy? After our arrival in Cornwall Mother had a letter from Pam. She was in the early stage of pregnancy and frightened to death by the whole idea. John was away flying, they had rooms in Shrewsbury, would Mother and I please come and help her? So yet again we bought the *Lady*, found a furnished house near Shrewsbury and Mother wrote off and took it on a six months' lease.

I went for a last sad walk along the cliff listening to the sea birds crying, watching the gulls sail and swoop in the sky. I felt that I was leaving a place I loved very much. I had fallen in love with Cornwall.

We arrived at the house near Shrewsbury in late August. It was a lovely place and Mother was especially pleased with the wild birds that came to the garden – all the usual ones and also blue jays, nuthatches and a pair of great green woodpeckers. Mother had a wonderful way with birds and we shared these things as indeed we shared most things in life.

Pam now gave up the rooms in Shrewsbury and came to stay with us. John visited on his brief leaves – test pilots were working extremely hard at this stage of the war. Poor Pam, she was terrified of having a baby, almost afraid to move in case she injured herself. She lay in bed a great deal and would not take any exercise at all. This worried me. She would not even bend down to pick up a pin off the floor in case of injury and I was afraid that she would have a difficult labour through this total lack of exercise. The district nurse called in one day and I told her of my fears. The nurse went up to see Pam and when she came down she said, 'Don't you worry about her. People like her always fall on their feet. She will probably not suffer at all.' In fact the nurse proved to be right. Pam's son Rodney was born in February 1944 – he came into the world in exactly an hour and a half.

Mother by now had found a furnished house in Shrewsbury for Pam and her son, and Pam begged Mother to stay on for a few weeks to help her with the baby. As Mother and I would not be parted, we all stayed. A month later Andy became ill. She developed measles and a middle ear infection. Poor little girl, she cried ceaselessly with pain and had a very high fever. It was bitterly cold and actually snowing when Pam suddenly told Mother that we had to leave at once in case she or Rodney caught any infection. I begged and pleaded with Pam, told her I would isolate myself and Andy entirely, but she was adamant. So Mother phoned a guest-house we knew back in Gorran Haven, and we left in the snow the next morning. We travelled many, many weary hours on the train to St Austell. I held my poor little one all the long journey – she seemed semi-conscious with pain and the high fever. We got a taxi to Gorran Haven and late as it was I phoned the doctor, and he came in a short while. He said that Andy was very ill indeed and should not have been taken on a long journey. Mother and I sat up with her all that night. It was nearly a week before she was out of danger and the pain and inflammation in her ear subsided. I thought over and over again, 'How could it happen that a sick child had to make that journey in the snow?'

It was now spring again and we were back in our beloved Cornwall. Mother decided that a place of our own was better for Andy, and of course Flicka, so she rented a house in a little place called Watergate at the end of a creek which joined the tidal river running into Looe and out to sea. It was a lovely, remote place, only three houses, and for all shopping I had a two-mile walk through the woods alongside the river into Looe, which was a much bigger fishing village than nearby Polperro. There were large fishing boats called luggers and a few smaller ones which were toshers. Looe is built on two sides of the tidal river, East Looe and West Looe, and to cross from one to the other without a walk up and over the bridge carrying the road, I hailed the rowing boat which ferried people to and fro all day long. The fare was one penny and it was well worth the fare to sit in the little boat and chat to the old fisherman who rowed.

While we were living at Watergate, a friend we had made in Polperro came to stay with us. Peggy was ten years older than I, highly intelligent and a lover of books and music. Her parents had died in her childhood and wealthy grandparents had brought her up, firstly with an old family nanny and then an expensive boarding school. She had inherited a sizeable income from her parents, and as poor health kept her from being called into war work where all her unmarried friends were, she was rather at a loose end. Peggy and I had liked each other on sight. We shared a love of reading and country walking, and I was thankful that Mother seemed to enjoy her company too. Peggy stayed with us for several weeks and then departed for her grandparents' home at Sunningdale near London, and Mother had Andy and me all to herself again. Andy was by now two and a half years old, and Mother really worshipped her. In fact I began to feel that she was spoiling my daughter rather badly.

In October 1944 Mother began to think seriously of buying a house somewhere, where we could settle down permanently. I don't think it ever occurred to her that I might marry one day, and I felt sure that she would have rejected the thought as impossible. In her mind, I knew, we would be together for the rest of our lives. After a lot of searching and house-hunting Mother bought a small detached house outside Newton Abbot, Devon, and we moved in – Mother, me, Andy and Flicka, and all our luggage. We had moved eight or nine times since we left the farm in Shropshire and now it was good to look forward to a settled life.

Mother had arranged that our arrival by train from St Austell would coincide with the delivery by Pickfords of all our furniture out of storage. Andy and Flicka ran about the long garden while Mother paced out the size of rooms ready for the carpets to go down. At twelve noon we were eating our picnic lunch and up rolled the removal van. The men started to unpack our things that had been in storage for four years and we had a terrible shock. All Mother's lovely carpets and rugs were eaten away by moths, they looked like fretwork and were totally useless. Everything was damp and mouldy. Poor Mother just sat down and cried. The Pickfords men were almost as upset as Mother and did all they could to comfort her by saying that four years is a long time and storage in wartime full of hazards. It was early evening before the van left, and we were faced with the chaos that only a complete removal can bring. But we set up Andy's cot, put our bedding to air and then I bathed and fed Andy and settled her to sleep in her new little room. Mother and I sat down wearily to eat the cold food we had brought from St Austell; we were glad indeed to crawl into our beds very late that night. It took weeks to get everything in some sort of order. Mother still had a small amount of her capital left from the purchase of the house and we went to auction sales and bought enough carpets and rugs to replace the ones that had been casualties of the war.

Mother was very happy now, we had a settled home together and Andy was a continual joy to us both. Sometimes I was lonely though, wonderful as Mother was, and close as we were. I often longed for someone my own age to talk to, but as I never went out, it was not likely that our pattern of daily living would change. When Andy ran about in the garden with Flicka, I often thought how Dick would have loved her, she looked so like me, a little Leo. I wondered too where her father was, poor George somewhere in India (actually he was in Burma). Indeed I had no idea if he were still alive. Grandmother still lived in her flat and each week sent a local paper to me. She knew how much I still clung to the town where I had spent the years between the age of five and nineteen. Through the paper I saw that several of our old friends, the boys, had been killed, but so far Mother's Jack was not among them.

Throughout the winter and spring I began to feel more and more that it would be best if Andy and I had a little time away from Mother, who ran all our lives now and upon whom I was totally dependent. I felt too that Mother was becoming very possessive about Andy as she had always been about me, and this troubled me. My friend Peggy and I had been corresponding regularly since she returned to her grandparents, and now she wrote and said that she had at last decided to have a home of her own and was looking for an old cottage somewhere in Devon, a county she liked very much. She asked if I could look in our local papers and let her know if I saw anything good for sale. One day I saw a group of very old cottages for sale near Kingsbridge. They were 'in need of renovation', the agents said. I phoned Peggy at once. She came down the next day to stay with us in Newton Abbott, and she and I left Andy with Mother for the day and went to look at the cottages. The end cottage was vacant, the two adjoining smaller ones had been let to the same families for many years. Peggy decided to buy all three and turn the large end one into her home. The whole idea was most exciting, the cottage was in a dreadful state, with weeds growing up between the slate slabs that had been the floors, very few windows left, and not much roof either. But there were lovely old black beams in the ceilings and over the derelict living-room fireplace was a truly magnificent old ship's beam about twelve feet long. The village was charming, full of thatched cottages, an old pub and one little shop cum post office, as well as a beautiful church dating back to 1200.

Peggy was anxious to begin the renovation of her future home as soon as possible, and she found a furnished cottage in the village to live in in the meantime. It stood next to the churchyard, a delightful old place called The Quillet. As she had no practical knowledge about old houses or how to go about contacting builders, etc., and as she knew that through all the moves with Mother I knew something about these matters, she asked me if I would consider bringing Andy to join her at The Quillet for a few months. She was quite excited about the whole idea. I would help her with the decisions and arrangements for her new home and in return Andy and I would have a temporary home with her. I told her I would think it over, and Peggy returned to Sunningdale to pack her things to move into The Quillet.

The more I thought about it all the more I felt that this was the temporary break from Mother that was needed. Peggy loved children and Andy had shown her liking for my friend from the start. So one afternoon while Andy was having her nap upstairs, I told Mother all about The Quillet and Peggy's offer to me. Mother was at first horrified and then furious at the idea of our parting even for a few months. The storm raged all the evening and all the next day. I put Andy to bed early and told Mother that I was going to phone Peggy and accept her offer. She became very hysterical – I had never seen her so uncontrolled – and taking my father's loaded service revolver from where it was kept locked in a drawer, Mother ran up to the bathroom, locked herself in, and shouted, 'If you leave me I will shoot myself.' But I knew Mother too well and so I called out, 'Go ahead if you want to, I'm going out for a walk,' and out I went slamming the door loudly behind me. Anxiously I waited outside. Had I misjudged Mother? After all my Andy was asleep alone upstairs. I held my breath as I waited. Nothing happened, so I went for a long walk to give Mother time to calm down and when I returned she had gone to bed.

For the next few days Mother was cool and distant to me and extremely loving to Andy. The day before we left she said coldly, 'I have asked your sister to bring Rodney to stay for a while. She is not very happy in her marriage.' Cheerfully I told her that I thought it was a good idea, but how I longed for Mother to understand what I was doing, and throw her arms lovingly round me as she had done all my life. After all it was only for a little while I thought and then we would be together again. A taxi took Andy, Flicka and me to Newton Abbott station. Mother refused to see us off. She was still deeply offended I could see, but I felt sure that, being the wonderful woman I loved so much, she would soon get over her anger.

At first I missed Mother terribly and almost decided that I simply must go back home to her, but by now Pam and little

Rodney were there. Also I had promised to help Peggy. Mother's whole upbringing had instilled into me that it was unforgivable to break a promise to anyone. So I set my mind to finding a suitable builder for Peggy's cottage and to getting the necessary plans drawn up and passed by the local council. I was determined to keep the character of the lovely old stone cottage and all rebuilding was to be done with this in mind. Peggy gave me a free hand with everything. She was one of life's dreamers, very impractical and content to laze away her days in The Quillet with letter writing, reading and playing the piano in the corner of the living room. Andy was now three years old and soon made friends with the village children of her own age and they all played happily in the garden, while I laboured on in my fights with both the builder and the local council.

Living in The Quillet was fun. The dining room was alongside the graves in the old churchyard and we could read the inscriptions on the head stones while we ate our meals. There was a full peal of bells rung on Sundays for morning and evening service and at first we were nearly deafened by the noise, but after some weeks hardly noticed it at all, we had become so used to the sound. I wrote and told Mother that I had become engrossed in rebuilding Peggy's cottage, and that it would be necessary for me to stay on in The Quillet until the work was finished, as without my constant nagging the slow Devonshire workmen tended to stand about in a lazy dreamlike state. Everything in the West Country moves at a snail's pace at the best of times and these were decidedly not the best of times. All the younger, more active men were away in the services and the older ones preferred what they called 'the old ways', which boiled down to never doing today what they could possibly put off to tomorrow.

Mother wrote back and said that she had decided to sell the house in Newton Abbott and move to a little fishing village the other side of Kingsbridge, taking Pam and Rodney with her. I felt that in taking Pam under her wing, Mother was having a dose of conscience for the years Pam had been on her own. Mother went on to say that Pam's marriage seemed to be crumbling. I felt rather sad at this – it seemed such a pity. For all his rather dour Yorkshire ways John had seemed devoted to his little son on the few occasions when I had seen them together. Mother said that she had taken the cottage in that particular village because it had a good bus service to Kingsbridge, and as that was where I took Andy for shopping we could often meet for lunch or tea. When I read her letter I realized that the love between us was as deep and strong as it always had been. But it was because of this that Mother had taken a dislike to Peggy. I am sure that she realized that without my friend's offer we would still be in Newton Abbott, so she refused all my invitations to visit The Quillet. However, I took Andy to see her and Pam and Rodney sometimes in their cottage by the sea. I think that John came there once or twice on a brief leave, but it was quite obvious that Pam's marriage to him was past mending.

While we were in The Quillet Easter came, and in the weeks leading up to Good Friday Peggy and I listened to a play on the wireless each evening. It was Dorothy Sayers's *The Man Born to be King*. Right from the first episode I was deeply affected – it was all so terribly real. Evening after evening I cried my heart out at the words of Jesus and his disciples, this Jesus who Mother had always told me was 'just a good man'. Now at last I knew that was not true, this Man, this Son of God come down to earth, had done all this for *me*. As Good Friday and the crucifixion came nearer I was so upset that Peggy begged me not to listen any more. But I had no choice – God himself was speaking to me. The play was so terribly real that I could almost see the blood and the sweat and the carrying of the Cross along the hot dusty road. The certain knowledge that Jesus had suffered for me, for my sins, was almost more than I could bear and I knew that love like that transcended any human love, and all I could do was to give my whole heart in return.

So I became a follower of Christ, but I was alone. Peggy had not felt at all as I had, and it did not occur to me to read the Bible or go to church even then. This thing that had happened to me so totally unexpectedly and so suddenly seemed a private thing, for just Jesus and me. But I knew that the burden of my sin in having Andy had rolled away and I was free from all guilt for the first time. One day I was digging in our little vegetable patch when I felt a great stillness in the hot sunshine. Looking up I saw for a few seconds the tall figure of Jesus standing a little way away. Then I was alone and went on digging – it all seemed perfectly normal to my untutored mind. When I was alone in bed at night and Andy was asleep, I prayed and talked to God, but for many years I did no more than just that.

Peggy's cottage was almost ready. It was May 1946, the war in Europe had been over a whole year and it was over with Japan too. Mother phoned one day and told me that Harry, an old friend of Pam's, was coming to stay. Pam had kept in touch with a lot of her old friends and especially with Harry's sister. A week later, the phone rang. It was George, my Andy's father! He had returned on the boat from India in company with Harry, and heard from him that Mother and Pam were in Devon, and that I lived nearby with a daughter aged nearly four years old. Acting on a wild hope George had travelled with Harry to stay with Mother and Pam. Would I meet him in Kingsbridge the next morning? I left Andy with Peggy, caught the bus to Kingsbridge, and when I got off at the terminus there stood George in his uniform. He was a Captain in the Sixth Gurkha Regiment, now on demob leave. He gazed at me with the most intensely blue eyes I had ever seen except when I looked at Andy. We went to a little tea shop for coffee and he asked very tactfully about Andy. I was not going to tell him anything yet; but we arranged that he could come and stay at The Quillet for a few days. I knew Peggy would understand.

The next day I met his bus in the village and as we walked along the lane Peggy appeared with Andy who rushed up to me. George dropped his bag, caught her up in his arms, and held her as if he would never let her go. He bathed her that night and when she was in bed we strolled along to the pub for a drink, my first since the war started. George took my hand, told me that he knew now that Andy was his daughter and asked me to marry him at once. But I felt very uncertain. I liked him so much, he was a fine man I felt, but I was not yet in love and I did not want him to marry me as an obligation because of Andy. So I told him that I wanted him to wait for a year and then see if he felt the same way. He had to go to London to get a job anyway. I would stay on in the new cottage with Peggy.

George stayed with us at The Quillet until his leave ended. We decided to go to the victory dance in the village hall on 6 June, Victory Day. I had not been to a dance since before the war and never with George, who looked quite stunning in his uniform with the black pips of the Gurkha Regiment on his shoulders. We were enjoying ourselves very much; we seemed to dance together perfectly. Then there was an 'excuse me' dance and a large fat local girl wearing a tight turquoise blue silk-type dress cut in on me and grabbed poor George. As they danced past George and I exchanged anguished glances, whereupon a stout matron next to me said, 'Go on, me'dear, you cut in and get him back.' I was so naïve that that had not occurred to me! The dance ended at midnight, it was a perfect June night, the sky full of stars, and we strolled down the lane to The Quillet hand in hand. Suddenly we stopped without a word, and George took me in his arms and we kissed. I knew then that he really was in love with me, but I still wanted to wait, and to be sure that it was right for us to marry. I knew that for me marriage would be for life, the single-mindedness of my love for Mother and also for Dick had shown me that when I loved anyone it was for ever – unchangeable, unmovable – and for ever.

George returned to London, was demobbed and set about finding a job to support a wife and child. He was a talented artist and had qualified as an art master just before the war, but now in the year after the war teaching was so poorly paid it did not seem to have any future for him. He finally got a job as a visual artist in a big advertising agency and lived in lodgings in London near to his work. He wrote to me two or three times a week and his letters became so familiar that the old postmaster who delivered them would say to me, 'Another letter from the

Major, me'dear'. George had been given the honorary title of Major on leaving the Gurkhas. He had been with Wingate all through the Burma Campaign against the Japanese and was badly wounded twice. Out of all our old friends before the war, he and Harry were the only two to live through to the uncertain days of peace. Mother's Jack had gone too and I felt very thankful that at least two of the old crowd were alive.

Mother did not take at all kindly to George's proposal to me or the fact that I now told her that he was Andy's father. She had never liked him very much and had thought that when the cottage was finished we would take up our life together again. In fact Mother did everything to persuade me that George would not be a good husband or father (how could she know I wondered?), and, of course, she stressed the difference in our former social backgrounds. This latter seemed absurd somehow – surely the terrible years of war had removed such false barriers, but apparently not – so far as Mother thought. But I was determined this time to make my own decision, painful as it was. Anyway Mother was committed to staying with Pam for a while as my sister was involved in divorce proceedings, and Mother was able to provide some stability for poor little Rodney. I loved my mother as I had always done with complete and total devotion, but I had grown up a lot more now and my devotion was no longer a blind one. I could see that Andy needed her father more than she needed her Grandmother.

In early September Pilgrims was at last finished to my complete satisfaction and Peggy too was delighted with the result. So we moved out of The Quillet, and into Peggy's new home. It was a truly lovely place now, and over the old front door which we had managed to rescue and repair climbed a huge old wisteria, its main trunk as thick as my wrist. It must have been nearly as old as the cottage itself. This was a happy time. Peggy and I shared the running of Pilgrims, I did all the cooking and shopping and she was supposed to do the cleaning but it was done in her usual vague way. Having been brought up in a house with four servants this was her first experience of housework. Andy had a best friend in the village now, Gillian, they were both four and a half years old, played 'house' with their dolls, and ran in and out of Pilgrims all through that lovely long summer. Children were safe in those days, we had yet to see the time when even in a village a child could be murdered a few yards from her home.

Mother had by now become reconciled to the fact that I might marry George next spring. We were once more united in our deep love for each other and I often took Andy for the day to the very old cottage where she lived with Pam and Rodney. The children played happily together – there were only eighteen months between them. Mother was horrified by what she called Andy's appalling Devonshire accent. 'How is the poor child ever going to be accepted in a decent school?' she wailed. Dear Mother, she always dramatized everything; even ordinary daily events could become transformed by her adjectives – the day was 'boiling hot' or 'freezing cold' or the rain 'poured in torrents'. This dramatic way of thinking and speaking were very much a part of her love of attention and was to last all through her life.

Because Mother had given up her struggle to be the only person who mattered in my life, to have my exclusive affections, she and Peggy had become friendly once more. So sometimes Mother came to Pilgrims and she and I took Andy for walks in the lanes with their banks and hedges so full of wild flowers. We taught her to know and love star of Bethlehem, Germanda speedwell, ragged robin, lady's slipper, and wild arum amongst the many flowers we recognized. Mother lifted her up to peep into the first nest she had seen, with the four bright blue eggs of the blackbird. So my little daughter learnt one of the most important lessons in life, an awareness of things around her and a love of the beauty and wonder of the countryside, something that was to remain with her into adulthood, so that she in turn taught these things to her own little ones. The unbroken chain of love and caring for the world in which we live can go from generation to generation, if there is a wonderful woman like Mother to forge the first link.

Autumn came and Christmas grew near. Peggy decided to

spend the holiday with her grandparents and as George would have the holiday free, he was to join Andy and me at Pilgrims so that we could get to know each other a little more, as an indication as to how it would be to share married life together. Mother would be with Pam and Rodney and Harry was joining them. Pam's divorce was about to be finalized.

Two weeks before Christmas heavy snow began to fall. In a matter of days we were completely snowed up in the now famous winter of 1946, the worst snow in the West Country for nearly a century. No food came into the village except milk which was delivered by farm tractor. Even the postman could not bring in the mail. The children loved the deep snow and spent all their time tobogganing down the hill outside Pilgrims. George and I made frantic telephone calls to each other as to whether he would be able to get to us for Christmas, but he vowed that no matter how difficult he would be there. 'I'll walk if I have to,' he said, little knowing how true that would turn out to be!

Two days before Christmas the road between our village and Kingsbridge was made safe for traffic, and so Peggy left for Sunningdale. But the road in the other direction from where we lived to Dartmouth was still closed with snow drifts up to twelve feet deep, and as it was fifteen miles away George's arrival seemed impossible. But the spirit that had taken him through the jungle in Burma was still there, and so on Christmas Eve he arrived in Dartmouth by train, loaded with gifts. When he inquired about some sort of transport to our village, he was met with amazed laughter. 'No chance,' he was told. 'No one can possibly get through yet.' So picking up his heavy suitcase George began to walk. He started out at 2 p.m. and struggled on through snow waist high at times. The moon came out, it was freezing cold and he became more and more exhausted. But he had been a Chindit for four years and added to that his love for me and Andy made anything possible, so he plodded on and on. He eventually staggered up to Pilgrims at 11 p.m. that night, utterly worn out and soaking wet from the deep snow. It had taken him nine hours to walk twelve miles. But a hot meal in front of a big log fire soon revived him, and we set about decorating the tree I had set up in a corner of the living room. We finally finished at 3 a.m. and fell wearily into our beds. The room was truly beautiful with the firelight flickering on the white walls, black ceiling beams, and catching the lovely decorations that George had made.

When Andy came down on Christmas morning and saw this fairyland with her gifts waiting by the tree, she was beside herself with excitement. We were a very happy little family that wonderful first Christmas together. Only one thing saddened me, George could not share my new-found love of Jesus and my close relationship with him. He seemed to have lost all faith in God during the war. I could only hope that in time he would find the peace and joy that knowing God brings.

After the holiday he went back to London, by bus to Dartmouth this time, the snow having been cleared, and Peggy returned to Pilgrims. She now asked an old school friend whose father was a vicar to stay for a holiday. Noreen herself was a true Christian, and while she was with us Peggy too came to know and love God and to accept Jesus as her saviour. It was wonderful to be able to share the joy and sense of freedom and adventure that a new Christian discovers.

The spring came, as only spring in the West Country can come, with long warm lazy days, much earlier than in the rest of England, and all the wild flowers filling the lanes with their sweetness, and the apple trees bursting into creamy pink blossom. By now I had decided to marry George. I was not in love with him – that came later – but I had great affection and respect for him. Andy was devoted to him and he her complete slave. We decided to be married in a register office, as we already had a child. A church wedding seemed hypocrisy to us both. Peggy was to keep Andy with her while George and I had a brief honeymoon in Ireland, and then we would move to a small house we had found to rent just outside London. Peggy had given us the bare essentials of furniture as a wedding gift and my darling mother had promised us all our linen, blankets and so on. We also had a substantial cheque from Grandmother, so we felt that we were a very fortunate young couple. We had both suffered hardships and loss in the war years, but now a new life was to begin and we were full of hope for the future.

We were married on a lovely summer day. A neighbour looked after Andy, and my beloved mother and dear friend Peggy were able to be present. After the ceremony, Peggy brought Andy to Kingsbridge station, and they stood together in the sunshine as our train started to move. The sun shone on Andy's blonde curls, she waved vigorously, and as the train carried us away George and I hugged each other. Our married life had begun.

Part Two

I cannot praise a fugitive and cloistered virtue, unexercised and unbreathed, that never sallies out and sees her adversary, but slinks out of the race, where that immortal garland is to be run for, not without dust and heat.

John Milton

All, everything that I understand, I understand only because I love.

Leo Tolstoy

Chapter 4

George and I set up home in the house we had agreed to rent in Amersham, just outside London, and George returned to his existing job. Andy was now over five years old and I arranged for her to spend mornings only at a small local school. She already loved books – Peggy and I had taught her to read before my marriage – so her first days at school were happy ones.

She was a self-reliant little girl. One morning during the summer holidays she announced that she was leaving home for a while. Very seriously she packed a bag of sweets, an apple and a bottle of water into her school satchel, kissed me goodbye, and walked off down the road. I did not want to interfere with something that seemed to mean so much to her, but I ran upstairs and watched anxiously from my bedroom window which had a view of the whole length of the quiet tree-lined road. Andy walked slowly right to the end of our road. Then she paused and sat down on the kerb. She sat there for about fifteen minutes eating her apple, then she took a drink from her water bottle, fastened it back in her satchel, got up and walked solemnly home. She came round the side of the house into the back door and called out, 'I'm back, Mummy.' I replied calmly, 'Oh good.' And that was the end of leaving home.

In February 1948 George came home one day and told me that he had been offered a wonderful chance to go and work in Durban, South Africa, on a year's contract for an advertising agency. If he accepted we would sail in early April. Ever since boyhood he had wanted to go to Africa and I could see that this opportunity meant a great deal to him. But I was secretly appalled by the thought of leaving Mother. I phoned her and asked her over for the day – she was now living in Sussex with Pam and Rodney – and when she arrived I poured out all my misery. I had thought that she would try to persuade me to stay in England – she had always bitterly resented anything or anyone causing us to be apart for long – but to my surprise she told me that I should agree to live in Durban for a year.

'After all, you chose to marry George,' she said. 'And now I think you owe him this time in Africa.' I should have known that my wonderful mother would say the right thing. We decided that if possible Mother would join us in Durban for at least part of our stay there.

The three of us sailed from Southampton in the *Cape Town Castle*. It was a lovely sunny afternoon, a perfect spring day, and I wondered sadly if Africa could ever be as precious to me as England was. Mother did not see us off – we had said our good-bye in private. I could only cling to the hope that she would indeed be able to follow soon.

Life in Durban was very pleasant. With the help of a mortgage from George's firm, we bought a large bungalow in a place called Hillary, on a hillside outside Durban. I was glad of the breeze on the hill – the heat was just starting to be oppressive. All the houses and bungalows were built up from the ground on concrete pillars as the white ants or termites ate everything not made of concrete. There were ant hills everywhere, even under the houses. There were also large flying ants which were attracted by the lights at night. As soon as they flew into the light, their wings dropped off and the bodies fell on the floor. Fortunately we had wire screens for the windows and the ants fell on to the *stoep* to be swept up by the natives and roasted. They were considered a great delicacy.

I had been told by the wife of one of George's colleagues that

I could not move into a house without at least one servant. It just wasn't 'done'. So I interviewed several Zulu and Bantu women, and then Lena came to see me. She was Bantu, aged forty, very quiet and I liked her at once. I arranged for her to meet us at our new house in two weeks' time and I gave her two weeks' wages in advance as she had no money at all. Our colleague's wife was outraged at this and insisted that I would never see Lena again – but I knew she was wrong. She arrived at our new house the day we moved in. Her living quarters consisted of a stone hut called a *kyah* in the garden. I had bought a bed, a chair, a rug and a small dressing table with a mirror for her. My new neighbours, who called before we had even unpacked, were very annoyed at what they called my 'pampering a servant'. Apparently their house girls slept on a sack in their huts without even the luxury of a bed.

In the cool of the early mornings I would drive George to work, with Lena in the back of our car, and then with a large basket balanced on Lena's head, we would walk through the many stalls in the market and buy paw-paws, grapes, peaches, avacado pears and Queen pineapples – delicacies then unknown in post-war England – for one shilling each. There were all kinds of fresh vegetables, fish, and big, black lobsters. I hated plunging the lobsters into boiling water. I would take a cowardly stroll in the garden whenever we had them for supper, leaving Lena to deal with them.

Andy made friends with a little native boy called Michael. They were the same age and played together every day. One Sunday, George and I took both children to the beach at Umshlanga Rocks for a picnic and a swim. The children were paddling in the rock pools when I suddenly heard a shout: 'Get off the beach, you nigger child. This beach is for whites only.' Looking up in amazement, I saw two schoolgirls standing on a rock a few hundred yards away. They were shouting at Michael. Without a word he turned sadly away and began to walk up the beach. I ran and brought him back. I was furious. His mother and father were Zulus and in my opinion the beach *belonged* to that once-proud race. This was their Africa after all; it was we who were the interlopers.

The general election had taken place just after we arrived in Durban. Everyone had gone to bed confident that General Smuts's United Party would be returned to govern once more, only to wake up next morning to the devastating reality that South Africa now had a Nationalist government. Their first action was to release all the people interned during the war for pro-Nazi and anti-British actions. They were now committed to a policy of increasingly strong apartheid throughout the country. Ineffectual as Smuts may have been, at least his party did not pursue racist policies, backed up now by the Dutch Reformed Church. In their so-called Christian eyes, men were by no means brothers.

Ill-health forced me to cut short my year in South Africa. Soon after Andy's birth, I had developed an unusual blood disease, leucopenia; the primitive antibiotic I had been given plus the puerperal fever had injured my bone marrow, affecting the production of the white blood cells. My consultant in England had advised George to take me to South Africa where I could eat plenty of meat as protein was a great help in combating the disease. However, he failed to tell us that people with leucopenia cannot always stand great heat. Now, in Durban, the temperature was increasing rapidly. One particular day a hot wind blew across the city and suburbs, killing all the chickens at once. As the summer approached, I began to feel really ill. Now our doctor told us that I would never be able to live through the tropical heat of summers in Natal and advised me to return to England. George still had three months of his contract to fulfil, but he booked a passage home for Andy and me. We were to sail from Cape Town so that I would not have to face the sea trip round the African coast. Andy and I were to travel on the Orange Express, a forty-eight hour train trip between Durban and Cape Town. George saw us off. I felt very sad and I knew he did too, but we could not risk my becoming even more seriously ill. Poor little Andy cried bitterly as she clung to her darling Dadlings, as she called him. We waved until he was out of sight, alone on the platform. It was our first parting since our marriage.

It was on the boat trip to England that I realized for the first time that I had truly fallen in love with George at last. Now my marriage was what I had always known marriage must be for me – indestructible, unchanging and for ever. I had loved George for a long time, but loving and being 'in love' as well make a very big difference. I knew that he had been hoping and waiting for me to feel the things for him that he had always felt so strongly for me. I wrote him a long, long letter, and told him what had happened to me – that I had fallen in love with my own husband. I posted it in Teneriffe.

We arrived in England just before Christmas. It was bitterly cold after the warmth and sunshine of South Africa. We had arranged to stay with friends in Surrey. Mother could not have us as she was still with Pam and Rodney, but the day after our arrival I went to see her. It was a wonderful reunion.

Early in the new year I became suddenly very ill with my leucopenia and had to spend three long weary months in a private nursing home run by nuns. They were wonderfully kind and gentle, but my recovery was slow, hampered by my fretting for George and concern about Andy, who was staying with family friends in Surrey and attending a weekly boarding school in Guildford. She was brought to visit me some weekends, but cried and clung to my hands when it was time for her to leave. She had to be removed by force. She, who had always been secure, was now suddenly insecure and uncertain, apart from her father and from me. I knew how she was suffering and suffered with her. When I recovered I asked Peggy, who was still living in Devonshire, if Andy and I could stay with her again to wait for George's return. He was due home any day now. So we went back to lovely Devonshire, and when we saw the banks yellow with primroses, Andy and I hugged each other in the joyous expectation that our unhappiness was over for good.

The weeks slipped by almost unnoticed. Andy and I were enjoying the lovely summer weather with all the wild flowers that she loved so much, and it was wonderful to be with Peggy again to share our prayers and Bible reading. Andy was a temporary pupil in the local school and when one of the children asked her what her father did in the war (they were all trying to out-do one another in glory), she told them that he had learned to blow perfect smoke rings and had played the piano in Chittagong! When Andy related this at tea time, she said, '*That* squashed them, Mummy. They were very impressed by what Daddy did. Their fathers had only flown planes and things like that.' Peggy and I fell about with laughter.

George's contract in Durban had been over for many weeks now but there was no sign of his return. He had written frequent long, loving letters at first, but now his letters became brief and more and more infrequent and I began to be very worried. I was writing to him weekly telling him of my deep new-found love for him and how much Andy and I missed and needed him. I felt that there must be something seriously wrong. By now I had no money in England, all our capital was tied up in our house and car in Africa, and as George's allowance had stopped I was forced to draw National Assistance, most of which I gave to Peggy for our food. I insisted that we could not be kept indefinitely by her, generous friend that she had always been.

At last, six months after our arrival in Devon and nine months after our leaving Cape Town, I wrote to Grandmother, who still lived alone in her little flat in Cheshire, and asked her to lend me the fare to fly out and see George. She agreed at once, and urged me not to delay any longer.

'Foreign countries are full of temptation for unattached young men,' she counselled wisely. So I cabled George to say that I was flying out in a week's time and had a cable by return, 'Sailing for home next week.'

Ten days later I received an air-mail letter from him posted in Cape Town on his way home. It was full of love and hope for the future. 'Now that you truly love me we will be a real family at last,' he wrote. I could hardly wait to greet him. Peggy was to keep Andy while I met George off the boat train in London, and I had planned a few days alone with him before collecting her. I went up to London the day before he was to arrive and booked a double room in a pleasant little hotel overlooking Hyde Park. Then the moment that I had so longed for came and I was waiting at the station barrier. Suddenly George was there, tanned and fit. He gave up his ticket and I rushed into his arms. I told him about the hotel and we took a taxi there, but there had been a telegram waiting for George at Southampton to say that his father had died and the funeral was in two days' time. We sat by the gas fire in the hotel bedroom and I said how sorry I was about his father and that of course we would both go up to Birkenhead the next morning. I went to put my arms round him, but he turned away, lit a cigarette and told me that he wanted a divorce. He had fallen in love with Andy's pretty young school mistress in South Africa.

I was stunned, so shocked that I could not speak. I felt as though I was dying inside. After a while I began to talk to him, to George, my husband, the man I loved, Andy's father. I told him that I understood fully how sad and disappointed he had been, alone in Durban, and that I knew that it was only natural that he had needed female companionship. I said that we belonged together; we always had – only I had not fully known this until we left Cape Town, and I told him definitely that I would not consent to a divorce at present.

'Get a job in London again and we will make a home together for Andy,' I said, with a calmness I was far from feeling. 'If you ask me again in twelve months' time I will set you free.' I was so totally sure that by then he would have forgotten this young girl and be my beloved husband again.

We slept on opposite sides of the bed that night. I lay awake until dawn, numb with misery and sudden shock, the most dreadful shock I have ever had.

The next morning George went to Birkenhead alone – to his father's funeral – and I started to look for a place where we could live near to London. I found a flat on Richmond Hill and phoned George to arrange to meet him there after the funeral. He sounded very reluctant, but I was my mother's daughter, with her strong will, and I insisted that he should at least try to take up our life together again, for Andy if not for me. I asked Peggy to bring Andy up to London the next day. Like a true friend, she did as I asked without asking any questions, and Andy gave George a rapturous greeting.

It was only a week until he once more had a good job in advertising and we three settled down to a more or less normal life. Andy was eight that year. On her birthday, George took many photos of his very happy little girl in her blue party dress with her halo of blonde curls. Very slowly he began to thaw towards me, and I knew that my faith in our love for each other had been justified.

In Richmond I began to attend the Baptist Church run by the Reverend Alan Redpath. I took Andy with me; George had still not found his own belief in God in a personal way. Now I felt that I wanted to start a Christian community, a place where followers of Christ could be together and share their lives. Like a wonderful answer to prayer, I heard through Peggy of a large old manor house to let near Sevenoaks, Kent. There were ten bedrooms, various sitting rooms, a huge kitchen, and a large lovely old garden completely enclosed by a high wall. I was sure that this was the place we were looking for and rented it on a year's lease. I already had two young couples from the church congregation who were ready to join us, then along came an elderly friend of Peggy's. In spite of all George's doubts (which later proved justified) I had the bit firmly between my teeth and went ahead at full speed. Somehow we found enough furniture (once more my dear Gran helped us out) and on a crisp and lovely day in early December 1950 we moved into our new home. The house was a rambling old Elizabethan mansion, with central heating and hot water provided by a terrible old boiler which burnt coke and sat in an outhouse like some fat old monster. It was poor George's job to stoke and maintain this temperamental machine, and a formidable task it was all that winter. We had divided the house up into private sleeping and living quarters with shared bathrooms (there were two); at first we shared the big old kitchen, but women find sharing a kitchen amicably is almost impossible, so the men converted two other rooms into kitchens for their wives, and all was well.

Just before Christmas two unexpected events took place, both very unhappy. First, my darling mother once more slipped a disc in her spine and, as this was the fourth time this had happened, the surgeon she consulted insisted on taking her into the London Hospital in Whitechapel and fusing the bones of the spine together. This was a painful operation and afterwards Mother was to spend three months in hospital in a plaster cast from hips to armpits, to allow the bones to knit together. A week after Mother's operation, Pam phoned me in a terrible state. She was crying hysterically. Rodney's father, John, had been killed in an accident in Scotland. He was still flying, this time for the Admiralty, and was walking away from the plane he had just landed when an incoming aircraft had a burst tyre on the runway, skidded round and ran over him, killing him instantly. Pam said that he had intended to join her and Rodney for Christmas, with the possibility of a reconciliation. Now poor Pam was in a state of shock. I rushed down to Sussex and brought her and Rodney back to the Manor for Christmas. I knew Pam could not manage without Mother's support at such a time.

In the new year Pam went to live with a friend in Sussex. She could not keep the large house she and Mother had been renting. Now that Mother was to be so long away, I suggested to Pam that we should keep Rodney with us for a year to give her a chance to organize her life again. Pam agreed. Rodney and Andy were very fond of each other. He was nearly seven and she was now eight years and four months. They shared a room and were like brother and sister.

Rodney took some time to settle down. The morning after his mother left, I gave him a boiled egg which he threw on the floor. He refused to eat 'such muck', as he called it. The same thing happened with the rice pudding for lunch. Andy watched in horror while Rodney threw his helping across the table. It was a long tussle between my small nephew and me and it was fortunate for him that I love all children so much and understand them so well. As time went by, however, he began to eat all I put before him and ran wild with Andy in our big garden. On hot week-ends George put the lawn sprinkler on and the two children ran naked in and out of the cool shower.

When Mother's time in a plaster bed ended, she too spent several months with us at the Manor slowly recovering her strength. She loved the old house and shady garden, and of course being with me again. It was a great joy for us to be together – like old times – but once she was fully recovered she felt it her duty to rejoin Pam and help her find a place where they could make a home for Rodney. I tried to persuade her to remain with us, we were so happy together – but when Mother made up her mind about anything, she was unmovable as a rock.

In the weeks before Christmas 1951 Pam wrote to say that she and Mother had found a cottage to rent in Sussex. She came to fetch Rodney. When they were ready to leave, I carried Rodney's suitcase out to the car. He flung his arms round me and burst into tears.

'Please, please let me come again soon,' he begged, but I looked over his head at Pam's face. As we waved good-bye from the gate I felt that Pam would not want to part from Rod again.

Earlier that year, in September, I had decided that as a practising Christian I should do as Jesus told all believers to do and be baptized. I affirmed my faith in the Baptist Church which Andy and I went to on Sundays. Andy and Peggy came to the service and saw my total immersion in water in the same way that John had baptized Jesus in the River Jordan in the New Testament. I wished very much that George could join in my beliefs, I loved him so deeply, but it still seemed too big a step for him to take.

Our Christian community at the Manor had not really developed in the way I had hoped it would. A few people (including George) were doing all the work and the others just idling. We were supposed to grow all our own vegetables and fruit, but it seemed as though only George and I ever did any real gardening. So when our lease for the Manor was nearly over, George and I decided not to ask for a renewal. We were both worn out by the big old house and garden. I think that we both realized that our going abroad again was inevitable sooner or later – we both loved to travel – so we now rented a modern house in Sevenoaks. The various members of our little community-that-never-was went their several ways.

For the past two years I had been suffering from an over-active thyroid. I developed a large swelling in my neck, a very rapid pulse and my hands shook badly. My doctor wanted me to have an operation but I was not willing to agree to enter hospital. However, at a medical conference in London I had heard of a new radio-active treatment which was being used in Sweden – it was considered too dangerous for use in England. I decided to try to get to Sweden somehow and have this treatment. I told George all this, of course, and then a wonderful thing happened. George was offered a very good job for a year in an advertising agency in Stockholm. This time I had no doubts about leaving Mother for a year. My need for treatment was too urgent.

We sailed from Tilbury in October 1952. Stockholm is built on thirteen lakes, all connected by bridges, and was a breath-taking sight at night when all the lights were reflected in the water. We found a flat in Grev Magnegarten, just off Strandvagen, which is a kind of promenade along a lake, with quite large cargo ships moored alongside. I began the difficult task of shopping in a city where all the nearby shopkeepers spoke no English and I spoke no Swedish. Even buying simple items such as bread and milk was a horrendous task. As for buying toothpaste and, worse still, toilet paper – I found it almost impossible. Then there was the laundry. We could not wash and dry clothes in the flat, so all our things were collected and delivered by a laundry van, and the poor driver suffered greatly I am afraid. I would say to him the only whole Swedish phrase I knew, '*Jag skule vilya ha min twät idag*,' which means, 'I want my laundry today,' and from him would pour a torrent of Swedish, whereupon I repeated my phrase even more firmly. This went on for several weeks, the poor man became more and more depressed, and I more and more frustrated. George's English-speaking secretary happened to be there one day, and she explained to me that the torrent of Swedish from the van driver simply meant, 'Certainly, I will bring it today!' So she advised him just to say, '*Ya, ya,*' to me, and we all heaved a sigh of relief.

As the autumn and winter closed in on us, the days became shorter. It was dark in that flat now from three in the afternoon to 10.30 next morning. The weather became more and more depressing. It rained almost incessantly, and the electric light was on in the flat almost all day. A fellow Englishman who also worked for the agency told me that the Swedish autumn is well known for its depressive quality, and he said there were many suicides during this season because of the weather, but he may have been joking.

In early November, I made an appointment to see the consultant I had met at the medical conference in London. He was at the famous Karolinska Institute, reputed to be one of the finest hospitals in the world. He examined me and agreed to give me the treatment I was so anxious to have, a very large dose of radio-active iodine. He told me to come in two weeks' time for this, and then issued a stern warning: 'Under *no* circumstance must you become pregnant for at least a year. You must promise me this.' I laughed and told him that there was no chance of that at all. George and I had wanted another child ever since our marriage, but we had now given up all hope.

So my great day came. I went along to the hospital and was given a small glass of colourless, tasteless liquid which the doctor handled with tongs. He wore a lead apron to safeguard himself. My symptoms were intensified at first but at the end of three weeks, I began to feel very, very much better and the swelling in my neck began to disappear, but a week later, the week before Christmas, my period failed to arrive. I thought this might be the effect of the treatment and carried on decorating our flat and wrapping gifts for George and Andy. I had already posted parcels to Peggy, Mother, Pam and Rodney. However, by the time my period was three weeks late, I had developed a bad pain in my back. I phoned George's secretary and asked her to find an English-speaking doctor for me. I went along to him the next day, taking a specimen of my water as he had requested. Back at the flat I took boiling hot baths to try to help my period to arrive and to ease the really bad pain. Two days later the doctor phoned – the test on my water was positive. I was pregnant! He was very alarmed and arranged for me to see my former consultant at the Karolinska at once. He urged me to go by taxi.

I was shown into Professor Wynblad's room and he was very, very angry indeed. He walked up and down and, in his sparse English, he reminded me of my promise to him before he gave me the dose of radio-active medicine.

'You fool, you will have a deformed child now, almost certainly a cretin,' he shouted.

He wanted to terminate my pregnancy there and then, but I refused. We had longed for this baby for so long. Nothing was going to rob us of at least the slim chance that it might be normal. I was kept in bed for two months, not even allowed to put a foot out, and had twice daily injections of a hormone to try to stop my threatened abortion. Then the pain in my back went and I was allowed to return to the flat.

Andy was wildly excited by the thought of the coming baby. She was a wonderful help. I was often very sick in the mornings, and she would bring a bowl of warm water and sponge my face tenderly. She went each day to do the shopping at the little local store, armed with a list written in Swedish by George. Our little daughter was by now ten years old, and growing up fast.

I dreaded the thought of having the baby in hospital where no English was spoken. My recent stay had been a nightmare. Every time I wanted anything it took so long to find the only nurse who understood a little of my language. Also I longed to be with Mother again at that time. So my patient, understanding husband suggested that I should return to England in the spring, taking Andy and arrange to have Mother with me. He had to finish his contract, of course, but this meant that he would be with us in the October, a month after our baby's birth. This time I knew that all would be well with George. We were a very happy little family, our happiness completed by the hope of a normal, healthy baby.

Mother had managed to rent a flat for me in an old house in Tonbridge, Kent, once more through our old friend the *Lady*. I found a good private school for Andy. She needed a school with small classes as she was behind her age group because of all our moves. She hated the school. Every morning she cried and begged me to keep her at home.

'I want to look after you and the baby,' she pleaded, but in vain. Much as I loved her, I knew this was something she had to learn to accept. Within a few weeks, however, she had a 'best friend', Bernadette, who often stayed with us for weekends. One day I was in the kitchen and I saw a basket going up and down on a rope in front of the window. Andy's bedroom was overhead, and she and Bernadette were giving rides to our very unhappy cat.

Bernadette's mother was a state registered nurse and she and I became friendly. However, she expressed great concern about my coming baby and told me that she felt sure that I would almost certainly give birth to a retarded child. This opinion I felt she could have kept to herself – I was worried enough already.

Mother did not come to live with me as I had hoped. She remained in Sussex with Pam, but visited us two or three times weekly. She did come to stay for my confinement, arriving a few days before the baby was due.

Once more my child was delivered with forceps. Just before I went under the anaesthetic there was a robin sitting on a bough outside the window, singing his lovely autumn song. We had agreed to call a boy-child Robin, so I felt that this must be a good omen for my baby's normality. When I opened my eyes the sister was holding out a little bundle, a tiny exact replica of George – our son Robin. As far as we could see, he was a perfectly normal baby, in spite of Professor Wynblad's forebodings. But we had yet to discover if his brain was normal.

A few weeks after Robin was born, George arrived from Sweden. He was thrilled to have a brand new son, but seemed a little put off by Robin's wrinkled, screwed-up face – he was a very plain baby. George had never lived with a very young child before. Andy was initially delighted with her new brother, but after George's return she began to grow jealous now that her father made such a fuss of him. George did not realize this, and was continually saying, 'Be quiet, you'll wake the baby.' One evening I heard her crying in her room. I sat down on her bed, she flung her arms round my neck and said, 'Mummy, I'm so wicked. I pray every night that Robin will die. *Why* did you have him, wasn't I enough?' Of course I reassured and comforted her, but I know now that that was not sufficient. I should have asked for medical help for her. Such deep jealousy at eleven years old would not go away by itself. In my ignorance I thought that she would grow out of these feelings, but I was so wrong. They grew deeper and deeper, and after this one outburst, Andy kept them buried away out of sight.

Chapter 5

With the arrival of Robin, our family was complete. As the months went by so it became apparent that my son was mentally normal, in fact very intelligent for his age. We now felt that the time had come to buy a house and settle down in England. In March 1954 we bought a house in Sevenoaks with our capital saved from Africa and a mortgage. But no sooner had we finished unpacking and settling in than George came home one evening and told me that he had accepted a job in Cape Town on a two-year contract and we were to sail in early June. We decided that we would let our new home furnished so that it would be waiting for us when we returned.

Mother spent a day or two with us before we left, but it was a strain. She interfered with George's treatment of Andy and Robin – he was ignoring Andy and spoiling Robin, she said. In spite of this, we once again asked her to join us in South Africa for a while and she promised to come if it could be arranged. Unlike me, Mother did not enjoy the idea of foreign travel and I thought it unlikely that she would really make the voyage.

Being in Cape Province was totally different from living in Natal. The climate was dry and sunny, not oppressive as in Durban. There was a far less strict colour bar in many ways; people of all colours used the buses and the same shops, both of which were forbidden in Durban. The majority of non-Europeans in Cape Town were Cape Coloureds, a mixture of Hottentot and Malayan, with a dash of the blood of the old Dutch settlers, and their skins varied from very dark to almost as fair as mine. They were a very independent people, who looked down on the African native races, the Zulus, Bantus, Xcorsa. Many a Cape Coloured girl 'passed for white' as they called it, meaning that she lived and worked undetected amongst Europeans.

There were frequent cocktail parties in George's new agency, and at one of them a secretary calmly told me what I thought was a shameful story. Nora said that some months earlier she had become very friendly with another young girl who had joined the staff. They had lunch together every day and the girl was a frequent visitor at Nora's flat. Then one day she asked Nora to come to her home for Sunday lunch. When Nora arrived the door was opened by a Cape Coloured woman, whom Nora presumed was a maid.

'Imagine my utter horror when my friend introduced her as her *mother*,' Nora said. 'I picked up my gloves and ran out of the house, and the girl never came to work at the agency again.'

Nora said that she had been so conditioned by her upbringing that she would have been physically sick had she sat down to lunch with a coloured woman. She knew that there was something wrong with such total prejudice but was not able to change it.

While we were living in South Africa this time, the Government brought in the Pass Laws, which have been so rightly and bitterly criticized all over the world. The new laws meant that all non-Europeans must carry a pass on them at all times, stating their name, address, place of work and their race. The latter had been established by the enforced production of birth certificates going back three generations. If you were found by police to be without a pass (searches were frequent), no explanation or excuse was accepted, you were marched straight to jail. One of George's colleagues told him that one week-end he sent his native garden boy to buy some cigarettes at a little shop two streets away, and the unfortunate man left his jacket on a garden seat with his pass in the pocket. He did not return, and it took his employer many weeks to trace him to where he was being held in jail. The police had only to walk to the house where the native said he worked and had left his pass, but they preferred to throw him into prison. He would have stayed there indefinitely had not his employer cared enough to look for him. It is no wonder that African native jails are bursting at the seams.

We rented a house in Hout Bay and the news of our arrival had gone round the native girls – several called asking for work. I did not see one I really liked until Ivy came one day. She was a Bantu, aged twenty-four. Her mother had been a teacher in a Bantu missionary school, so Ivy spoke good English. The Government were closing all the mission schools, as they did not intend to allow the Bantu people to be educated above the level of 'hewing wood and drawing water'. In other words, above servant level. Ivy was unmarried, but she had a six-month-old baby, Stephen, living with Ivy's mother in a native village outside Cape Town. She loved chidren and carried Robin round on her back in a kind of sling, as all native women carry babies.

One afternoon the weather turned chilly and I decided to light a fire. I knelt down and was putting paper and wood in place, when Ivy came hurrying in.

'What are you doing, Madam?' she asked. 'Madam must not do work like that.' I explained that in England during the war all housework was done by 'Madam'.

'Surely not washing clothes and cleaning floors,' Ivy said in horror. She could scarcely believe that white people could possibly be forced to do such menial tasks.

When I went shopping, Ivy told me to ask for 'girls' meat' for her – all women servants are known as 'girls' – as her diet was mealie meal and girls' meat twice weekly. I tried to give Ivy the same food that we ate, but she was quite firm in her polite refusal and each day cooked a pan of mealie porridge for herself which she ate both hot and cold.

Not long after she arrived, she had flu. I insisted that she should stay in bed and I took her food in to her, to her acute embarrassment. I asked her if she would like something to read, thinking of lending her one of Andy's books. To my surprise she said, 'There is a book in the sitting room I would like, please Madam. I saw it when I was dusting.' It was *Mr Polly* by H. G. Wells. And yet even educated Ivy was full of the contradictions I seemed to meet everywhere in this fascinating country. She told me one day that her baby Stephen was very ill with gastro-enteritis which was a killer disease amongst both native and coloured babies. There was an almost total lack of hygiene or sanitation in the villages and compounds where they lived outside the city. I had seen the shanty town in one part of Cape Town, hovels made of bits of cardboard and corrugated iron, just thrown together, garbage lying everywhere, and stray dogs and small children sitting about in the dirt. I gave Ivy the week-end off to visit Stephen, and when she returned on Monday she told me cheerfully that Stephen would soon be well.

'My mother, she arranged for a sheep to be sacrificed,' she beamed – Ivy who read H. G. Wells and went to the local Baptist Church every Sunday. But the sheep didn't work and poor little Stephen died a week later. Our local European doctor happened to be having dinner at our house a few days later, and I mentioned the death of Ivy's baby.

'Good,' he said, 'that's one less black brat to grow up.' He was not invited to the house again.

It was while we were in Cape Town that Mother wrote to tell me that Pam was about to be married to a local farmer whom she had met through attending horse shows and the local hunt. Pam wrote to me too, joyful letters about her coming marriage. It had all happened very suddenly. Her future husband was very well off and kind to Rodney. They were married in the spring of 1955 and both Pam and Rod now had a secure future.

When George's contract ended in June 1956, he was asked to stay on for a while and offered a permanent job as personal creative assistant to the 'old man' with a view to running the agency when he retired. It was an attractive prospect, which we discussed a lot over the next few months. But it was a difficult decision to make for two reasons. The first one was that Grandmother had been writing to me for months begging us to return home. She had given up her flat in Cheshire as she was not really able to look after herself and had moved to a guest-house in Tunbridge Wells. Mother, since Pam's marriage, was renting an unfurnished flat nearby so that she could at least keep a watch on Gran. They still seemed to hate each other, however, and quarrelled all the time. Gran said she hated her lodging and could she live with me for her remaining years – she was eighty-five – as she had always loved me dearly.

The second reason concerned Andy and Robin. We had a wonderful life in Cape Town, with all the fresh fruit and other good food, plus the perfect climate which enabled us to spend so much time outdoors, swimming, surfing and enjoying the kind of life that could not be ours if George worked in London again. Andy was nearly thirteen and like an awkward, long-legged colt. She had her father's deep blue eyes and blonde hair down to her waist. Robin was talking fluently by now; in fact he hardly paused for breath all day. His little body was plump and brown – he was a very winning little boy. But it was the development of their characters that was to me the cause for concern. They were both waited on hand and foot by the servants. One day I saw Robin, aged nearly three, clap his hands and say sharply, 'Come here, boy,' to a man old enough to be his grandfather. Andy had a less demanding nature, yet even she just dropped her clothes everywhere and a maid ran her daily bath for her. If we were to live in South Africa for the next ten or twenty years, I felt that their sense of values would be all wrong and they would not have the ethics that are the only hope of a solution in maintaining the standards of behaviour without which all nations are surely doomed.

The Cape seemed to us both to be an earthly paradise, the beauty of the mountains and sea, the lush growth of trees and flowers, and the wonderful sunny climate even in wintertime. But there were so many man-made problems to consider. In such a country, with its friendly, smiling natives and coloured people, life should have been so good, but how could it be when there was so much cruelty and oppression?

Now it was once more spring in Cape Town, and surrounded by all the loveliness of the wattle in bloom and the vines shooting up in the dark soil of Constantia Valley, we made our decision. I wrote home to Mother and Grandmother telling them that we would be sailing in November, leaving the hot sunshine of the Cape for cold and foggy England. On our last evening, George and I drove alone up to the top of the 'Neck', where the road dips down towards Hout Bay, and we stood looking across all the unbelievable country spread out below, dotted with little farms and houses. We felt very sad and reluctant to be leaving, but we knew that for us it had been the only thing possible. Perhaps the political system would change in a few years time, justice and compassion would begin to emerge, and we could return to this wonderful and much-loved country.

As soon as we were back in England and settled in our house in Sevenoaks, dear old Grandmother came to live with us. When George and I drove to Tunbridge Wells to fetch her and her belongings, she was really pathetic. She thought that we were taking her to live in an old people's home and tears ran down her wrinkled cheeks. We tried to reassure her, but she was not able to believe us until she was installed in the ground floor room I had made ready (our former dining room) and Robin and Andy greeted her lovingly.

Gran was not able to climb stairs now and as we had no washing or bathing facilities downstairs, we felt that we would have to find a bigger house to meet her needs. Also Andy and Robin were growing up and needed more space. Once more I went house-hunting and we found a large old house in a little village between Sevenoaks and Tunbridge Wells. Our move to Rhoden, as it was called, pleased Mother greatly as it was only a short bus-ride away from the flat where she was now living since Pam's marriage.

Before we moved, George and I had decided to foster a little coloured boy whom we had seen in our local Dr Barnardo's (ever since Andy was three or four we had always held a

Christmas party for a group of children from Dr Barnardo's). We felt that this was in some way a gesture for all the native and coloured children in South Africa who were suffering so much because of European prejudice and oppression – a very small thing to do, but better than nothing. Phillip's father was a Nigerian student in London, his mother an English nurse, and as they were unmarried, Phillip had been put into Dr Barnardo's at a few weeks old. Now he was exactly the same age as Robin and we were determined that they should be brought up as brothers. We hoped to adopt Phillip legally at a later date. So when we moved to Rhoden our family consisted of Andy, aged nearly fifteen, Robin and Phillip both four years old, Grandma now aged eighty-six, and our two Pekingese dogs.

We had arranged for Gran to stay in a small private nursing home in Sevenoaks while we actually moved house. She had fallen one night at home getting out of bed and cut her forehead and we thought that she would be safer at night during the upheaval. However, she made a great nuisance of herself while she was there. Just as Mother's obsession was suicide, so Gran's was changing her will, which she had done at least once a year since Grandpa's death so long ago. Now she wanted to change her will again and the matron at the home begged me to help so that there could be some peace for the nursing staff. So I asked Gran's solicitor to call, and of course she discussed it all with me.

In the existing will, Mother had the income for life on a third of the capital, and Pam and I the income only on the rest, the entire capital being tied up on the great-grandchildren. For some time, there had been trouble between Pam and Gran. Now Gran decided that she wanted to cut Pam out of her will entirely and leave the interest for life to Mother, with the whole trust to come to me when Mother died. But I told her that no matter how she felt, Pam was still her granddaughter, and I urged her to leave something to her. Eventually Grandmother made her will in the nursing home, with her solicitor and doctor present. She left the interest on all her capital to Mother for her lifetime, £2,000 pounds for Pam and the rest to me, both on Mother's death. The matron said that from that moment on Gran was satisfied, and there was once more peace all round for her remaining four weeks' stay with them.

In the new house I made one of the entertaining rooms into a bed-sitting room for Gran. It looked out on to the old-fashioned rose garden – I knew how much she loved flowers. Robin and Phil shared a bedroom. To my surprise it was Phil who was jealous of my love and attention, not Robin. In fact I had to restrain Rob from giving in to Phillip all the time. They both went to a small nursery school in the mornings, and George and I were looking forward to adopting Phillip, when out of the blue I had a letter from Dr Barnardo's saying that his mother now wanted to visit him. Of course this had to be allowed, but Phillip had never seen her, and called me 'Mummy', as Robin and Andy did.

This young woman, whom I shall call Doris, told us that she was thinking of marrying a London bus driver – not even Phillip's father. We now learned that she had three other children, all by different men. Two of the children were living with her and one was in care. She remarked casually that she would probably take Phil away from us if she did marry, and as soon as she left (Phillip was very confused and upset) I wrote a strong letter to Dr Barnardo's, asking them if they could prevent this woman, who was a total stranger to Phil, from taking him away from the security of our home and our love. But the reply was negative. Legally she was his mother, and we could only hope and pray that she would care enough for the child's happiness to leave him with us.

It was now 1958. Grandmother had been with us for nine months and was eighty-seven years old. She became ill quite suddenly, with acute kidney trouble and senile dementia, which meant that she sometimes became confused and would get up and wander about at night. One night she tried to climb the stairs, but I heard her and put her safely back in bed. I had engaged an elderly trained nurse to care for Gran at night and I looked after her in the daytime. On her bed-side table she had a little bell which she could pick up and ring if she wanted me at any time of the day or night. She loved what she called 'our little talks', and often decided to have one when I was serving a meal or in the bath. Robin and Phillip were always taken in to say good-night to her, and on her good, lucid days, she chatted away to them and kissed them both. She never once mentioned the difference in the colour of their skins. I used to wonder if she even noticed it.

Poor little old lady, she was quite tiny and during her days as a hospital matron had looked very like Queen Victoria. Now she became totally incontinent and her bed had to be changed at least twice a day. Because she was wet so often, she developed a very nasty sore on the base of her spine from lying or sitting in bed so much. Her doctor told us that it was really a breaking down of skin tissue due to old age. The sore became extremely painful during the last weeks of her life, and the doctor prescribed a strong painkiller, but even so Gran suffered a great deal. While the nurse slept in the day, my sturdy daily help Florrie helped me to lift Gran out on to her commode so that she lay in a wet bed as little as possible. Sunday was the nurse's day off and as Florrie did not work week-ends, George and I had to manage alone. Grandmother loved George, and she was so ashamed and apologetic when he lifted her out of the wet bed. She had always been a very fastidious person and the poor dear seemed to be in her right mind just when George had to lift her. She suffered more and more, both physically and in her wandering mind, and I prayed and prayed that she would die peacefully and soon. I thought, and still think, that it is so wrong for the very old and incurable to linger and suffer this way.

Then one bright and lovely October day, my dear Gran died, so peacefully and with her hand held closely in mine. I knelt at her bedside while she slipped away, and asked God to take care of her. A few days before her death, she had suddenly sat up straight in her bed, and with a look of joy on her face said very clearly and firmly, 'Jesus loves me.' I replied, 'Of course he does,' and she had sunk back into her semi-conscious doze.

I phoned Mother to tell her that Grandmother was gone, and she came the short bus journey to help me with all the things that have to be done when someone dies. We were standing by the study door, with Gran's coffin on the table, and I told her that Gran had made a new will before coming to live with us, a fact that Gran had made me promise not to reveal to anyone until her death. When I explained all this to Mother, she became very, very angry. She started shouting that Gran was a wicked old woman, an evil old woman, in spite of the fact that Mother was much better off under the new will. She would, however, now have no power over the distribution of Gran's estate. Also she was furious that Pam would only finally receive £2,000, although she knew that Pam and Gran had not got on well.

I was deeply shocked by this behaviour. It was so unlike Mother as I knew her; but she was changing in some way. We were no longer so close and she seemed full of a bitterness against life that I had never seen in her before. Of course, she was now living on her own and her health was poor. She developed Paget's disease (which she was to suffer from for the rest of her life; she became a registered addict for the drugs she had to take). She was becoming neurotic and complaining and altogether rather difficult to deal with. But I remembered a quotation that Mother had drilled into me in my teens:

> 'Love is not love that Alteration finds.
> No, 'tis an ever-fixed mark, that looks on tempests
> and is unchanged.'

And that was the way I still felt about her now.

Because Gran had stated in her will that she wished to be cremated, two doctors had to sign her death certificate. Her own doctor had already examined her. The day of the cremation I broke down completely. Dear Gran's coffin stood open on the table in our little study. I had picked a red rose earlier that morning, a last bloom before the frosts. Now it was in Gran's clasped hands. Her face was so peaceful, I knew that she was safe. The undertaker came to screw on the lid. Mother went with George and me to the crematorium. Pam was already there with her husband. We did not speak to each other and sat in different parts of the little chapel.

After Gran's funeral, I stood looking out of what had been her window. The roses were all dead now, and the hedge draped with lacy spider's webs hung with drops of November mist. I thought about the person who had been my much loved Grandmother. On my long childhood visits to her and Grandfather, I had followed her as she took the cook to the pantry every Monday morning and unlocked the door from the bunch of keys she always carried clipped to a belt round her waist. Then she would give the cook the rations for the coming week, for the cook, the parlour maid, the housemaid and the lowest being in the house, the kitchen maid. Gran would dole out tea, sugar, and margarine (the staff never tasted butter), which had to last them for a week. In no circumstances were they given any more before the following Monday. The food for the family was given out to cook every morning, again by Gran with her keys. The gardener, who was known as Baker, brought his own lunch, although I expect cook secretly gave him the odd cup of tea.

Gran had been obsessed by economy where there was no need for it at all. Grandpa had been a very successful doctor, but she had doled out everything as though there were an impending famine, even soap, toilet paper and so on. When Grandfather had retired and they moved to St Annes-on-Sea, they took with them an elderly Irish maid called Molly. Gran removed the electric light bulb from Molly's room and gave her a candle to carry up each night. And yet she had loved me so much (I suspected only me) that I had only to ask for something, and it was mine. I turned from the window, crossed the room and locked the door behind me. There were too many memories there for it to be used again yet.

The strain of the last few months of Gran's life, and the grief I felt now that she was gone, plus the long period of running a large house with Andy and the two little boys, all added up to a breakdown. Our doctor insisted that I should go away for a complete rest. I left the house and family in the capable hands of Jean, our nanny/help, and Florrie-the-daily, and went up to stay with Peggy, who was now sharing a house with a friend in Yorkshire. My three weeks' break passed all too quickly. We went for long walks on the moors and the cold northern air of November did a lot to heal my body and spirit. Peggy, her friend and I did some Bible study together, and prayed together. I returned home rested and refreshed in every way.

After my return, Phillip's mother arrived. She took away the screaming, terrified little boy who tried to cling on to Robin and to me. With Gran dead and Phillip gone, the house seemed too big and I had no real need of Jean, our nanny. George and I discussed moving again. He was all in favour of a smaller place. The house and our need to employ people to help had been swallowing George's salary almost before it was paid. I was no good at managing money anyway. Mother had not taught me anything about budgeting in my youth. We finally decided to move to Tunbridge Wells, where Mother had her flat. She seemed to have settled down and was enjoying life. Her chief occupation was watching the lovers in the adjoining park through her binoculars from her bedroom window.

Andy was now sixteen. We planned that she would attend the Tunbridge Wells School of Art. She had shown the promise of real talent as a painter very early on – when she was seven, in fact. Her teacher had shown me two of Andy's paintings, one of a squirrel and the other of a tree. She had suggested that we should consider sending Andy to an art college if she continued to paint so well. It looked as though Andy had inherited her father's gift and I had two artists in the family. Now we showed some of her paintings and drawings to her headmaster, and he agreed that she should continue with painting.

Sadly for her, though, art would always be second best. When she was fourteen I had taken her, on the advice of her ballet mistress, for an audition with Madame Ninette de Valois. Andy longed with all her heart to join the Royal Ballet. After a lengthy and careful inspection, Madame de Valois had taken me aside and asked Andy's exact age. When I told her, she said regretfully, 'I'm sorry, but although your daughter's dancing is excellent, she is already the maximum height we accept, and at fourteen is obviously going to grow taller.' Poor Andy, she cried for weeks and scorned my suggestion that she might like to train as a ballet teacher. It was all or nothing for her, as it had always been for me. So she reluctantly agreed to spend a year at art college and if she liked it to continue her studies there.

She had been brought up a Christian. We attended the Baptist Church in Tunbridge Wells together and now she felt ready to do as I had done so late in life and be baptized. Our pastor, who was a genuine believer, arranged for this to take place on a Sunday after evening service. Andy was very popular at the local college and five of her closest friends attended the service, but once more George felt unable to join us. Total immersion in the Baptist Church is always a moving experience, either to be part of or to witness, but I have never known it to be as it was on that Sunday. Andy stood in the water with our pastor and affirmed her faith in Jesus Christ. A total hush fell on the packed congregation and I knew without any doubt that we were all in the presence of our Lord. To confirm this wonderful feeling, all five of Andy's friends went up to the altar as Andy left the water and asked if they too might be shown how to follow Jesus. They all came from broken homes and were what was then called 'art student hippies', but in the course of the next few months all five were baptized and gave their hearts to Jesus as Andy and I had done.

In 1960 George decided that he could no longer travel to London – a journey of one and a half hours each morning and evening – and that we must live nearer to his work. I was reluctant to leave Tunbridge Wells as we now saw quite a lot of Mother. She had lunch with us every Sunday and Andy did all her shopping for her on Saturdays. However, George was determined, so once more we moved, this time to Richmond in Surrey. Andy had done two lovely oil paintings of the trees in our garden and these hung in our new flat, a reminder of the beauty of the Kent countryside.

Andy continued to study art in London. When she was eighteen, she started to share a flatlet with a fellow student.

In 1964, when she was twenty-two, she married a boy she had met through Richmond Drama Group. They had known each other for about a year.

They had only been married a month or two, however, when Andy told me that she was going to have a baby, and to my joy her first daughter was born.

It so happened that not long before Andy's marriage I myself had become pregnant, at forty-eight years old. The whole family had been wildly excited at the thought of a new baby. Andy had started knitting baby clothes and George's managing director had toasted him in champagne and sent me a dozen red roses. But I developed the same bad back pains as I had had in Sweden when Robin was coming. I explained all this to my doctor and begged him to give me the same injections that had prevented my abortion the previous time, but he would not listen seriously at all. I lost my baby in the fourth month, a great grief to us all. I cried for weeks and could not look into a pram – every new baby I saw should have been mine. Now I looked at Andy's baby girl and without realizing it, I thought of her as the baby I had lost. I was supremely happy whenever I could see her. She was a lovely little girl, with Andy's blonde hair and her daddy's dark brown eyes. In a few weeks she could wind us all round her little finger.

We had a wonderful Christmas that year. There was a fireplace in the big L-shaped living/dining room, so we were able to have the yule log fire that I loved. George and Rob had put up and decorated a lovely tree. Andy and her husband brought the baby to see us to complete our joy. In the spring Andy had another little girl, but we were never again to have such a wonderfully united Christmas.

In the following February, George and I were sitting up in bed reading one night, when he suddenly said, 'I have left the agency and I'm not going back!' He had suffered a massive coronary in 1964 and for a long, long week, I think the longest week of my whole life, he had hovered between life and death. He had recovered slowly – but it was six months before he had been able to return to work. He had smoked between fifty and sixty cigarettes a day for years – it seemed almost a part of being in advertising – but from the day he had entered hospital he never smoked again. Now, however, his heart had been troublesome again and he had been unwell for several months. George worked far too hard, and as Creative Director had no less than six television commercials going at once, which entailed a good deal of pressure. But when he calmly told me that he had left advertising for good, I was astonished. It was so totally unexpected.

He now proposed that we should make a permanent move to Cornwall. For several years we had rented a cottage in Mevagissey, a little fishing village, for our summer holiday, and in 1961 the owner had given us the first option to buy it. It had always been a secret dream of mine that we should own it, and my dream had come true, as so many of my dreams have done all my life. We had bought the cottage furnished and I let it through a local agent. We now began to settle all our affairs with the knowledge that from now on we would be living in Cornwall. It was a terrible grief to move so far away from Andy and the children, but we hoped they would be able to come for visits. Sometimes we love too much, and without enough thought; this has always been my weakness, and in the end my downfall.

Chapter 6

Robin was fourteen when we first moved down to Cornwall. He and I were very close; one of our chief ties was our Christianity. In 1964, when he was eleven years old, Robin had been to a Billy Graham crusade in London and had given his heart to Jesus Christ as Andy and I had done. While we lived in Richmond he had been in the Covenanters, and, most wonderful of all, while we were living in Mevagissey, he had chosen to be baptized by a genuine Christian who lived near Truro. This took place in a very large deep pool at Constantine Bay and was a most moving event. I found my son a tower of strength in many ways.

He was also a highly intelligent boy. When we lived in Richmond he attended a small school where there were only twenty pupils, all with high IQ levels. He had previously been in a couple of secondary modern schools – he had never taken the 11-plus because of illness – but had been unable to study because of the rowdy element in the overcrowded classes. This had caused him great unhappiness. When we moved to Cornwall, we were anxious that he should not have to return to a secondary modern school and arranged that he should study for O-levels at our local technical college.

George and I had accompanied him to the interview with the principal of the college. In the course of our discussion, the principal happened to remark to George that he was looking for an art master to start the department of art and design at the college, which had just been reorganized into a college of further education. I told him that George had qualified to teach art before he joined the army at the beginning of the war. Nothing more was said at the interview, but within a month of Robin's starting as a student, George had a letter from the principal asking him to join the staff to build up the art department. It was to be on a part-time basis at first, so should not cause George any strain. He was getting bored sitting at home all day, so he readily agreed. By 1970 he was teaching full time and had worked the department up from nothing until he had twenty-eight O-level students, twenty-five A-level students and two adult evening classes in painting.

We now found that living in the cottage during the summer was becoming an unexpectedly unpleasant experience. We were right on the harbour and in July and August the crowds were unbearable. People threw fish and chip papers outside our door, there were several very nasty fights between gangs of leather-jacketed youths on motorbikes, and by the end of September the village was one vast rubbish dump. During the winter too I saw things that sickened me – local youths throwing stones which broke a seagull's leg, and one horrible day I found a live seagull nailed upon a shed door in the village. On Guy Fawkes night, fireworks were thrown through old people's letter boxes, scaring them badly. I realized how much the village had changed since we first came there to stay for our holidays fifteen years ago.

Because of this, we decided to move and in the spring of 1970 put the cottage up for sale. We found a buyer very quickly. Instead of looking for another house straight away, we bought a caravan on an attractive site near the old town of Lostwithiel. This would give us plenty of time for house-hunting. We moved in the week before Whit. It was lovely sunny weather that week-end and on the Sunday I strolled up the road to look at the beautiful church which dated from the eleventh century.

Just below the church, screened by a tall hedge, I saw a most interesting house. The part I could see looked to be Georgian and as it appeared to be uncared for, I began to get ideas. On the Monday I walked up to the little shop-cum-post office and talked to the elderly lady sitting behind the counter. I was to grow very fond of her in the days to come. I asked her casually about the house below the church. I had a job to conceal my excitement when she told me that the owner was a recluse, who wanted to sell part of the building. The old lady was not fooled by my manner.

'Why don't you knock on the door and ask him?' she said shrewdly.

I went up the short, overgrown drive to a battered yellow door. I knocked and knocked and was just giving up hope when I heard about half a dozen locks being undone (the owner had a mania for locks and bolts I found later). There stood an elderly man in shirt sleeves. Very politely I told him that I had heard he might like to sell part of the house.

'I want to sell it all,' he said abruptly. 'Come round the side and I'll meet you at the front door.'

I walked round the house and then caught my breath. It was unbelievable, a once-in-a-lifetime house. It was built of mellow Cornish stone, around three sides of a very large terrace only half paved. The sheer beauty of the house was a dream come true. But there were tall weeds everywhere and the large lawn in front was uncut and turning into hay. The owner now came out and told me that he had seen a bungalow which he wanted to buy; if I wanted the house I must decide quickly. I ran all the way back down the hill to our caravan, so excited that George could hardly understand me.

'We *must* have it. It's just perfect. Please come and look at it now,' I panted. Back we went. The taciturn old man showed us over the inside of the house this time. There were nine bedrooms, one terrible antiquated bathroom with a bath standing on legs in the centre of the room, a big, farmhouse-type kitchen, two large entertaining rooms, and several stone-paved dairies.

The whole place was in a shocking state. I saw George's face getting longer and longer. At last he said, 'We must talk it over and let you know in a day or so.' The owner grunted and then closed the door with its many bolts and keys. We went back to the caravan and sat down.

'No way am I going to take that house on,' George said very firmly. 'I am *not* going to tackle a task like that.'

But I had fallen in love with the formally gracious building and the acre and a half of unkempt, old-fashioned garden. The price the man was asking was very low indeed, although it would take quite a lot of money to put the house right again. Fortunately my husband loves me very much and he also knows that sometimes my bright ideas do turn out the right way. The next day I walked up to see the owner of what was already our house in my mind and told him that we would buy right away. In early September, the house was finally ours.

The week before we moved in, Andy came to spend a brief holiday (she was about to go abroad). She and Rob had a lot of fun camping in the house overnight, sleeping on the kitchen floor. She loved the house as I did. With all my heart I wished that things were different, that she and my darling grandchildren did not live so far away.

That winter George and Robin worked on our house every spare minute they had. On moving in and trying to open the windows, we had found that they were all nailed up. When we removed the nails, fifteen rotted windows had fallen out. Now these were replaced and the marathon task of redecorating began. In every room the walls had been given a coat of green colour-wash and everywhere the lovely old woodwork was painted in dull brown. By Christmas time, George and Rob had made the drawing room, two bedrooms and the big kitchen habitable. By autumn 1971 the whole house was looking lovely.

I now renewed my plea to Mother to come and live with us in Cornwall. She loved the country and birds so much. It would be easy to give her her own rooms in this large house; she could have as much privacy as she wished yet be able to join in our family life. But once again she refused, saying that to leave Sussex and join me might upset Pam. But Pam and I had been on friendly terms for some time now. I had stayed in her house several times during the past two years. Although we had always had disagreements, once the argument was over we gradually became friendly again. Even the matter of Gran's will had been settled between us. I had agreed to pay Pam £1,000 on Mother's death as a gesture of goodwill. I could only think that Mother's refusal to leave Sussex was another example of her playing out one of the little dramas she loved so much.

In the following year, with the work on the house completed, I now began to think seriously about going into a business which had always fascinated me and about which I knew a fair amount because of all our many, many moves. I wanted to start a property company, but instead of the rabbit hutches other companies were building, I wanted to build some houses of quality, houses that people would still be glad to own in fifty or even a hundred years' time. I had already seen the piece of land where I wanted to start building. It was in a little village called Lerryn, on a very pretty river. The land had outline planning permission for six houses, but I wanted to give each house a little more garden. In my mind I saw five well-built, attractive dwellings there. The land was due to come up for auction in a few weeks and would probably fetch about £25,000. There was no time to waste if it were to be mine.

I went to see a very good accountant I knew in Plymouth to ask him how to go about forming a property company. Mr P. always seemed to know all about everything; in fact I privately called him 'Mr Fix-it'. He advised me to go to see a young solicitor, who was a partner in a firm in a nearby town. In the meantime, Mr P. set about registering the company for me. The solicitor suggested that I should finance the project through a loan from a merchant bank. He explained that such banks provided finance in one of two ways: they either asked for a share in the company being formed and a percentage of the profits, or they made a straight loan at a pretty high level of interest. He gave me the name and address of Cannon Street Acceptances Ltd, a merchant bank in London.

The next day I went up to London. At CSA I met Mr S., the new-business manager, and outlined my proposal. My accountant had estimated that to build the kind of houses I had in mind would cost roughly £18,000 each. He had agreed with me that they should sell readily at about £35,000. I explained these figures to Mr S., showed him a small plan of the land, told him its expected price, and asked him for a loan. Mr S. did a few figures on paper and then offered me a loan of £100,000, repayable in twelve months' time. This really took my breath away. The man had never seen me before. I was an elderly woman with no previous business experience, and he calmly lent me £100,000.

All the financial arrangements were to be done through my solicitor, or rather my company solicitor as he had now become. My accountant had by now registered the name of the new company as Patterson Properties Ltd. He was a shrewd man and had told me to make it a limited company so that if I did get into financial trouble, any debts would be purely and simply the company's and nothing at all to do with me as a private person. But trouble looked impossible in those halcyon days. It was late January 1973; 1972 had been a boom year for land and property and the rise in values seemed set to continue. When the land was auctioned I bought it for £25,000.

My solicitor had advised me on securing a good architect, a pleasant Scotsman who designed five lovely houses for me, incorporating a lot of my own ideas. They were all to have four bedrooms, and a bathroom and separate lavatory upstairs, and downstairs a really big dining/living room with service hatch into a good-sized kitchen. Just inside the back door there was to be a cloakroom and shower. We planned magnificent stone fireplaces in the living room and picture windows, one of which would slide right back to give access to a wide paved terrace at the back of the house where the stream ran down the side of the land. Each house was designed with a double garage, and it was my idea to have up-and-over doors both ends of the garage so that the owners could drive in and straight out again without having to reverse.

Our detailed plans were not passed until the late spring. We had bought the land in January and by now interest was mounting on the £25,000 we had paid for the land. I set to and hired a foreman and eight building workers to start on our houses. I knew nothing about the actual details of building, but I trusted my architect, who came out to inspect weekly, and my foreman, who had been well recommended. I provided a small old caravan on a corner of the land as a site hut where the men could also eat their lunches on wet days. There were plenty of those that spring and summer. I was now renting a small office in the local town, and I engaged a young girl to handle all the wage packets and business letters. George had been forced to give up his teaching which had become very much full time and too great a strain. Robin was taking his A-levels, but he helped me in the holidays. George was drawing sick pay and we lived on that plus what I was able to earn by buying and selling antiques in a small way.

That year was one of the wettest summers on record and work on the site was continually held up by heavy rain. The roadworks on the little road to serve the five houses were also delayed because I had insisted on changing the route slightly so that we could keep a magnificent old oak tree – it seemed wrong to cut down a tree that was over a hundred years old. However, by late summer, we had two houses almost completed, the men worked so well. One of our suppliers told me that I was known as the 'Lady Builder' everywhere. The fact that I was at the site every day in heavy gum boots and that I paid the men myself on Fridays caused some surprise.

Ever since we started work on the site, we had been required to submit a monthly certificate to CSA as to the exact amount of money spent on materials, wages, etc., and this had to be signed by our architect before we drew on our loan facility. Then out of the blue I had a phone call – the managing director of CSA and his assistant were to land by helicopter in the field next to our site to take a look at the progress of our work. The field was full of cows, but the farmer was very helpful and removed them, and the men and I laid out a big cross in white material to show the helicopter where to land. Fortunately it was a lovely sunny day and the whole of Lerryn School was brought to see this spectacular event. Half the village turned up too. The big man, Mr D., inspected the two houses and our plans for the others with great thoroughness. He was very impressed and congratulated me on our team of workmen. But he reminded me that time was nearly up on our year's loan, it was shortly due to be repaid, and as yet we had not sold a house. Then off they went.

We pressed on with our building. My architect pointed out that we would have completed and presumably sold the houses during the next few months, and would need more land if Patterson Properties was to continue to function. He added that if the boom continued land might be very hard to find next spring. We imagined a satisfactory profit on Lerryn when it was all sold and I wanted to put most of the profit back into the company. I drew no salary, although I was on paper the managing director. All the money was to go into the company at first. George and I were now having a struggle to make ends meet, but of course that was nothing to do with the company. So thinking of our need for land again in the fairly near future, I did as most building companies do, and found a really exciting piece of land for sale, up on the side of a hill at Polperro. The land sloped steeply, and had magnificent views out over the harbour and sea. It was reached by a small lane that went with the land. This time there was outline planning permission for twelve houses on the two and a half acres. Again I did not want to build like that. Instead I drew up plans with my architect for only seven really outstanding houses and once more rushed up to London to CSA. The land was coming up for auction and I was told it would fetch around £40,000. I produced a feasibility report on the proposed development to submit to CSA. Included in that was a statement from a well-known firm of estate agents that the seven houses would, in their opinion, easily sell for £47,000 each.

This time I saw the managing director of CSA. I was also introduced to another man whom I was told was a representative of the National Westminster Bank. I was a little surprised; I did not then know that CSA was one of several subsidiaries of the Nat West. I explained my proposed plans for buying the land at Polperro and also that we should have a decent profit from Lerryn after we had repaid the original loan of £100,000. We now had prospective buyers for two houses and were fairly confident that we could begin to repay the first loan soon. The managing director said that he was very pleased with our Lerryn project. After a close inspection of our facts and figures, both for current expenditure and final estimates, he agreed to lend Patterson Properties another £128,000 for the Polperro development. But he said that CSA would perhaps require some extra security besides the mortgage they already held on everything at Lerryn and would hold on the Polperro land.

The day after I arrived home I contacted the agents for the Polperro land and offered £45,000 to save the land going to auction. My offer was accepted. We now owed CSA £228,000, or would do so if we drew on our facility to the full. My solicitor then told me that CSA did indeed require more security. They wanted George to give them a charge on our home, on which we had spent so much hard work, and on our final small amount of capital. The house had been valued for some time at £45,000. My solicitor urged me to get George to sign the document. George went into the solicitor's office and signed – there seemed to be little risk; there were as yet no dark clouds on the horizon. On the contrary, CSA were encouraging me to carry on building. Both George and I also signed what our company solicitor told us was a form of 'personal guarantee'. We did not bother to read it fully; the solicitor earnestly assured us that he had inspected it thoroughly and that there was no need for us to worry at all, it was all in order. I took two of my workmen off the site at Lerryn and they began to clear the land at Polperro.

We were now past the time for repayment of our original loan from CSA and they began to press me for payment. We had three houses almost finished at Lerryn, but in spite of extensive advertising, we had not yet found even one firm buyer. The houses were on a lovely site, they were very well built, and greatly admired by all who saw them, but the boom was over and house prices had begun to drop. The hold-up of the wet summer meant that we had missed the market at its peak. Our actual debt to CSA at that time was the £100,000 original loan plus interest which had been used to buy the Lerryn land, build the houses and buy enough materials to finish the project, and the £45,000 purchase price for the Polperro land against our new loan facility of £128,000 for its development.

Most building firms seemed to be slightly in the red on their first venture and to recover on their next, so we were not really worried. We knew that the houses at Lerryn had at least a market value of around £30,000 each and our big profit would come when we built at Polperro. Because CSA were now pressing our company for repayment of the Lerryn loan, I asked my accountant and architect to put all these facts in the proper order and on Wednesday, 27 September 1974, I took my statement up to London to put before a meeting at CSA. The man from the Nat West was again present. I discussed my figures fully with them and they agreed to give us more time to sell the Lerryn houses. The managing director told me that they were very satisfied with what they had seen of the houses already built and urged me to carry on building.

I returned home that night and paid my usual visit to the site at Lerryn the next day, Thursday. To my surprise, I saw the CSA new-business manager, who had been present at the meeting in London the day before. He was walking round the houses with a stranger. Feeling slightly alarmed, I asked what on earth he was doing there as we had only parted yesterday afternoon. He replied that they were only looking round and he remarked that I was 'doing an excellent job'. I paid my men as customary the next day, Friday, and we closed the site down for the week-end. Then I went home to Lanlivery Manor for tea.

George, Robin and I were watching the six o'clock news on BBC television that evening when we suddenly heard the following statement: 'Today one of the large merchant banks, Cannon Street Acceptances, went into voluntary liquidation and a receiver has been appointed.' We were so shocked that we could only look silently at one another. Patterson Properties was finished, wiped out in a simple news bulletin.

Part Three

Necessity is the plea for every infringement of human freedom. It is the argument of tyrants; it is the creed of slaves.

William Pitt, 18 November 1783

We must not forget that when every material improvement has been made in the prisons, when the temperature has been rightly adjusted, when the proper food to maintain health has been given, when the doctors, chaplains and prison visitors have come and gone, the convict stands deprived of everything that a free man calls life.

Winston Churchill, 1910

Chapter 7

So on Friday, 29 September 1974, the only source of finance to the property company was frozen by the voluntary liquidation of the merchant bank who were supplying our loan. I not only felt shocked by this sudden action, I began to feel very angry too. This event must have been known to CSA months ago, and yet they had encouraged our company to go on building, running up more and more bills with our suppliers of building materials, and worst of all, had agreed to lend the company yet another £128,000 for Polperro.

On Monday I went to the site in Lerryn earlier than usual, just as our building team were arriving for work, and sitting in our little site van, I told them exactly what had happened. I told them that I wanted to try to find another source of finance so that we could keep on building, and I explained that it was not even certain that their wages would be paid on the coming Friday. By this time, I had no capital of my own, but intended to try to raise some somehow. The men unanimously told me that they would carry on during the coming week and wished me luck in my efforts. They were an unusually good group of workers.

I went to see my own private bank, where I already had an overdraft of about £1,000, and asked the manager to increase my personal overdraft to at least the sum which I knew would cover the men's wages and our urgent company bills for supplies. After a lot of persuasion, he reluctantly agreed, but only on condition that I signed a charge on my reversionary interest in Gran's trust. I now owed a considerable sum on the trust, as I had been borrowing smaller amounts over the years. Somehow I had never managed to handle George's salary properly, and had always been in debt to either our bank or Gran's trust, the loans on which would be repaid when Mother died and Grandmother's trust was paid to me.

Then I went to see the manager of the bank our property company used, which ironically was the Nat West! I asked him to lend Patterson Properties enough money to finish our building at Lerryn, so that we could then offer the completed houses for sale. We only needed about £15,000, and he agreed to ask the area office of the bank in Launceston to agree to this.

My last call was to our company solicitor. I asked him to find out at once how much the mortgage on Lanlivery Manor was, held as security by CSA, the form that he had not only allowed, but urged George to sign. He said he would find out right away, and he actually said that he thought it was about £12,000, which meant that we could easily raise more on a house valued at £45,000!

In a few days the area head office of the Nat West refused to help. My personal loan from my own bank was only enough for the men's wages and some pressing bills. On the Friday afternoon, I paid our men, and they helped Robin and me to close the site, put up barriers, and make the houses as safe as we could. The men all offered to return to work if I did succeed in refinancing our company and we shook hands all round.

I still hoped to do a rescue operation somehow, but all avenues were blind ones. I could not find any sum large enough to finish our project, and I put an advertisement in a national newspaper offering Patterson Properties for sale as a going concern. With our Lerryn Houses and Polperro land, the company was still a viable proposition. My company solicitor suggested that I should put his firm's telephone number in my advert, and he would deal with replies. I very foolishly agreed.

He phoned me next week, and said that there were fifteen replies, which was excellent considering the fact that the property market seemed to be very much in the doldrums. But I never did have any contact with any of the replies. He told me that one by one they had dropped out. I was still trusting his actions, so all I felt was great disappointment.

Now came the greatest blow of all. The solicitor told me that he had discovered that CSA held a charge over the *whole* of our home and also on any private money we had. I told him that we had no private money, Patterson Properties already owed us £15,000, the very last of our savings invested in the company when it was formed. Then he said, 'Yes, but what about your reversionary interest in your grandmother's trust. If your mother were to die now, they would take that too.' I now learnt that when George and I signed the personal guarantee form in the solicitor's office, we had given CSA a charge of first call not only on our home, which was all we had left, but also on anything we might receive in the future, including Gran's trust money.

Christmas came and went. Robin and I made it as cheerful as we could. George did not yet know the full extent of our troubles and I knew what a terrible shock it would be to him. I wished with all my heart that *he* had been in charge of our family finances and not allowed me to over-rule him and handle our income when we were married. I realized yet again what a curse it was to have inherited the dominating traits of three generations of self-willed women. Just after Easter 1975, Patterson Properties was put into liquidation. We could not pay our bills, and the high interest on the loan from CSA was mounting daily.

By now I was very worried about Mother. In fact her sufferings were far more important to me than our desperate financial plight. To me people came a long way before money.

During 1974 Mother was living in Haywards Heath. She had a large bed-sitting room in the home of a nurse, Mrs Wilkins, and her family, and seemed fairly happy. She still insisted on staying near to Pam which I felt was to compensate for Grandmother's cutting down Pam's share in her will. I often talked to Mother on the phone and in my weekly letters about her coming to live with us in Cornwall, which she loved almost as much as I do, and I think that she was seriously considering this move.

While Mother was living with her, Mrs Wilkins became very alarmed by Mother's constant talk of suicide. Apparently when Mother's hot milk was taken in to her at night she almost always said, 'Well, Mrs Wilkins, I don't think I will be here in the morning. I'm going to change my world tonight,' and similar remarks. Mrs Wilkins informed Mother's doctor of this and also warned him that Mother had a large bottle of sodium amytol sleeping pills – 'Enough to kill half of Haywards Heath,' the anxious woman said. The doctor told her not to worry as he knew about the tablets and also knew Mother well; there was no need for any alarm. However, Mrs Wilkins, who was really concerned about Mother's constant chat of suicide, spoke to Pam.

'My mother has talked like that for nearly forty years. She doesn't mean a word of it,' Pam replied. Had I been asked I would, of course, have said the same. Dear Mother, she was as close to me as ever, but I could see that to outsiders she was becoming a problem. They did not understand that her constant grumbling and pessimistic outlook were just her way of wanting attention. Both Mrs Wilkins and Mother seemed to feel that a parting loomed on the horizon.

On 19 March 1975, Mother got out of bed in the morning and had a bad fall. She told me later that it was a blackout. She fractured her hip badly. Pam phoned me and told me that Mother had been rushed to Cuckfield Hospital and was to have an operation the next day. I was frantic and asked Pam if she could put me up if I came to Sussex.

'There's no need to come,' Pam told me. 'I will phone again tomorrow.'

The next morning Mother had a six-hour operation to pin her hip; she was nearly eighty-six years old. When I talked on the phone to the sister in charge, she told me that Mother was in shock. She was, in fact, suffering withdrawal symptoms, for she had been taken off the drugs she was regularly prescribed.

They kept her in the recovery room overnight and the next day she was well enough to be moved back to the ward. I spoke to the sister every day and she assured me that Mother was recovering slowly. I also wrote to her and sent her flowers. Pam still felt that it was not necessary for me to travel up to see Mother.

The day after Mother's fall I had talked to Mrs Wilkins on the phone. She said that she had given the big bottle of sodium amytols to the ambulance men when they took Mother to hospital – poor Mother's security as she called them. Later she said she gave them to Pam. She also told me that Pam and her husband had packed up all Mother's belongings, including her furniture, as she would not be returning there. For some time before this Pam and I had veen trying to get Mother into St George's Retreat, a private home for old people, set in twenty acres of lovely grounds including a farm. Mother had been very keen to live there.

'It will be lovely to walk in the grounds and feed the birds. The nuns who run the place are sure to be patient, kind and dedicated women,' she'd said. So Pam now contacted the Reverend Mother, whom I had also seen, about a place for Mother when she came out of hospital. They agreed to take her and once she had recovered she moved there just before Christmas.

So Mother went to live at St George's Retreat. We wrote to each other every week and I phoned the Reverend Mother, Sister Leonie, every week-end to ask for news about Mother's health. Mother's letters were not at all reassuring. It seemed that the operation wound on her hip was not healing and that her other hip had now broken open where it had been pinned after a bad fall ten years ago.

Summer came, a terrible summer of drought and baking heat and Mother's letters became more and more distressing. In one she wrote, 'I'm not making any progress. It's a Herculean task to get across the room, walking with my Zimmer, and the nights are hells of pain.'

On 6 June I drove up to London with my son Robin. We stayed the night with friends and then, in the scorching heat, we went to have lunch with Pam and her family on our way to see Mother and then home. Pam said that we would only have a cold lunch as they were all off to Plumpton Races at 2 p.m., but her housekeeper, Mrs Cox, provided an excellent meal. Before lunch Pam and I sat and talked in her sitting room while Robin and his cousin Tam, who was a registered radio ham, examined Tam's latest radio equipment. Robin and I left to visit Mother just before Pam's departure for the races.

The heat was almost unbearable and poor Mother was in a very unhappy state. We talked for about an hour and a half and she told me that she thought one of the nuns had been unkind to her. It was obvious that there was some friction, but Mother could be very difficult at times.

'They are going to cut my leg off,' she said. Poor Mother, she clung to me when we left and privately I made up my mind to take her home to Cornwall as soon as she could make the long journey. Before Robin and I left I insisted on seeing the Reverend Mother, and told her that as Mother's next of kin I would never agree to the removal of her leg. She laughed heartily, and said it was not true at all.

'Old people talk like that because they want you to go home and worry about them,' she remarked, but she did not know of the deep love between me and Mother and just how terribly worried I was.

When I got into the car to leave, the heat and the glare were worse than ever, and then I found my sun-glasses were missing. I could not drive all the way to Cornwall without them, so back we went to Pam's house, to see if I had left them there. But Pam's daily help, Doris, utterly refused to let us in. To my amazement she said she had been told on no account to admit anyone. I pointed out that I had had lunch there and that this was my sister's house, and after a lot of argument Doris let us into the hall. She and Robin stood by the door and I went into the sitting room. There were my sun-glasses, down the arm of the big chair where I had sat and talked to Pam. We were in the house about three or four minutes and then left to drive home.

We arrived about 8.30 p.m. and at 9 o'clock Pam phoned.

She was angry that I had gone into the house while she was away. In vain I tried to explain that I was just looking for my sunglasses, but Pam told me I was never to visit her house again.

In August I went to London to train as a sales representative for *Encyclopaedia Britannica.* I stayed at a small hotel, all expenses paid, and went for daily training at head office near Oxford Street. I had a week's training in the suffocating heat of London, and returned home on a Saturday. On Sunday evening I went out and sold a full leather set of *Encyclopaedia Britannica* for cash to a nursing sister. I had never sold anything in my life before! So I started working very hard and selling very successfully. I believed in the value of what I was offering, I like people, and those facts, coupled with my contagious enthusiasm, enabled me to be named 'Representative of the Month', then 'Representative of the Future'. By November I had won many major awards and seemed on the way to a new successful career at fifty-nine years old! In this way, I hoped to repay all our personal debts.

But selling during that terrible summer of 1975 took its toll on my health. The earth was cracked and parched and as I drove about the heat was almost unbearable. I had terrible headaches and, of course, added to all this I was still fighting legal battles to keep our home from being seized by the merchant bank, and to find some way to rescue our property company. Several other small companies in Cornwall and Devon had managed to find other sources of finance after the collapse of CSA, but so far I had had no success, and CSA still held the first charge on our house and my interest in Gran's trust, as no settlement with them had been reached. However, my work for *Encyclopaedia Britannica* began to get our personal affairs in order. We had also sold almost all our antique furniture and paintings and so on. I knew that if I continued to sell so successfully, we would be completely free of personal debts very soon. We only owed between £200 and £300.

As if I were not already labouring under a well-nigh intolerable burden, poor Mother was never out of my mind. She wrote to tell me her hips were agony. Her letters became more and more distressing. In one letter she said, 'I've never suffered such pain, Pam told me not long ago that I am neurotic from head to foot and have been ever since I was a child! She wouldn't give me any help.'

In another letter she wrote:

> I don't know what happened to Pam . . . I did also ask her to bring me a bottle of Codein . . . although by repeated Dr's orders I should have 4 doses every day, I'm lucky to get it 2 or three times, and have sometimes had only one . . . Nights are worst, because I have to be in bed by 8 p.m.

Further down her letter Mother said, 'Please remember, *don't mention me* in any way to Pam,' and at the very end of her letter, 'Don't mention me to Pam, only stirs up bitterness.'

She also said that she had no place to put anything I sent her, the nuns kept her room free of everything except the bare essentials. She made me promise not to send a card or my usual Cornish calendar at Christmas. In a letter in September she wrote, 'Now please don't forget, *no* Xmas card or anything, it will only distress me if you send and I can't.' Of course, I kept my promise and didn't send her anything.

She had never got over the removal of her big bottle of sodium amytols, her 'security'. Now she could not rest until she had something similar tucked away safely again. She was writing every week, begging me to take her some of my own sleeping tablets. She made me promise not to say anything of this to anyone:

> Now I urge you never to speak to one person about helping me out in case you ever get the chance, not even George or Rob, because at once you are in that person's power. Of course, cremation helps to make it safer, but if you ever have the chance and are this way, put some in a screw of tissue, don't bring a bottle which could be traced.

Even in the grip of so much pain, Mother had not lost her love of intrigue and drama. This extraordinary behaviour was typical of the streak of eccentricity which went right back to Great-Grandmother, who had lain in the wet orchard in her nightgown, through Gran and her uncontrollable tempers, and even to Mother's obsessive and abnormal character. Because I loved her so blindly, I had accepted the strange way in which Mother thought and behaved, her passion for churchyards, for instance, and constant talk of things like suicide, madness and death.

With so many worries, such unbearable pressures all round, I don't know how I kept my sanity during that time. On 18 September we had some friends to dinner. I broke down in the kitchen and told Daphne of Mother's letters, despite her injunction, and that I could not resist her pleas much longer. My friend was horrified and begged me not to do anything to endanger myself.

On Sunday, 2 November, I phoned the Reverend Mother at St George's as usual and she told me that Mother was going into hospital on Tuesday to have her two abscesses opened up and cleaned. My poor darling mother, how she must have been suffering. I did not dare tell the Reverend Mother of Mother's letter begging me to help her. On Wednesday, 5 November, I phoned Cuckfield Hospital and was told that Mother had had the operation on both hips under an anaesthetic and was very poorly. I did not know how to bear the thought of her suffering – I felt so helpless – and made up my mind to do as she asked and replace her 'security pills'. At least I could do that much for her. I wrote to tell her that I was bringing the tablets she wanted to keep. A week later I received my awards from my sales work, a full set of the *Encyclopaedia Britannica*, champagne, a pewter tankard and a lovely little clock. It all meant nothing with Mother's plight on my mind day and night.

On 27 November I had to go to London to see our solicitors about the way in which the merchant bank was treating us. I spent the night at the little hotel where I had stayed for my sales training. The next day I travelled to Sussex and to St George's to see Mother. I took with me a few Panadols to try and ease her pain, as she continually told me that she was having no proper medication. I also took about fifteen of my own sleeping pills wrapped in tissue. She was overjoyed to see me and we talked of all our happy times together in the past. I told her that I had never forgotten that she had saved my life when Andy was born. She then asked me to give her the tablets. She put them away in the pocket of an old coat at the back of the wardrobe (she had a private room as a paying patient).

'I am *so* thankful,' she kept telling me. 'I feel so much better now that I have those to keep in case I get very old and become like a vegetable.'

We said a tearful good-bye. I hated leaving her again, but she seemed so much happier now that her precious 'security' was tucked away safely. Of course, neither of us knew that for weeks my sister had been intercepting and opening our letters to each other, and had actually taken them to the Sussex Police in the October, a month before my visit.

I now had two rather puzzling letters from Mother, one 'to keep', and one 'to burn'.

St George's Retreat,
Burgess Hill,
Sussex.

Dear Yo, 30:11:75

I am so glad you got here, for somehow, I do have one of my hunches that I am going downhill. I never told anyone, not even the Dr and as I was in bed with bladder inflammation no one knows. It was two of those queer falls in one night – out for over an hour, but I was lucky enough to fall across that huge long basket chair. I've never told Pam of it, but lately I have that same feeling. You see I never want to have another turn and then perhaps lie like a log for years, just an expense and liability. I don't know if you ever knew, I don't *think* Pam did, but not very long before Pup died we talked of all the many many nights I'd sat by you children in W. Kirby, and he gave me an unopened bottle of strong sleeping tablets saying he knew how level headed and careful I was and there might come a time when I'd give anything for a night's sleep, and he couldn't help me. Do you know I still had them unopened at Ockley Lodge and when I was going into Cuckfield with that distended abdomen I was worried because of course my room was unlocked. So I kept, I think, round about a dozen or so, and flushed the rest down the lavatory. I still have the few, nobody has ever found them or tumbled to them, there are not so many now, but I just want to warn you that if I have the pluck I shall try to take them. Yo I can't bear it much longer. Last night at 4 a.m. I woke and could have screamed with the pain in the left (good?) hip, what's the use. I feel sure you *and* Pam wouldn't want me lying helpless in such pain for years and I'm *not* getting better. My true love to everyone, and tell George I do appreciate the welcome and friendship he's always given me. Oh if only you and Pam could again find some form of friendship! There's some pain tablets in my handbag a friend brought some months ago at my request but I couldn't take them, too big and can't break them. But they are harmless. *Don't* come all this way just for a few minutes' funeral service. Love to all. Think of the future not the past, and tell Robin 'have guts and perseverance!!'

Love Mumie Narns.

This letter was very much Mother in her 'Agatha Christie' role. The second letter was enclosed in the same envelope. It said:

My dear Yo,

Thank you for letter. Three days after you came the Rev. Mother came to see me and was so affectionate and friendly. She mentioned that she had seen you for a short time, and as near as I remember said 'Your daughter is very worried about you, and it's so natural, as she can't get to see you as it's such a distance, and she is so anxious in case you became helpless or something like that – worse than you are now. I want you to write and reassure her every care and help you *could* have would be given to you. Nobody can bear your pain but you know and several here know that you are my special patient, and I would see that every help was given to you.' I'm still going by ambulance 3 times weekly to therapy, but on Wed 17th I see Mr Richards and I'm going to ask to drop it. It all, including the bumpy ride, makes the pain so much worse. With this I shall post the letter you should keep locked away, in case you need it, but *burn* this part immediately. A kindly person I met at therapy and talked quite a lot to gave me a bottle of some white tablets for pain to try, and I found them very helpful. My nice Sister – I think the one you met – breaks them in 2 for me but very reluctantly, as the first 2 nearly choked me! But if that were known she would be severely punished so *burn this.* I'm awfully frightened to die, in case it's wicked, and I don't want any more punishing, I've had enough. I'm staying here for Xmas because I can't manage Pam's at all, what's the good of going if I can't see the dogs and horses, and someone would have to fetch and bring. Beside one can't hide pain and they have enough worries without having Xmas Day spoiled. I don't expect I'll write again before Xmas, not even a card, and don't forget your promise likewise to me. Explain to Rob about Xmas. He'll understand. This is why I tried to do a little extra last Xmas.

My love to you all. Just drop a card if you sell house, oh how I'd love to see the birds and animals! If only your family and Pam's could get friends again! . . . But it's sad for the children. forgiving types. But it's sad for the children.

My love. Mumie plus Narns.

On Christmas Eve I was making mince pies in the evening when Pam phoned. I had not heard from her since the sunglasses episode in June. She was extremely angry again and said that the Panadol pain killers had been found in Mother's work basket, and how *dare* I interfere with the treatment she ha dat St George's. I replied that as far as I could see Mother was having no proper treatment. If she were, how could she have needed an operation on two abscesses on her hips eight months after her fall and arrival at St George's? Pam slammed down the phone and I did not hear her speak again until she appeared as chief prosecution witness at my trial fourteen months later.

I felt very sad that Christmas Day. Although Mother still had her 'security' pills tucked away, I knew how much she was suffering and at her age it all seemed so wrong, especially when so much of her life had been spent in helping others. Now it seemed there was no help for her.

At the beginning of January I had a frantic letter from Mother telling me that on 28 December she had been taken by ambulance to the hospital for treatment on her two unhealed hips, and the nuns had searched her room, found the pills and removed them. It was, so she wrote, the first time she had left her room since I gave them to her on 28 November.

'*Why* did they search my room?' Mother said. We learnt later of course that through Pam's reading of our letters the nuns knew exactly where to look. Now Mother was frantic and begged and implored me to take some more to her! In another letter she told me that on 2 January she had had a fall in the night getting out on to her commode, and had lain on the floor for several hours unable to reach a blanket or eiderdown, shivering with cold until the night staff found her, and tucked her up with a hot water bottle. Mother also said that she had a severe bladder infection, and I was so worried by all this that I at once phoned the Reverend Mother. She told me that Mother had had a slight fall, there was no need for me to be alarmed and her small amount of bladder trouble was yielding to treatment. No mention was made of the discovery and removal of the pills, and there was certainly nothing said about her being in a coma.

Mother's letters continued. She told me that her nights were 'Hells of pain', and that she was not even given the medicines ordered by the doctor who visited St George's once a week, and that she simply could not bear the thought of her future at St George's in such pain. Mother now wrote letter after letter begging for her 'security' pills again, and saying things like, 'God bless you if you can manage it, darling, but be very careful, you must not get caught,' also, 'Can you put some in a little box?' and so on. I could see quite clearly that as well as her obsession with the pills, Mother was getting a lot of enjoyment out of the intrigue. She had always loved her little dramas and I did not grudge her this small thing, God knew she had little enough to brighten her life.

I was to work on the *Encyclopaedia Britannica* stand at the Ideal Home Exhibition opening in London on 22 March. I was still selling very successfully in spite of all my appalling worries, but on 19 February I went to bed with a very bad attack of flu. The newspapers said that there were over a million cases of the virus now, and I was one of them. I had a high fever and bad cough, and the prospect of the Ideal Home seemed very slim indeed. However, on 23 March I recovered enough to get up and stagger to London to stay at the same small hotel where I had stayed for my training. I started selling at the stand the next day from 4 p.m. to 9 p.m. and actually sold a full leather set for cash! But I felt really weak and still had a really bad cough. The next day I did the shift from 10 a.m. to 4 p.m. and once more sold a set for cash, then back to the hotel and simply fell into bed. On Saturday, 27 March, I again worked from 10 a.m. to 4 p.m., made two more sales and left ten minutes before a bomb exploded just near our stand, injuring eighty-four people, some very seriously. My husband had heard about it in a news flash, and phoned my hotel, frantic with worry. He wanted me to go home at once, but I had given my word to stay on for another week. (All the years of Mother's training had made it impossible for me to break a promise.) But I did feel very shocked, it had been so close and I still had a bad cough and was weak from my flu.

The next day was 28 March, Mother's Day. I woke feeling very tired and unwell, but I had written to Mother and promised her that I would be with her on this Sunday. I made my way to Victoria Station, where I bought a big bunch of daffodils, a book of puzzles which I knew Mother liked, and also the *Sunday Telegraph* as she always enjoyed doing the crossword puzzle. I had to get a taxi from Burgess Hill station as there was no other way to reach St George's, and I was there about 1.30 p.m. To my surprise the front door was locked, the first time I had found this, but a nun I did not know soon came and took me to see Mother. Her private room was quite large but rather gloomy, and on this lovely sunny day all the curtains were drawn over the windows. Mother and I kissed each other, we were so happy to be together again. She loved the gifts I had brought, especially the early daffodils. Knowing how much she liked the sun, I pulled back the curtains and we sat down for a long talk. Mother told me that the week before my visit she had been taken out of her room and kept in another room all afternoon with Pam, as 'her floorboards needed repairing'. Neither of us knew that, during that time, the police had dressed up as plumbers to bug the room. About an hour after my arrival Sister Bernadette, a nun whom Mother liked, brought in a tray of tea for which I was grateful; I had had nothing to eat or drink since an early breakfast.

About halfway through the afternoon Mother asked me if I had brought 'the things', and I reassured her that I had. She told me that this time she had a really safe place to keep them. I said, 'Yes Mummy, don't make a mess of it this time,' referring to the previous occasion when the nuns found the pills. Mother assured me that she would not, and then asked me to help her to pin them to her vest which she wore under her nightie.

'Pass me those teeny weeny safety pins on the window ledge, I have been keeping them specially for today. I always dress and undress myself, so they cannot ever be found here,' she told me happily. Then patting her chest she said, 'I feel so much better now.'

I again asked Mother to come and live with us in Cornwall; privately I was determined that she should, even if I had to do a lot of persuading. We talked about the last time that I had left her the pills in November, and after Christmas the nun had searched the room and taken them away.

'I went to my pocket and they were gone. I nearly went mad, so when Sister came in – what do you think I had for lunch today, some jelly. Fancy having some jelly,' said Mother.

Just after 3.30 Sister Bernadette came in again and asked me if I would like a lift to the station as a car would be going soon.

'Yes, darling, save the taxi fare,' said Mother. I asked the nun to let me know when the lift was ready.

All the afternoon we had talked in our usual way, the way we had talked to each other for over fifty years, a private family way of talking. About suicide, death and cremations, all interspersed with remarks about the birds feeding outside, and my dress creasing when I sat down. To an outsider it would have seemed a very strange conversation indeed, even a crazy one, but then neither Mother or I are exactly like other people. We congratulated each other that our family doctor had 'eased Daddy out' when he was dying of cancer. Mother also mentioned Pam. She had told Mother that there was a streak of madness in the family.

At 4.15 Sister Bernadette came in to say that my lift was ready, so I kissed Mother, and we joked about our next meeting. She said that she might be fit enough to dance a jig. Poor darling, she was so brave in spite of all the pain in her open abscesses and the Paget's disease in all her bones.

I was shown out of a side door, and the nun pointed to a well-dressed woman standing by the drive.

'There is the lady who is giving you the lift, good-bye,' she said, and she quickly went inside and shut the door. As I went up to the woman, she indicated a man coming out of the same side door and said, 'This is the gentleman who is giving us a lift.' The man had a small case in his hand and I thought that he was probably a lawyer who had been to visit one of St George's 200 patients. I told the man how grateful I was for a lift to the station. The woman climbed into the back of the car and I sat beside the man. We drove round the grounds, he said that he thought that he had lost his way and we chatted about how beautiful the grounds were. After about eight minutes he found the right driveway and we came out on to Ditchling Common about four miles from where my sister lives. As he stopped the car for traffic approaching from the right, the man turned to me.

'Mrs McShane,' he said, and he paused. I was thinking that as he knew my name he must know Mother too, when he continued, 'We are police officers and you are being taken to the police station.'

I was utterly astonished. I told him that there must be some mistake as I had been told that we were on the way to the railway station. He said that there was no mistake and we were now on the way to the police station. I asked him *why*, what was I supposed to have done, but his only reply was that he could not tell me anything until we reached the police station. I sat in shocked and terrified silence. It seemed incredible that anyone could be abducted under false pretences like this – surely it couldn't happen in this country?

When we reached our destination and got out of the car, I saw that it was indeed the police station. I was told that this was Burgess Hill. I was taken upstairs and ushered into a small room with a table in the middle and one or two chairs. A man came in who, I was told, was the chief superintendent. He sat down across the table from me. When I asked him why I was there he said it concerned my mother. He asked me a lot of questions about her, but I refused to answer. I did not want her to get into any trouble at St George's.

Then he asked me if my grandmother had lived with me before her death. Had I persuaded her to alter her will? Had she died in my house from a fractured skull? I told him that the only fact that was true in all that was that Grandmother had lived with us for the last eight months of her life. I told him that during the last two months I had employed a resident night nurse as Gran was totally incontinent. In fact, I pointed out, Grandmother had died of kidney failure and old age at eighty-seven years old. But it was as soon as he mentioned Grandmother that I realized that all these allegations must have come from my sister. Suddenly a lot of things fell into place – how the nuns and Pam had known where to look for the first lot of Mother's pills in November, and why Mother had written and told me that she could not understand how Pam knew everything that was said in our letters to each other.

The chief superintendent kept banging on the table, shouting, 'I'm convinced you wanted to get your mother to kill herself so that you could get the money.' He meant Gran's trust. This was a ridiculous suggestion. Part of the trust had been swallowed up in the property company and CSA still had first charge on the rest. I had known for a long time that I would be lucky to receive a fraction of the full amount once our affairs were settled.

While he was questioning me, the chief superintendent told me that the police had my whole afternoon's visit with Mother on video tape. I did not believe him. I told him he was lying. No one could have bugged my mother's private bedroom in that way without her permission.

I was by now utterly exhausted. I had been kept in the room and interrogated for over five hours. I told the superintendent that I had some letters from Mother to me. I felt sure that when he read them he would understand everything. I asked if I could phone my husband.

'No phone calls,' I was told.

I was then driven back to my hotel in London. The police searched my room and at 10.30 p.m. we started a long drive to Cornwall. I was put in the back of the same small car in which I'd been abducted from St George's and the same man and woman got into the front. I told them that I suffer from car sickness. But it didn't seem to matter. We drove all night. The man chain-smoked. I asked him if he could possibly smoke a little less as I still had a very bad cough and the smoke made it worse. He refused.

We arrived at my home at 4.30 a.m. George answered the door. I explained as gently as I could what had happened, not wanting to shock him because of his bad heart. He took the man and woman into the kitchen while I fetched about twelve letters, all that I had kept from Mother, and I gave them to the man. He then told me to sign a form stating that I was on bail for £250 for two months. But I had no idea whether I was being charged with anything. I don't even recall being told I was under arrest. Then, the two went to our local police station at St Austell to rest and eat. They picked me up again at 10.30 a.m. and took me back to Burgess Hill station – the right one this time. I caught a train to London and returned to my hotel, worn out and frightened and still not understanding what was happening.

Chapter 8

The day after my return from Cornwall I went to my solicitor in London and told him everything. Then I went back to my selling at the Ideal Home Exhibition. I travelled home the following Sunday, the day after the exhibition closed, having sold six full sets of *Britannica,* in spite of all I had been through! I must have inherited at least some of Mother's unbreakable spirit. For the next few weeks I went on with my sales work.

It was a great sorrow that the condition of my bail was that I could not see or even write to Mother. I wondered how she was. Did she know what had happened to me? Had the shock of what had happened had a bad effect on her already poor health? I heard nothing more from the police but I talked on the phone several times to my solicitor, who was having great difficulty in getting in to see Mother. The nuns blocked him all the time. However, he had had a letter from Mother saying that I 'was in no way to blame, it was all her idea,' which of course was true. She also told him that she had not known that her private room had been interfered with by the police.

On 20 May, worn out by anxiety and the terrible heat again, the hottest May for two hundred years, I phoned my solicitor's office. My bail expired at the end of May and I was very worried. His secretary told me that he had left a message saying that I need not go to Burgess Hill to surrender to my bail after all. I thought this meant it was all over and cried and cried, then went to bed and slept for sixteen hours. Next morning I had a phone call from him. It was not over yet, but the police had now extended my bail to 20 June, a month from then. So I continued my sales work in the roasting heat and despite terrible headaches – I was the family breadwinner now.

On Saturday, 5 June, I was at home. It was two weeks since the solicitor had told me that my bail had been extended for another month and a few days after my sixtieth birthday. I had been out selling earlier in the day, and was having a cup of tea with George and Robin. It was 5 p.m. There was a knock on the door. Two plain-clothes detectives and a uniformed police woman identified themselves and asked if they might come in. I said that they could. Then the older man, an inspector, told me that I was under arrest on instructions from the Sussex police. I felt very sorry for him. He was so obviously embarrassed at having to take this action and said that he could not understand why I could not remain in my own home until the Sussex police collected me. I was a well-known local citizen and not likely to run away. I went upstairs, accompanied by the woman police officer, put a few toilet things together and was then driven to St Austell. It was 6 p.m.

In the police station (where I was well known through my constant rescuing of lost cats and dogs) I was taken to a very old tiny cell. It was 6 ft wide and 7 ft long and contained an iron bed bolted to the wall, with a foam pallet, and an open lavatory right up alongside the head of the bed. It smelt rather badly as it had no cover. There was a small barred window high up in the wall, so dirty that no light came in, and an electric globe in the ceiling covered with wire mesh.

'*Please* don't shut the door. I have claustrophobia. I won't be able to bear being locked in this small space,' I appealed to the inspector. But he told me regretfully that he had no choice, the door must be shut and locked. But he was very kind and said that I could phone my husband later and ask him to bring my pillow (there wasn't one supplied) and an extra blanket for the coming night. I was then stripped and searched by two female officers – a stupid indignity at my age, I felt. The heavy metal door clanged shut and I was alone.

I fought hard against my rising panic. To occupy my thoughts I set about making my cell a little better. I folded the one grey blanket and laid it over the open lavatory to make a sort of table by the bed. On this I put my Bible, a book I was reading and the tin mug of water I'd been given. Then I sat on the bed, took up my book and tried to read. But unless it has ever actually happened to you, you will never really know the terror and anguish of being locked in a small cell behind a heavy metal door, with its tiny peep-hole through which you can be spied on at all times, even while using the lavatory. The whole incident was so unexpected and so frightening. My bail had been renewed until 20 June, so why was I now locked in this cell? I *still* had no idea what I was supposed to be charged with.

During the evening I was let out and taken to the front office. A sergeant who knew me asked what on earth I was doing there. I phoned George and he and Robin brought me a pillow, a blanket and some Hovis and honey sandwiches for my supper. I could not eat the thick doorsteps of bread and margarine I had been given. We kissed good-bye and then I went back to my cell to wait for the Sussex police to fetch me. I was eating my bread and honey when an enormous centipede crawled across the grubby stone floor. It must have been eight or nine inches long. I yelled and banged on the door and then yelled some more. Eventually the prison matron came, opened the door, took one horrified look at the insect, and promptly squashed it. I had to take certain tablets at night for migraine and also for sleeping. The inspector had checked this with my doctor on the phone and George had been allowed to bring them. The matron now gave them to me.

Sunday morning came. It was so grey in my cell that I did not know if the day was wet or sunny. At lunch time I was given a tin plate, with a revolting mess of meat and potatoes, and a plastic spoon with which to eat. By now I was past eating anything. The hours dragged by and still I was locked in. I had been allowed to keep my watch only because of the kindness of the inspector.

At 6 p.m. on Sunday, after I had been in my cell for twenty-four hours, the Sussex police arrived. It was the same man and woman as before and they put me in the same little car and we drove off to Burgess Hill. They refused to talk to me or tell me why I had been treated in this way.

'You are our prisoner,' was the only remark the woman made. The whole twenty-four hours had been like some horrible nightmare. I felt I might just as well be living in pre-war Nazi Germany or present-day Russia. Could things like this really be allowed to happen in England?

We arrived at Burgess Hill Police Station at 11.30 p.m. I was deeply thankful to see my solicitor waiting for me. He had just returned from a holiday and George had only managed to contact him late on Sunday afternoon. The man read out the charge. It was the first time that I actually learnt that I was being charged with anything. He then told me that I must appear before the magistrate at Haywards Heath Court next morning. My solicitor, who lived about five miles away, asked if I could be released into his custody for the night and spend it at his home. This was refused. So I was once more locked in a cell for the night, no pillow this time and only one grey blanket. The next morning I was driven in a police panda car to the Magistrates' Court and charged. It was read out in complicated legal terms – that I had aided, abetted, counselled or procured an attempt by Mother to commit suicide and that I had maliciously caused her to take something noxious. What it really boiled down to was that I had tried to harm my mother. This was an absurd charge. Of course I pleaded not guilty. I was again given bail on condition I did not write to or see Mother unless her life were in danger. Then I left with my solicitor who drove me to his office in London. I later caught the 5.30 train home to Cornwall. It had been the most terrible thirty-six hours of my not uneventful life. I did not know then that much worse was to come.

On 14 June my solicitor phoned. He had at last managed to see Mother. They had had a long and friendly talk. Mother had again said that this whole thing was entirely her fault. She was worried because she had written several letters to me and my solicitor told her I had not received any of them. Presumably they had been intercepted once more, although no one had any legal right to prevent Mother writing to me. (It was a condition of my bail that the Reverend Mother should read any letters.) This seemed quite a serious matter, so the solicitor wrote to Pam asking her if she knew about the letters. He received no reply.

The anxiety I felt about Mother increased. She was totally isolated from me. For the first time in my life we were not able to communicate at all. I realized more and more how much I had always loved her. I think that when she looked at me she saw herself, or an idealized picture of herself, all her hopes and dreams centred in the greatest love of her life. But that was far from my sister's picture of our relationship. Now I longed to see Mother, to reassure her, to see for myself that she was not being treated as harshly as her previous letters had indicated.

On Thursday, 15 July, I suddenly had a strong feeling that something was very wrong with Mother. We were so close – we had often known by intuition that the other was in trouble. Now I could almost hear her voice. I phoned the Reverend Mother in the evening and was told that Mother was indeed not very well.

'We think she's a little anaemic,' she said. In fact Mother suffered from pernicious anaemia; before going into St George's she had been having two injections a week for this condition for several years. Surely this must have been in her medical notes at St George's?

The next day I felt ill with absolute certainty that something was very wrong. We decided that George and Robin would drive up and see her – they would go on the Monday to avoid the heavy week-end traffic. I again phoned the Reverend Mother and was told the same thing – 'Not too well.' I did not tell her of my family's intended visit. George and Robin set off at 5.30 a.m. on Monday, 19 July. When they arrived at St George's they were shown into a room and kept waiting for nearly an hour. Unknown to them, the Reverend Mother informed the Burgess Hill police that they were there.

A detective sergeant and a detective constable duly arrived and ordered George and Robin to leave. They stated that Mother was a prosecution witness, which was totally untrue. George went to a local call box and phoned our solicitor, who in turn spoke to the Public Prosecutor's Office. He was informed that the police had no right to intervene in this way. George and Robin returned to St George's and the men from Burgess Hill were removed. Still there were long delays. One nun came in and told them that Mother was too ill to see them, but George kept insisting, his suspicions thoroughly aroused by now. At last the Reverend Mother appeared and stated that Mother had collapsed and been rushed to hospital on the previous Friday.

George and Robin set off for Cuckfield Hospital. There a young doctor told them that Mother did not wish to see them. Robin insisted that his grandmother would want to see him. The doctor went away, then came back and said that Mother still insisted upon not seeing anybody. My son would not accept this and asked for a note from his grandmother to this effect. Thereupon the doctor then said that my mother was in fact too ill either to write a note or to receive any visitors except Pam and her housekeeper, Mrs Cox. By now both George and Robin were convinced that they were being deliberately kept from seeing my mother and, upon being pressed further, the doctor admitted that he had been instructed not to let them in. As it was early evening they left for home, George phoning me first to tell me the whole story. I at once contacted our solicitor who in turn spoke with the hospital administrator. As a result, when I phoned the hospital that night, the young doctor apologized and said that he was now allowed to tell me that Mother was very ill indeed and having blood transfusions. I asked if I should come, a condition of my bail stated that I could see Mother if her life were in danger. He asked me to phone the next day as he could not make the decision at the moment. I phoned on Tuesday evening. He told me that Mother was worse and he thought I should come.

The next morning at 5.30 Robin drove me up to Sussex and we saw Mother in the hospital. She was in a public ward. I stood by her bed and held her thin, frail hand, Robin stood at the foot of her bed and my sister sat in a chair nearby. Mother was semi-conscious. She had a needle in the vein in her arm attached to the blood-transfusion machine. After a while she opened her eyes and I gave her the red rose I had picked that morning, her favourite flower. She smiled weakly at me and I held her head and gave her a little drink of tea that a nurse handed to me. We stayed for about an hour. When we were leaving I said, 'Don't forget I came, will you darling.' 'I never forget anything, my dear,' she replied quite firmly. The tears ran down my cheeks, and we walked slowly out of the ward. I did not know then that I was never to see Mother alive again.

My solicitor was waiting outside the hospital. He was furious at the way I had been treated.

'This is now a whole new ball game,' he said. But it wasn't, it was the same old ball game, as I was to discover.

Throughout June and July I had worked hard at my selling, but in September I had a letter from *Encyclopaedia Britannica* suspending me from my work pending the outcome of the trial.

Mother had returned to St George's. She managed to smuggle out a letter (the last one I ever had from her) through my solicitor. She said, 'I will be glad when our case is over, and I can see my daughter again. . . . I *will* see her, even if I have to crawl outside on my hands and knees.'

She also said that she liked and trusted my solicitor, Mr B. 'He is a good friend,' she wrote. Mother was my chief defence witness and she gave Mr B. a very clear statement about why I had given her the pills. She said that I was in no way to blame, the whole thing was her idea. She actually said that she had 'persuaded me against my better judgement'. But she was virtually isolated. It seemed so wrong that Mother should be kept a prisoner in this way. In fact on my solicitor's last visit to her, Mother told him that she could not talk to him any more or 'I am to be turned out of here,' she said. Indeed, without my help, there was no way poor Mother could move from St George's and of course I was still not allowed to see her.

I was becoming more and more worried by the fact that it was now late August, yet no QC had been engaged for me, although Mr B. told me that he had been informed that my trial might be the second week in November. I decided that I should change solicitors, but we had no knowledge of legal people in London. In desperation I very unwisely phoned a man who had introduced himself at Lewes Crown Court in July when I had applied to the court to allow me to visit Mother. He worked as a reporter and had offered any help I needed. I now asked him if he knew a reliable solicitor in London and he gave me the name of a friend of his, 'a real live wire' he told me. I had to go before a judge at Lewes Crown Court to change solicitors. It was now 12 November and I had been on bail since March.

After the court hearing I was pestered by reporters all wanting my 'story'. I did not want to talk to anyone. I travelled back to London by train with a very friendly young girl who said she worked for Yorkshire Television. Her name was Di Burgess. We discovered that we shared a love of cats. She told me that her TV company was thinking of making a documentary on the problems of people in retirement who had been ruined by the failure of several merchant banks. She asked if George and I would be willing to take part in the filming of the documentary. I told her I would discuss it with George. Poor George, he was now very unwell and so worried about me. In early December Di Burgess paid us a visit. She seemed so friendly and anxious to help and she too was concerned about the fact that I *still* did not have a QC to defend me. We agreed to take part in the documentary.

Mr R. seemed no more successful than Mr B. in getting a QC to defend me. I was now so worried that I decided to take things into my own hands. I talked on the phone to a friend in Richmond, a retired solicitor. She gave me the names of several leading Queen's Counsels and I started phoning their clerks in London. This is not allowed really, all contact has to be through a solicitor, but I was pretty desperate by this time and I have never been bothered very much by what is 'done' and what is 'not done'. I spoke to the clerk to Sir Peter Rawlinson. I'm afraid I let him think that I was speaking for my solicitor. The clerk told me that he knew about my case and that Sir Peter would like to act for me but could not do so until the week following 25 January. My trial was now set for 24 January. The clerk tried to persuade the clerk to the court at Lewes to put my trial off for a week, but this was refused. The next day or two I phoned several more leading counsels' clerks – but because of the nearness of the trial no one was free to take my case.

On 14 December Di Burgess, the girl from Yorkshire Television, arrived at Lanlivery Manor with her boss, Mr John Willis, and a camera crew to film George and me and our house. I signed a contract for two days' filming in our house and was paid £250. The two days were chaos, men and wires all over the house. We all went to Lerryn to film our property company's now-abandoned site. Once or twice I was asked to comment on my forthcoming trial, but each time I refused to discuss it at all.

On 21 December I went to London and at last found a QC who could take my case at this late date. He was Mr S. I phoned my solicitor and told him that I had found a QC for myself. Mr R. made an appointment for me to see Mr S. after Christmas.

Two days before Christmas, while I was icing the cake (the sky can fall, I would still keep our family Christmas intact), I had the most wonderful surprise – Andy phoned. She was at London Airport! Bless her loving heart, she had spent all her savings to fly home to be with us, to give us her love and support for my coming trial. On Christmas Eve George and I met her at our local station. My darling daughter looked as lovely as ever. *What* a welcome we gave her, we all loved her so much for her unselfishness in flying 12,000 miles for a family Christmas. So in spite of the misery surrounding me and my concern for Mother, we had a joyful, peaceful Christmas Day, and for a few hours I could forget the terrifying ordeal facing me in January.

On the last day of December, Andy and I went to the sales in Plymouth. While we were out I had a bad fall and injured my right hip. So I hobbled about on crutches for the next few days;

a fall at sixty years old is rather a shock to the system. The entry in my diary for New Year's Eve reads, 'Thank God 1976 is over, the worst year of my whole life I think.' It was a good thing I did not know what 1977 had in store.

By the end of the first week in January I had a competent Junior Counsel, Mr P.B., who had been recommended by our retired friend in Richmond. On 10 January he, Mr R. and I saw the police video-tape for the first time in Mr R.'s office in London.

It was now clear that a week before my visit to Mother on 28 March, on the day when she had been told that her floorboards needed repairing and had to spend an afternoon in another room while the work was supposed to be carried out, the police had dressed up as plumbers and installed their latest 'toy', a tiny video-camera, over Mother's wardrobe and a tiny bugging device under her table. The Reverend Mother had co-operated with them in an amazing way, allowing them to invade my mother's private room. The police later justified their action by stressing that their chief and foremost duty is to prevent crime, yet they made no attempt to prevent my taking the pills to Mother, thereby committing an illegal act. On this occasion not only was no effort made to prevent the crime, the scene was actually set up for it to take place. The Sussex police *wanted* to film my handing over the pills – I was the 'patsy' or 'fall guy' in American parlance. Suicide itself is no longer against the law, but old people are by law denied the means by which they can choose themselves whether they wish to live or die.

The day after we saw the film, I met my QC, Mr S., for the first time. Present at the meeting were my solicitor, Mr R., and my Junior Counsel, Mr P.B. I was horrified to hear that Mr S. had no intention of challenging the police invasion of Mother's room. Apparently such activity is not against the law. Nor did he intend to challenge the way in which I had been abducted from St George's under false pretences or ask how such activities could take place in a Roman Catholic retreat. He warned me that if I pleaded not guilty and was convicted, I would probably be sentenced to five years in jail. If I was to plead guilty, however, the fact that Mother had actually *asked* me to help end her life of suffering would act as a powerful mitigation and there was a strong possibility that I would only get a suspended sentence. I was truly shocked that such a proposition should be made to me, and told Mr S. this in no uncertain terms. He advised me to think it over carefully and let him know my decision on Monday.

My solicitor drove me to the flat of a friend in Knightsbridge where I was staying and on the way there I broke down and cried. He too told me to think things over carefully.

'If you go to prison the shock will probably kill your husband,' he said.

I went back to Cornwall the next day. I had made up my mind that I could not plead guilty to something when I was *not* guilty. It was against my whole moral code, the code that dear Mother had so firmly instilled into me all my young life. So I told George and Andy of my decision. They agreed wholeheartedly.

'Always remember Sir Thomas More, Mummy,' said Andy. But I had no wish to lose my life as he had done.

The next day, 13 January, I phoned Mr R. and told him of my decision. He reluctantly agreed to try to find another QC. On Sunday, 16 January, Mr R. phoned and said that he was hoping to secure Mr John Lloyd-Eley. It did not come about, however. Instead, at the last minute my solicitor managed to engage Mr Gerard Wright. I met him only once before the trial – in London. We only spoke for about fifteen minutes.

Mr R. did manage to see Mother before the trial started and served a subpoena on her in case we should want her to speak on my behalf in court. She had accepted it willingly. He said that although her mind was very clear, she was now very frail indeed. But I knew Mother so well. I knew that like Grandmother and Great-Grandmother, she had such determination and such a strong will that nothing would prevent her from speaking in my defence if I asked her to. In fact, I could see her putting even the judge in his place, and thoroughly enjoying a part in a real-life drama, after all her years of imagined dramas and intrigues. With that thought, I prepared to face my trial.

Chapter 9

I said good-bye to my dear family and our much-loved animals (we now had five cats and two dogs), took a last look at the frosty garden which I had created out of the wilderness seven years ago, and caught the train to London. It was Sunday, 23 January. The trial was to start the next day. I travelled on to the small hotel in Lewes where I was to stay during my trial. Di Burgess from Yorkshire Television had promised to pay my hotel bill in return for my giving the first chance of my story to her boss after the trial if I were acquitted. This was only a verbal 'gentleman's agreement' – I just hoped she would keep her word. I had no money for an hotel, however small.

On the Monday morning, leaning on my stick, I limped along to the Crown Court. My hip was still very painful. I had to push through all the press and TV cameras outside. While I was standing waiting in the entrance hall the court usher came up to me and said, 'Would you like a chair, Lady Purchas?' I explained that I was not the judge's wife, only the accused on trial. Then my Junior Counsel, Mr P.B., arrived with Mr Wright, my Queen's Counsel. A young woman was with them. She introduced herself as Mrs T., a part-time worker in my solicitor's office. Her real profession was nursing. Mrs T. told me that my solicitor had been called abroad. She was to attend throughout my trial.

Everyone filed into the court. It was the famous (or infamous) court room No. 1, where so many murder trials had been held, the former happy hunting ground of Judge Jeffries, known as the 'Hanging Judge', a room full of the echoes and atmosphere of the sum total of misery and despair that had surely soaked into the heavy wood panelling on the walls. I felt that over the door should be written, 'Abandon hope, all ye who enter here.' The press box was full, of course. Then I saw the jury. There were four young women, almost certainly housewives and mothers, and I felt pretty certain that they were not going to want a long a difficult trial. I have since learnt that jurors can be changed in certain circumstances, but I was given no opportunity to discuss the possibility.

Judge Purchas came in and sat down in his red robe. He had been a civil judge and this was to be his first criminal case. I was sitting in the dock, of course. I had passed very close to Pam to reach my allotted place. She had her housekeeper with her, without whom she had scarcely moved for the past twenty years. I looked at my sister to smile, but she stared straight ahead. How sad that we, who had played together as children and grown up together in the same house, should now be separated by so much bitterness. Then the prosecution QC, Mr Roger Frisby, rose to his feet to open the Crown's case against me.

The whole prosecution case was based on two things: the police secret video-tape, without which they didn't have a case (or so their solicitor had told my solicitor) and my alleged financial motive in wanting Mother to kill herself. The really tragic point was that I *could* not have had a financial motive. We still had no settlement of our affairs with CSA. Had Mother taken the pills (which I am convinced was not her intention at all) and died, every single penny of Gran's trust would have gone straight to the receiver for CSA under our personal guarantees which were still in force. Putting it cold-bloodedly, it was in my own interest at that time to keep poor Mother alive, at least until we were released by CSA and that still looked a remote possibility in the distant future.

But all this was ignored by Mr Frisby, naturally enough. He

had to present quite a different picture of my intentions. At first he told the jury that I would have inherited 'the bulk of Mother's fortune' if she had died – in fact he meant Gran's trust; Mother certainly had no fortune of her own. He later corrected this but kept on stressing that I was over £200,000 in debt. That debt was the debt of Patterson Properties Ltd, a company debt; it was not my personal debt at all. However, CSA still had the charge on our house and my inteerst in Gran's trust. Our own small private debts were almost cleared by my successful work for *Encyclopaedia Britannica* and we would have been entirely free from them had I not lost my job through this trial. Mr Frisby also said that Mother was a 'devout Catholic', but in fact she hated the Roman Catholic Church. He did say one very true thing, and that was that Mother was 'not the type to kill herself'. After forty years of her obsession with suicide and death, this was surely obvious to anyone who knew her well.

However, Mr Frisby spoke most convincingly and eloquently, although I had been told that he was a sick man. I now found out just what a terrible creature I was, how greedy, callous and even depraved. Of course, he was only doing what he was supposed to do on behalf of the Crown – to make my character as black as possible. And he certainly succeeded.

When I got back to the hotel just after 4.30, there on the reception desk was the local *Evening Argus.* It carried a big splash across the front page – a picture of me going into court and some of Mr Frisby's very uncomplimentary remarks. I went and sat in the lounge and at once the manageress came and asked me to pay the bill in advance, 'under the circumstances,' she said coldly. I told her that my friend would be in soon to pay the bill. I was very relieved when Di Burgess did indeed arrive and kept her part of our 'gentleman's agreement'. The national news came on the television set, and there I was once more, limping along to the court with my stick. The newsreader gave extracts from Mr Frisby's opening speech. The next day the newspapers carried headlines such as 'Amazing court story of alleged bid by daughter to persuade her rich mother to kill herself' and in letters two inches high:

'DEAR MUM, TAKE THESE DEATH PILLS'. This was in the *Sun*. In actual fact, those words were never used in court, either by me or by anyone else.

Day after day the trial continued. All the time the prosecution referred to my 'wealthy mother', my desire to inherit a large sum of money – I could see that the jury were being skilfully indoctrinated with my financial motive for giving the pills to Mother.

The police were called to state how they took me from St George's but before they gave this evidence, Judge Purchas sent the jury out and warned the press not to report this part of the proceedings. The two police detectives said that I had been properly cautioned in the car as we were leaving St George's. When the judge called me into the witness box I said very firmly that this was not true. I told the judge that at *no* time had I been told that I was under arrest or cautioned, that had either of those things been said to me. I was intelligent enough, in spite of the shock, to demand the right to phone my husband or my solicitor. However, the judge told me that he preferred to take the word of the Sussex police.

The jury came back and the trial proceeded. My sister was called as the chief prosecution witness. When my Counsel cross-examined her she said that she had challenged Gran's will because she was 'not satisfied by the circumstances of her death.'

'And I am still not satisfied,' she added.

Then Mr Wright asked her about a letter which she had written to me during my time in Cape Town. In her letter, Pam had said that if she died with the birth of her baby by her second husband (like the rest of our family she too talked a lot about death), she wanted me to take Rodney to live with us so that I could bring him up.

'If you mistrusted your sister and did not think she was a good person, why were you willing to give your son into her care?' Mr Wright asked. The letter in question was handed to Pam. Although it was not at first admitted, the letter was later admitted by the Prosecution to be in Pam's handwriting after it had been examined by experts. Pam also admitted that

Mother had talked of suicide for over forty years, and that Mother and I had indeed played this 'suicide game'.

'And a very dangerous game it is, I would take no part in it,' she added.

Mr Frisby had described what he called a 'dress-rehearsal for death', claiming that Mother had been found in a coma after my visit on 28 November. However, when Sister Benignus, one of the sisters at St George's, gave her evidence she said that she had made an entry in her patients' record book in which she recorded finding Mother in a coma on 29 November, the day after my first visit with Mother's precious pills. Now, under cross-examination, she said that she had made a mistake and that it was 29 December when she found Mother in a coma on the floor. The room had then been searched and the pills found in a tissue in a coat pocket in the wardrobe. But, from Mother's letter to me, written on 30 December, it appeared that the pills had been found and taken away on 28 December while Mother was away having therapy and that from our intercepted letters the nuns knew exactly where to look for the pills. The judge commented that Sister Benignus had an unreliable memory for dates and details, but the discrepancies in her sworn testimony made it appear that Mother had actually taken some pills in an attempt to commit suicide. If she had done so, it is unlikely that *any* pills would have been found.

Doctor Todd testified that on 1 or 2 January he had been called to see Mother as she had had a fall. He stated quite plainly that he had not seen any sign of a coma and that the fall was consistent with an old person getting out of bed in a sleepy state and in trying to reach the commode falling on the floor. This was exactly what Mother had described to me in the letter in which she wrote that she had 'lain on the floor frozen with cold, unable to reach my eiderdown or a blanket.'

It was stated by the prosecution that Pam had taken our letters to him for his advice, but Doctor Todd denied this. When asked if it was true, he said, 'No, that is not true.' At no time had he been told about the pills until he was shown them on his visit to my mother in January.

The press reported nothing of the fact that Sister Benignus admitted making a mistake about the date or that the doctor said that he could see no sign that Mother had been in a coma. No, they were much too busy with their headlines of 'Nurse Turns 'Tec', 'Don't bungle it Mummy'. Just as Mr Frisby's job was to secure my conviction, so the reporter's job was to sell newspapers. I was made to look more and more fiendish, the headlines more and more sensational. I was called many things – 'Angel of Death', 'Daughter of Darkness', and 'Daughter of Evil'. There was nothing, so it seemed, so diabolical that it could not be applied to me, nothing that I could do to prevent it.

Television screens were set up all over the courtroom to show the secret video-tape made by the police in Mother's bedroom. Everyone saw poor Mother pull up her nightdress and sit on her commode in what she thought was the privacy of her own room.

The last scene on the video showed poor Mother being stripped and searched by two nuns. I had not seen it before. She was crying out, 'No, no, don't take my clothes off, please.' It was dreadful to see her on the small television screen being treated in that way. I heard her pitiful cries of 'No, no, *please* don't. God forgive them, they know not what they do.' I heard her last brave, dignified words, 'You don't understand, my daughter gave me those because she loves me so much.' It was too much. I broke down in the dock, sobbing uncontrollably. The judge ordered a fifteen-minute recess. I was led out, blinded by tears.

'No, no, they can't do that to Mummy,' I was saying. Mrs T., my solicitor's representative, sat me down and got some strong coffee.

I learned later that the jury seemed very perturbed by my behaviour. Was it that they wondered at that moment if I could possibly be 'not guilty' after all?

The day before Mr Wright closed his case for my defence, I felt that the jury had been so indoctrinated by the very forceful remarks of Mr Frisby (I felt sorry for him, he looked so ill by now) that I needed my *only* witness, the only person, other than myself, who knew the truth. I passed a note to Mr Wright and he requested the judge to grant a fifteen-minute recess so that we could confer. Mr Wright, Mr P. B. and Mrs T. sat down with me in a small room. I told my counsel that I wanted him to call my mother to court. She had been subpoenaed and was fully prepared to come and speak for me.

'If you bring a frail old lady to court, it will be very bad for you. The jury will think how callous you are,' he told me. I was very upset and tried to insist on Mother being called. After all, she and I were the only people who really knew exactly what had happened. Mr Wright remained adamant in his advice not to call her. I was so ignorant of legal matters that I did not know I could have insisted.

The judge's summing up was so long and involved that I knew no ordinary man or woman, unversed in law as the jury must be, could only grasp half of what was being said. After the summing-up, Judge Purchas told the jury to retire and consider their verdict. Poor bewildered souls, the foreman came in two or three times that day to ask the judge to explain points on which they were confused. At 4.30 they returned and the judge asked if they were going to be able to reach a verdict that day. He had twice been asked by the foreman if he would accept a majority verdict and he had refused. He would only accept a unanimous one. So now, at the end of the day they were told that they must go to a hotel and be locked in until the next day's hearing. Judge Purchas told them that if they could not reach a unanimous verdict by the next morning, he would then accept a majority one.

I was alone now. My two friends and my vicar, who had given evidence as to my character, had gone back to Cornwall. They had told the jury of my kindness to many people in need in the past, and of my real concern for the welfare of old people but, of course, none of that was in the daily papers. So I ate my solitary dinner, then went up to my room, got into bed, and after my usual phone call to George and Robin (Andy had gone back to her job abroad by now), I tried to lose myself in the thriller I was reading. By a strange coincidence, a tiny place in the Lake District was featured in my book and I suddenly remembered a holiday we had had there, when I was thirteen years old.

Father's ship had been in dry dock for a re-fit in Barrow-in-Furness for about eight weeks, and we had all stayed in Ulverstone at first, then Father had gone back to sea, and Mother, Pam and I had spent another two weeks on a farm in the Lake District. Mother was not too well and said she needed some good farm food. The farm was owned and run by the Longmarsh family, surly father, tired and overworked mother, two sons Jeff and Abe (the latter was a big brawny young man), and a buxom sister, Flo, who waited on us in the dining room. Flo was unmarried but obviously in the last stage of pregnancy.

Just after our arrival Mother heard Flo crying in our room while she was making the beds, and the poor girl had poured her troubles into Mother's sympathetic ear. She had not told her family anything about the coming baby, and was fairly sure that they had not even noticed her condition! Mother urged Flo to at least confide in her mother, but the girl was very frightened and knew that neither she nor her mother stood any chance against the three domineering men.

Two nights later Flo started her labour. Mother heard her screaming and a terrible row going on in the kitchen, with men's voices shouting curses and abuse. Never lacking in what she considered to be her duty, Mother marched into the kitchen and demanded to know what was going on. Mr Longmarsh was purple with rage.

'I'm not having no strumpet in *my* house! Flo must leave at once,' he shouted. Mother told him coldly to stop the noise at once, and then she sent Flo up to her bed. Mrs Longmarsh scurried upstairs after Flo. Then Mother turned to full force of her anger on Mr Longmarsh and his sons. She demanded that one of them should go at once for the district nurse and when Mr Longmarsh tried to protest, she cut the ground from under his feet.

'How many young girls have you and your sons made pregnant?' she demanded. 'How dare you criticize Flo, when you are almost certainly worse than she is.'

She then turned her attention to Abe, who stood shuffling his huge feet, and fixing him with her eyes (as Mother could do so well) she said, bitingly, 'And who knows *who* has fathered this poor baby.'

The men were completely cowed, and Abe went at once for the nurse. Flo was having a bad time to judge by her cries. Poor girl, she was in labour all night. A young doctor came and went, and it was not until the next afternoon that the baby arrived, a lovely nine-and-a-half-pound boy, but stillborn.

All this had been very disturbing to a nervous thirteen-year-old child like me. I was very upset. Just before bedtime that night, Mother took my hand and led me in to look at Flo's little dead baby in a tiny coffin in the room next to ours. I had never seen anyone dead before, and this strange tiny waxy creature was to me a thing of horror. I could not go to sleep! Mother saw my distress during the early part of the night and, taking me into her bed, she said, 'You don't need to be afraid of that little baby. It's neck was broken before it was born.' As though this were some magic spell, all my fear fell away and I went to sleep thinking, 'Poor little thing, its neck was broken' – a comforting thought, given to me by Mother.

Now in my hotel room in Lewes, I thought of Mother lying in St George's in such pain, yet still with enough courage to be ready to stand by me in court, and I made up my mind that no matter what happened tomorrow when the jury returned, I would stand by what I knew to be the truth, with as much dignity and control as I could muster. I fell asleep at last with the remembrance of all the women in my family's past, their iron determination, their self-will even to the point of self-destruction. What a strange, strange heritage I had. In medieval times there could have been several of my family burned as witches!

A few days earlier in court, Mr Wright had asked Pam's

housekeeper about a curse that Pam alleged Mother had put on her and the farm. The woman had admitted that she knew of the talk of such a curse; that was supposed to be why all the animals kept dying. My last conscious thought was a mental chuckle, that even at eighty-seven Mother was still thought to retain her ability for working her magic!

Chapter 10

The next day, 10 February, was wet and raw. The whole world looked very grey. Maybe it always does when one faces the possibility of a prison sentence, however remote. It was still remote to me. There had been so much really firm evidence in my favour – the psychiatrist, Dr Low-Beer, had said that in his opinion Mother did not intend to use the pills, but was so obsessed that she would not rest until she had them; Mother's former landlady had told of the big bottle of sodium amytol which Mother kept always near at hand and of Mother's constant talk of suicide to her. And even Pam had said that 'it was a suicide game'.

As I walked along to the court, I wondered what Mrs Margaret Thatcher had really thought of my letter to her before the trial started.

Lanlivery Manor,
Lanlivery,
Nr Bodmin,
Cornwall.

The Rt Hon Mrs Margaret Thatcher,
The House of Commons,
Westminster,
London.

January 18 1977

Dear Mrs Thatcher,

I listened with interest and admiration to your broadcast on Jimmy Young's show last week and it is your views on personal freedom that prompt me to write this letter.

Last summer in Australia, you said that you felt the British people seemed unaware of the insidious encroachment on our freedom and personal liberty; and now, a really menacing event is about to take place.

Last March the Sussex police secretly installed a closed-circuit television camera over the wardrobe in the private bedroom of an old lady aged 87 years, who is a paying patient in a large Roman Catholic Retreat. When the patient's daughter (aged 60 years) visited her, the police recorded everything on this hidden television camera, installed without the knowledge or consent of the patient, who is mentally very alert, in fact she does the 'Daily Telegraph' crossword every day.

The Sussex police acted in this manner because the patient's younger daughter had been intercepting letters between her mother and sister, opening them and photocopying the contents over a period of some six months.

The patient had been begging her elder daughter to take her some sleeping pills, to keep locked away, in case she (the old lady) should ever find her suffering unendurable and want to end her life peacefully.

I am the elder daughter and I know that my mother is not at all likely to take her own life, in fact it is a fantasy of hers which has been going on for at least forty years.

Next Monday, January 24th, I go before a judge and jury, the case against me being based on the video-tape (sound and vision) obtained by the Sussex police.

Whether I am found guilty or not is of much less importance than the admission of this type of evidence, and the ominous fact that if the Sussex police get this admitted as evidence, we have the beginning of a complete infringement of our personal privacy and the police would begin to have almost unlimited powers.

I came to the House of Commons on November 12th 1976, and told my M.P., Mr Robert Hicks, all the facts and he was horrified.

Now I have told you, because I feel sure that you must feel very strongly that we *must* fight for our personal privacy and liberty; any other attitude makes a mockery of our fight against Hitler's secret police, and brings us in line with Soviet Russia.

I have admired you ever since you were Minister for Education, and I hope that before long our country will be in your capable hands.

Please watch my case, and speak out against the *method* of obtaining evidence, if you really value freedom.

Yours sincerely,

Mrs Y. T. McShane.

I wondered about the jury too, if they had been unable to reach a unanimous verdict late yesterday afternoon, would they now take the judge's offer and return a majority one? At the end of yesterday's proceedings I had heard my counsel and Mr Frisby discussing the definite possibility of a re-trial, which could happen if the jury refused to give a verdict today. I would welcome that, as *then* we could perhaps remove the trial from Lewes to London, a thing we had tried in vain to have done before. I went into the cold, grey stone building, past all the clicking cameras and excited newsmen, along the corridor which needed painting badly, and into the canteen.

The canteen at the back of Lewes Crown Court is small, and today it is crowded – reporters, people waiting for cases to be heard, and unmistakably a small group of CID men talking in a corner. I pick up my cup of coffee just as a court usher hurries in.

'The jury are returning,' he tells me. They have been locked in an hotel for the past thirty-six hours.

We make our way to the now familiar court room. I feel sick, but at the same time quite calm. I'm glad I packed my suitcase this morning in the small hotel where I spent the past two and a half weeks. Tonight I will surely be on my way home to Cornwall and this nightmare over.

As I go into the dock yet again, I make plans to see Mother as soon as the verdict is given. I'll get a taxi to St George's, I think, and this time the nuns cannot stop me from seeing Mother. I sit down in the dock, the barristers and counsels troop in. The court is packed with spectators again as it has been every day. This is an unusual trial and reporters now pack the press box getting their note books ready. As soon as the court rises they will make a dash for the phone boxes outside, and I see the headlines in my mind, 'Suicide Woman not guilty'. It has to be that, because that is the truth, and in spite of all that I have listened to for so many days now, I still believe that the jury must have seen my innocence.

'The court will rise.' In comes the fat little judge in his red robe, and I laugh to myself, remembering the day the trial started and the usher asked me if I were Lady Purchas! His Lordship sits down, we all sit down, and in come the jury. I look at them to smile – several of them have smiled at me during the trial – but now they avoid my eyes and look straight ahead. The judge asks for their verdict. Is it a majority verdict, or is it unanimous? To my surprise it is unanimous. Then the foreman steps forward. I feel sure *he* likes me.

I hold tightly to my little wooden cross that I have held all through the past days of uncertainty, given to me years ago by my sister, who has been the chief prosecution witness. The foreman of the jury reads from the paper in his hand, the court is hushed.

'We find the accused guilty.'

Someone at the back cries out, 'No, no,' and I am stunned.

'The accused will rise,' says the little man in the red robe, and I stand up and hold the edge of the dock. I look across at the jury in disbelief and horror. Haven't they heard *anything* I've said? Don't they know that I love Mother more than life itself? But the judge is speaking.

'You will go to prison for two years.' Surely that cannot be what he is really saying, to me, at sixty-one years old?

People behind me are crying out, and the judge raps his desk.

'Silence,' he says. 'The court will rise.' And in shock and disbelief I realize that he was indeed saying those terrible words.

Unobtrusively, two women prison officers appear, one at each side, and I turn to walk down the steps from the dock to the cells below, seeing a sea of faces. Some women spectators are crying and I wish I could speak to them.

Down below the court the white-washed cells are old and

small. One of the women officers takes everything away from me, even my little wooden cross.

'Sorry love we have to do this, it's the law,' she says, and I can see the compassion in her eyes. She is about five years younger than I am.

'I'll get your dinner now dear, it's half past twelve,' the other woman says, but I can hardly hear her. I keep thinking of Mother, what will happen to her now, with no one who loves her and will help her, she is already as much a prisoner as I am to be.

My solicitor walks in, in his black leather coat, and shakes my hand.

'Sorry about my suntan,' he says, 'I've been in Jamaica.' This is the first time I have seen him since before my trial; Mrs T., the nurse and part-time office worker, is the only representative from him that I have seen. I ask him to phone my husband and son in Cornwall. Will the shock kill my husband? I know how bad his heart is and how worried he has been.

Then they all go away and I sit alone, looking at the small, heavily barred windows which are below ground level. There is no daylight, only a bright naked light in the ceiling. I cannot cry, cannot feel anything, except a terrible sadness that because I loved Mother so much all my life I am going to prison, and perhaps will never see her alive again, my wonderful courageous mother, with her unbreakable spirit. She is very frail and old, and so helpless now. There is a quotation that says, 'For evil to succeed entirely, it is only necessary for good men to do nothing.'

Chapter 11

The cheerful blonde officer, who was nearly my own age, came and sat down at the little table. I was not now in the cell, thanks to her kindness, but in the small anteroom used by solicitors and police when prisoners are brought down from the court above. It was a room without windows, a naked electric bulb in the ceiling, and a small lavatory opening at one end. I asked her why we were sitting there, it was already 2 p.m. (she had allowed me to have my watch back). She replied that we were waiting for transport from Holloway to come and fetch us.

Time seemed to have lost all meaning in this dungeon-like place. The ceilings were so low that they pressed down on my head, and I felt stifled. There was no air or natural light; it brought to mind the dungeons and torture chambers of a past age. I asked the woman how old the building was. She did not know but said with feeling that it should have been pulled down long ago. What was happening in the world above our heads? What was George feeling? Did he know yet? These and a hundred other questions went round and round in my head. It seemed an eternity until at last at 5.30 (we had been waiting since noon) our transport arrived.

I was taken out by my present officer and the male prison driver, into a small mini-bus with heavy mesh over all the windows. But at least I could actually see out and look at the rain-soaked streets of Lewes, and then the places between Sussex and London. It was dark, but the street lights were on; people were hurrying home from work no doubt reading that the 'Suicide Woman' had been given a two-year sentence in prison. The woman officer was very good to me on the journey. She allowed me to swallow (dry) one of my special migraine pills. This was not allowed, but she took pity on my obvious suffering. Migraine at home is bad enough, but very much worse in a prison van.

We reached Holloway in due course. Inside the prison I was taken upstairs and handed over to a big, tough, black-haired woman officer, who took all my possessions, suitcase, coat, etc., and put me into a large room with tables and chairs. I crossed over and looked out of the windows. The room looked on to a concrete yard and other buildings opposite. There were no window bars, I was thankful to see. All the windows were made in a way that although they could be opened slightly, each section had an iron bar running down the centre, so it was not possible for even a head to get through. But many windows were smashed, the lights were on everywhere, and there was a constant noise, women screaming abuse at other windows, or trying to call out messages. The din was indescribable – women banging on the windows, and even glass breaking.

A coloured prisoner, a 'trusty' (or red band) brought in a plastic mug of tea (no sugar) and a plastic plate containing two thick slices of bread and margarine and a lump of cheese. I just sat and looked at it all, I was stunned and past all thought of food or drink.

Half an hour later the officer called me across the passage to a kind of office with a desk and filing cabinets.

'Stand on that and strip,' she said. I looked at her in disbelief.

'Well, get on with it,' she said crossly, 'You can leave your pants on,' the last with a sneer. I did as I was told, and standing on the towel took off all my clothes except my vest and knickers. She took each garment from me, and having searched it, threw it in a pile on the floor. Then she handed me a grubby blue towelling bath robe, and said, 'Go along to the end, for a photo and fingerprints, and *move*, I don't want to be here all night.'

The records man sat me in a chair, turned a very bright light on my face and took two pictures, one full face and one profile. Then he took my fingerprints. I went back to the office and was told that I could have three sets of clothing. The officer tried to remove my engagement and wedding rings, but after a great deal of effort with soap and water only the first ring came off – I had not taken it off since 1947. Then she said, 'I shall cut your wedding ring off.' I told her that she would have to cut my finger off, as I utterly refused to lose my wedding ring. I learnt later that legally she could not take any woman's wedding ring. Strangely enough, I kept my watch, but although I pleaded hard, my little wooden cross was not allowed. All my possessions, other than my three sets of clothes, were now packed in my case, and it was sealed up, and I signed for it.

I dressed again and was then sent along to the doctor, who proved to be an ordinary National Health practitioner from outside. He read my doctor's letter which had come with me, about the various pills that I regularly took – for thyroid and migraine – and also my sleeping tablets. He gave me one dose for that night, weighed me (I was then 11 st 6 lbs) and I was taken along to a cell. It is not really fair to call them cells at Holloway – they are all single or double rooms, with one or two bunks, a table and a chair, wash basin, and a small curtained-off lavatory. Normally they are as pleasant as any closed prison can be, but this was the reception block, and the room was so filthy that I did not want to put my bare feet on the floor. I sat on the single bunk and undressed. Then I crawled down under the bedclothes, and for the first time cried as though my heart would break. All the pent-up terror, loneliness and despair that I had felt for so many hours just flooded out, and I fell asleep worn out with weeping.

Next morning I was woken up at 6.30 by someone banging on the door which was then unlocked, and an officer told me to be in the dining room at seven for breakfast. I washed as well as I could in the dirty basin, dressed, and went out into the corridor. There was already a queue of women, all sizes and shapes, all ages, but mostly young, and with quite a few black or coloured girls. They were all shouting and laughing, and seemed quite at home in this dreadful place – the corridor was as filthy as my room. We were handed a bowl of thin grey porridge at the serving hatch, a plastic egg cup half full of sugar, and two slices of bread and margarine, then collected our mugs of almost black tea from a trusty operating a big urn at the end of the room. I went and sat down at a table. The noise was deafening. Suddenly there was a fight, one woman threw her porridge in another's face. It was not near to me and I was thankful to be out of the way.

After breakfast, we were all told to gather up our things (there were about thirty people, all admissions from the day before) and go along to a waiting room. Our belongings now included two blankets, two sheets, one pillowcase and a towel which had been issued the previous night. I saw that the old hands spread out a blanket, bundled everything on to it and then tied the four corners, so I did the same, and heaved my bundle along to the waiting room. We sat until our names and numbers (given on arrival) were called out, then we followed an officer to whatever prison block was thought suitable. I went with three other women to Block C4Y, which was called Assessment and, I learnt later, was considered to be the best billet, after the hospital of course, which seemed to be everyone's ideal. C4Y was up on the third floor, and I laboured as fast as I could up the stone stairs; I had already discovered that it was wise to do everything as quickly as possible, to avoid the displeasure of the officers, or 'screws' as even I began to call them.

We were met at the top of the stairs by a stout middle-aged woman with dyed blonde hair. She looked very tough indeed and glared at me in such a way that my heart sank even lower. She told us to dump our bundles inside the door to the corridor, which she then locked, and then ordered us to follow her along to our allotted cells. Two of the women were old friends, and joked and laughed with the officer, Mrs C. She put them into a cell together, so I plucked up courage – I felt really desperate – and asked if I could possibly have a cell to myself. Mrs C. looked at me for a long minute, then said gruffly, 'O.K., you can have number five,' and I felt so grateful that I would have some privacy, at least for a while.

I laid my things on the bottom bunk, then made up the top bunk, so that I would not feel quite so shut in – Mrs C. had locked the door and the cell was only about 8 ft wide and 10 ft long. Suddenly I felt my old claustrophobia in full force. I was frantic to get out. I began to cry hysterically. Try as I would I could not stop, and having no tissues or handkerchief, my nose ran as well as my eyes. Then God sent me the help he knew I needed so desperately. The door was unlocked, and in came a cheerful, fair-haired young woman. She put her arm round my shoulders, and told me that she was Sister Jennie, of the Church Army and working full time in Holloway. Gradually she calmed my sobs, and then told me that she knew that because of the bad publicity I had had at my trial there was sure to be some hostility among the officers, so she had talked to them and asked them to try to be a little more understanding. She had pointed out to them that to come to prison for two years at my age was a terrible shock, and she assured me that Mrs C. would do what she could for me.

I poured out all my terror of being locked in the small cell, and worst of all, I explained that I was sick with anxiety about George, and what had happened to him now I was sent to prison. Sister Jennie promised to see the welfare officer at once, and ask if I could speak to George on the phone. After asking Mrs C. to give me a pile of tissues, she left, and I sat down to read the Gideon Bible she had given me, and to draw strength and comfort from the unchanging word of God.

At 2.30 I was taken down by a red band, to wait outside the welfare office for my phone call to George. Lying on a window ledge was that morning's paper with a picture of me, and the headline: 'Angel of Death gets two years.' The reporter went on to say that when Mother learned I had been sentenced she had said, 'I am glad my favourite daughter has gone to prison, now I can sleep in peace!' It was so utterly absurd that had I not been standing in the cold grey prison corridor I would have laughed. After all her letters begging me to take the pills to her, and knowing how much she loved me, the words could not possibly have come from her, I knew.

The welfare officer called me into his office, asked me to sit down, and then phoned my home. Robin came on the line first and I had a few words with him. He said bravely, 'Don't worry, Mother, I'll take care of Father, keep your courage up,' and then handed the phone to George. I could not believe it, my poor husband was sobbing. He had been all through the war in India and Burma, been commended for bravery, and even when his mother died had not shed a tear. But now this brave man was crying, and he could only just manage to say, 'Darling, it's such a shock, such a shock.' Then he broke down completely, and put the receiver down. I was crying myself by now, and the kindly welfare officer sent for some coffee. When I had regained my self-control he said that he would arrange for Robin to bring George to visit me briefly on Monday. He said that if I could put on a brave front it might reassure George, whose heart trouble he knew about. How can I ever thank this kindly man, whose compassion meant so much to a family in deep distress? I can only hope that he may read this, and know how much a simple act of kindness was valued, and always will be. In fact, during this brief time in Holloway, I met nothing but kindness from both the welfare workers and all the officers, for whom I had nothing but praise.

Friday night came, and it was the most terrible night I had ever spent. No pills had been prescribed for the appalling migraine from which I suffered and none of my sleeping pills either. I had been taking Nembutal on a doctor's prescription every night for over twenty years, and I did not realize that what I suffered now were severe withdrawal symptoms, added to the migraine that descended in the middle of the night. No less than five times I rang my bell for the night officer, and begged and begged for something, anything, to ease my pain. She even sent for the night sister on duty, but I was only told, 'No, not unless ordered by the doctor.'

I will never forget those hours in my bunk, from lights out

at 9.30 to 6.30 next morning. Without the help of God I think I would have gone out of my mind. It was fortunate for me that the streak of family madness and instability had passed me by, or I would surely have tried to end my life in my mental and physical agony. When we were called at 6.30, I was grey with exhaustion, but by the grace of God, I had held on. Now my pains eased a little, and I could just manage to drink a cup of the almost black tea which seemed to be a feature of life in prison.

All the prisoners called the officers 'Miss'; so far I seemed to be the only one who asked their names and used them. Now one of the young women leaned across the table and said to me, 'Excuse me, Miss, but why are you eating with us?' I laughed (for the first time) and said, 'I'm not a "Miss", I'm just a prisoner like you.' The girl turned to her neighbour and said crossly, 'When she came in the TV room last night I stood up, I thought she was the governor.'

After breakfast I asked to see the doctor, and was told that no doctor was available until Monday, except in case of emergency. The officer refused to consider my needs as that.

On Saturday morning everyone cleaned her cell. There were about twenty cells and a large dormitory with ten to twelve beds, mostly occupied by the young girls. Almost everyone seemed to be in here for shoplifting, and I was surprised to learn that some of them had been here four or five times before. On Saturday afternoon we were taken out into the concrete yard for half an hour's exercise, but it was bitterly cold, and we were all glad to go back inside. Tea, the last meal of the day, was at five. Then we were locked in our cells until 6.30, when our doors were opened, and we could either lie on our bunks reading, or visit friends among the other prisoners, or we could watch the very old TV set in the common room.

Sister Jennie came to see me, and we had a long and comforting talk. She told me that many prayers were being said for me, and we arranged to meet in church the next morning. Night time came once more. We had a drink of tea and a bun at 8 p.m., and our doors locked at 8.30. Lights out was at 9.30.

I was so thankful that I was alone in my cell, and could say my prayers and read my Bible in peace, and try to gather my courage for yet another night of pain. But just before lights out Mrs C. came to my cell, and gave me one of her own migraine pills. She told me that she knew what hell a migraine was, but swore me to secrecy, as she could have got into serious trouble for helping me. How wonderfully God takes care of his own, even through the unlikely channel of a prison officer!

On Sunday morning about twenty of the forty or fifty women in C4Y went to church. The service was held in the brand new church which was not even finished yet. In fact New Holloway had only been occupied for two weeks before my arrival, and looking across at the old prison, with its tiny, heavily barred windows, I was thankful that at least I was in the new building. But although the move had been so recent, hundreds of windows had already been broken, wash basins torn from walls, and paint kicked off the doors – sheer wanton vandalism which only made life more unpleasant for the people who did all these stupid things. The morning service was spoilt for me by the regimentation of the women by the officers. Yet when I saw a nasty fight break out in one row of seats I realized that strict control was necessary here, even in church, so many of the women were very young and completely rebellious.

We were locked in our cells again after Sunday dinner, which was served at 11.30 a.m., and our cells were opened at 1.30 again. Those who had visitors (normal visiting hours were 1.30 to 3 on Saturdays and Sundays) were taken downstairs to the visiting hall. The rest sat and read or watched television. I lay on my bunk and slept until tea, which was at 4.30 on Saturdays and Sundays. I felt much refreshed by my long rest, and also my constant sense that even here, even now, Jesus was not far away.

On Monday morning we all went to the workroom at 8 a.m., and sitting at long tables, put plastic baby pants into bags. We were allowed to talk and even to move about from one table to another. Our work ended at 11.15, ready for dinner at 11.30. In the afternoon I did not go to work, but waited for my visit from George and Robin. When they arrived at the main gate the news was phoned to the welfare office, and I was taken downstairs. Just as they came into the corridor with an officer, I came along and rushed straight into George's arms. Nothing could have stopped me, short of a gun! We all went into the welfare office, and I sat and held George and Robin's hands and told them not to worry, I was fine, and felt sure that my appeal would soon be heard and be successful. George was shaking, he looked so drawn and ill. For the first time I wished with all my heart that I had ignored Mother's cries for help and stayed at home to care for my family. All too soon the visit ended. George was told that he and Rob could come for an official visit the next week-end, 'If your wife is still here,' the welfare officer said ominously. We all knew how important it was for me to stay in Holloway to wait for my appeal. I smiled and waved as they left, then went back to my cell for another crying spell. I was beginning to have a very sore throat and to lose my voice too. The doctor I had seen that morning had put me on to an antibiotic as my leucopenia made it difficult for me to throw off infections, but of course I had not told George and Robin any of that.

The next morning I saw the doctor again as he had requested, but now my voice was really gone, and I felt very unwell indeed. He told me to go back to bed and to see him again the next day. I was thankful to obey his orders. I think the strain and shock had caught up with me, I just wanted to sleep and sleep. On Wednesday I was told by Mrs C. that I was being transferred to Styal, a closed prison in the north of England, the next day, but when I saw the doctor again he said that I would not be going because I was not fit.

I was thankful to have a visit that afternoon from my Junior Counsel, Mr P.B., and Mrs T. They had come to discuss my appeal. Mr P.B. said that it was essential for me to stay in Holloway to be available for legal conferences, to prepare the grounds of appeal. I told him I was very much afraid of being moved so far away the next day, and he promised to petition the Governor at once to let me stay in Holloway. I told him that I could *not* accept prison for something I had not done, and he said that there was indeed a lot of discussion in legal circles as to whether a crime had actually been committed or not! After all, the charge had been 'Aiding and abetting a suicide' – but no suicide had taken place. Mr P.B. had lodged leave to appeal, and also an application for bail the day after my conviction, but I was unlikely to get bail when there was still such a witch hunt in the press. He and Mrs T. left with renewed promises to try to stop my removal, but it was many months before he was able to contact me again.

The next morning I saw one of the doctors and told him that I was supposed to be moved to Styal in Cheshire later that day. He said very firmly, 'In view of your age and this infection, I want you kept here for another week. It is a very long journey and you are not fit.' I was very relieved, and went to tell Mrs C., my officer, who at once went off to make enquiries about this. She came along to my cell, looked pityingly at me.

'I'm sorry, love. You're leaving at 2.30,' she said.

I did not then know that the Home Office rule is that no prisoner can be moved from one place to another, for whatever reason (even an appeal), unless a doctor has examined the prisoner and certified him or her fit to travel. That morning I had actually *seen* the doctor write 'unfit to travel' on my notes. In vain I tried to explain this to Mrs C.

'You're wasting your breath, flower. Someone high up wants you out, and out you will go,' she said.

Three women had come from Styal Prison to Holloway during my week there, two for their appeals, and one who told us gleefully that she had managed to convince the doctor that she was a 'nutter' and needed to be in the special wing in Holloway. All three women had told horrifying stories about Styal. They said it was known among prisoners as the worst nick.

I knew that if I were in Cheshire I would be out of touch with my legal advisers in London, and also my MP Mr Robert Hicks. I had seen Mr Hicks in the House of Commons before my trial, and had told him in detail how the Sussex police had invaded Mother's private room, without her knowledge or consent, to install their camera and listening device, and he had been horrified. He had written to George since my sentence and promised to visit me in Holloway. Styal would put an end to any contact with anyone, even people like the Council for Civil Liberties whom I felt sure must be very concerned about the police actions. It was doubtful if even George and Robin could travel the 340 miles from Cornwall for a two-hour visit.

So I was to be kept in a closed prison, cut off from family and friends, but there was nothing I could do about it, except pray, and trust that God had some purpose in this added injustice. After dinner as it was always called, I was told to get my bundle ready again, and was then taken back to the reception office where I had been on arrival. There were three other women going as well as me, all young, and all serving short sentences for shoplifting. We were not strip searched this time, just our belongings, coats and pockets. Then we were herded into a mini-bus which had come from Styal, with two officers. I still could not speak above a whisper, which seemed to annoy them both, but I felt too ill and despairing to care. The bus drove off through the rain-soaked streets of London. The rain lashed against the windows of the bus and I huddled into my coat on the back seat. The two screws sat up front, joking and laughing together. One of them, I found out later, was one of the more blatant lesbians in Styal!

We arrived at the prison at about 5.30, cold and stiff and tired. As the big gate was unlocked and we drove inside, I felt a wave of fear and doubt. It all looked so grim and forbidding after the cheerful lights of Holloway. We were soon in the reception room which looked even more dingy and unfriendly. It was a filthy and horrible place. The two screws told us to sit and wait, then a big black nurse arrived, who strip searched us each in turn and gave us each a blue towelling robe (at least these were clean here). We were weighed and told to dress again. Once more an officer went through my things, listed them all over again, and told me to sign for them. I again pleaded for my cross which I had held all through the trial, and was again refused.

Then I was told to stand in front of a desk, and recite my name and number to the young woman sitting there. I thought from her tweed suit that she must be a welfare officer. I could not have been more wrong. Miss B. was one of the five assistant governors, or AGs as they were known.

A very thin, ginger-haired young screw arrived to take me to my allotted 'house'. It was pitch dark and still pouring with rain, and she had to help me along. I could not manage my big bundle, which once more contained my bedding.

Styal Prison occupies what was a children's orphanage before the war. There are about thirty old red-brick Victorian houses, a small new hospital unit, and a large new administration block, as well as various smaller buildings containing the laundry, library, etc., all set in 47 acres of grounds, which look very beautiful to visitors, but give no hint of the suffering and degredation inflicted on those forced to live here. All this is surrounded by a 20 foot high double mesh-wire fence, which is patrolled at night by male screws. And of course there is the old stable block, Bleak House, but that is very different from the rest of Styal, and needs a much fuller explanation at a later date. There were also three LTI houses as they were called, which means 'Long Term Inmates', for prisoners serving three years and over. These women had many privileges. They all occupied their own rooms and could have their own curtains at the windows, their own bedspreads, even their own china and record players. They could make tea whenever they wished. Some were only serving the required three years, but there were quite a few lifers who had been in Styal for ten years or more. A sentence of three years was considered much better than one of two and a half years, because of the privileges it carried.

The thin screw, Miss A., and I eventually arrived at Size House. I was very glad to get inside out of the cold rain. The climate up here was so different from my beloved Cornwall, and much colder than even London. There were sixteen women living there and we arrived to find tea was over. It was now 7.30, but I was given a cup of tea and the usual two slices of bread and margarine, with some fish paste this time, but I was too tired to eat, and my throat was very sore. One of the older women, June, took me up to the dormitory where I was to sleep. There were four bunks and three single beds, but only a top bunk was unoccupied so I made up my bed there. We all had a small, formica-topped locker, and space for two coat hangers behind that on a hook on the wall, covered by a curtain. There were no curtains at the windows and, unlike New Holloway, there were thick iron bars both across and up and down, so that they formed little squares. They were fixed to the wall outside the window, so we could push the windows up or down to open them. There was lino on the floor; it was brown, very old, and cracked. A row of wash basins was in a room across the landing, and there were two bathrooms and two lavatories.

By the time I had made my bed and been told all the rules and regulations by Miss A., it was 9 p.m., and we had to go to bed. Each woman went into the office for a 'rub-down search', which meant the officer just patted our clothes (some officers patted the women's bodies too, for obvious reasons) and the prisoner's tobacco tins were locked in the office until the next day. But when we got upstairs, the six other women in my dormitory produced from the most unlikely places – their bras, pants, and even their shoes – what they called 'roll-ups', thin rolled cigarettes to be smoked after lights out!

I lay and read my Bible which I was allowed to keep. The other women ran in and out and chatted to each other; they had all been in Size House for some time and had formed firm friendships. Then Miss A. came up and put out the lights, went downstairs, and locked the door behind her. One of the women watched her walk away in the light of the tall standard lamps outside which line the roads connecting all the buildings and are left on all night. As soon as the screw was out of sight, they lit their roll-ups with matches also smuggled upstairs, and began to talk. There was one coloured woman in my room who was soon joined by a friend. Other women came in, sat on the beds, and made a great deal of noise. They began to tell very dirty stories, which I hate, so I put my head under the bed clothes and tried to go to sleep. At about midnight the room at last quietened down, and in a few minutes people were snoring loudly, but I could not sleep at all. It was all so strange and my throat hurt badly.

As in Holloway, we were all called at 6.30, but here there were strict rules. We had to be up, washed and dressed, and have stripped our beds, stacked the bedding neatly, and then be down to sign the book in the office by 7 a.m. – one minute late meant going to Bleak. Breakfast was at 7.30, and consisted of lumpy porridge with no milk, a half egg cup of sugar, a cup of tea and bread and margarine. Some days there was marmalade, and on Sundays an egg or sausage, and occasionally cornflakes with milk. The cooking in each house was done by two women picked at random. Some could not cook at all, but it made no difference, they were just told to get on with it, and we all suffered their efforts in the kitchen. Sometimes the food was totally inedible.

As this was my first morning, I had to see the prison doctor and the Governor, before joining what was called a 'work assessment party'. At 8.45 Miss A. took me along to the hospital block and I joined the queue to see the doctor. There was quite a large dispensary at one end of the corridor where three uniformed nurses were handing out medicines, and I felt hopeful that I would at least be given the things recommended in my own doctor's letter, which I knew had come from Holloway with my case history. At last it was my turn, and I was called into the surgery by a tall elderly sister, who treated us all as though we had done her a personal injury. The doctor looked up.

'Sit down,' he said, then opened my medical file which the sister put in front of him. He read my doctor's letter, grunted, and then said, 'We don't believe in unnecessary medicines here. All you will get is your thyroid pills.' The sister told me that was all, and I was sent along to the dispensary with a note about my Thyroxine.

Then I was directed to the Governor's office, where after another wait in a queue I was called into the holy of holies, the seat of supreme power in the whole prison of 290 women. I had already been told to state only my name and number, and stand to attention, so I did so. A grey-haired woman I later learned was the 'Chief' stood by the window; the Governor sat behind a large desk. She spoke quite kindly to me, and then said, 'A first offender of your age should automatically go to an open prison, but we cannot send you there while you are waiting for your appeal. When that is over, should you lose the appeal, you will at once be sent to an open prison.' However, as my stay in Styal became longer and longer, it became obvious not only to me, but to all those outside the prison who were concerned with my trial and removal to Cheshire, that it was the firm unshakable intention of the Home Office that I should be kept right away from any possible source of help.

Having been dismissed by the Governor, I returned to Size House and was directed to join the party of newcomers who were supposed to be in the process of assessment as to their suitability for various kinds of work. There were six newcomers including me, four of us from Holloway, and two from a place called Risley. There was an officer in charge of us, and she was supervising the cleaning of an empty house which had been repainted ready for another intake of prisoners. She was a kindly woman, and I was told to get a cloth and clean the windows. The screw, Miss C., told a younger woman to help me. The work was done very half-heartedly – even the officer did not seem to care if anyone worked or not – and later I learnt the reason for this. The so-called 'assessment party' didn't mean a thing; a board of officers met weekly, presided over by the AG whom I had mistaken for a welfare officer on arrival, and they made up their minds what work we were all to do as soon as we arrived. Suitability had little or nothing to do with where we found ourselves working.

We went back to our various houses at 11.45, dinner was at 12.30, and on arrival at Size I discovered one of the most petty and stupid rules in Styal. No woman was allowed to go upstairs between making our beds at 7.45 a.m. and bed time at 9 p.m. without special permission from the officer in charge. Most times this was refused I found. Going up the stairs without permission led to Bleak.

During the dinner hour I was called into the office, where I stood in front of the desk at which sat Miss B., the AG who wore tweed clothes. I now learned that I was in her row of houses, and therefore in her charge. My fellow prisoners had warned me that Miss B. was not a person to be taken lightly. She asked me a few questions, to which I knew she already had the answers in my open file on the desk, and then asked me where I would like to work. I told her that I was a keen gardener and would like to join the workers in the grounds here. She suggested that it would be best to wait until the weather was warmer, as I was sixty years old. I never did get to work outside. I then asked her if I might put my name down to go to an open prison (the other women had briefed me on this) and she repeated what I had been told by the Governor, 'No one on appeal goes to open prison.' She then warned me to obey the rules at all times, and not to become too friendly with my fellow prisoners.

'They all come from a very different background, and are mostly thieves,' she said, which I thought a strange way to help me to 'settle down' in Styal, as the Governor had urged me to do.

The last meal of the day was tea at 5 p.m., and then we were free to amuse ourselves as well as we could. There was a duty rota on the wall, two women to wash up and sweep the dining room each day, and the rest of us either read or watched the old television set in the common room once the washing up had been finished. At 8 p.m. we filed into the dining room once more for a bun and a cup of tea, but our cooks were pretty hopeless and the buns too hard to bite or even break. So from tea time until breakfast at 7.30 the next day we went hungry. This happened fairly often if the cooks could not do their job properly.

Saturday morning we got up at 6.30 as usual, and then instead of going out to work, we were all given jobs cleaning Size. Mine was to scrub my dormitory and Miss A. told me to be sure to move the lockers and beds and scrub behind them. I stood looking in dismay at the large room, when June came in and whispered, 'Don't take any notice of her. We never move furniture out when she's on duty. Wrap a wet floor cloth round the sweeping brush, and just go over the floor.' So I did and nothing was said. That was my first lesson on how to survive in

Styal. Dinner was at 12 on Saturdays because visiting was from 1.30 to 3.30, and on Saturdays only. At 12.30 there was a mad rush for the bathrooms. Only women who had visitors were allowed a bath, the others washed if they wanted to, and were then ordered downstairs again until bedtime.

I put on my check suit, the one I had worn all through my trial, and the only decent warm clothing I had here. The other two sets of clothes I was allowed were slacks and sweaters, which I needed for everyday use.

Three of us had visits, and we sat anxiously waiting, then at 1.35 my name was called, and Miss A. took me up the long road to the big hall where visits were held. I wanted to run all the way in my anxiety to see George and Robin, but Miss A. restrained me. Then we were at the door to the hall, and the screw gave me a 'rub down' search, and asked me if I could see where my visitors were. The big cold hall was full of tables, and at each metal table were three chairs – only two visitors were allowed without special permission. There sat George and Robin looking anxiously around for me. I ran to the table, they stood up, and I hugged and kissed them both, then sat opposite to them, as the rules demanded, and held their hands across the table. There were officers standing at intervals all round the hall, and upon the raised stage at one end sat the AG, Miss B., and two other senior officers, with a silver stripe on their sleeves. There were also two very big male screws standing by the main door.

Our precious two hours passed all too quickly. It had taken Robin seven hours to drive here in our little old car – George was not well enough to drive – but despite the distance Rob assured me that they would visit again in two weeks. As a first offender, or 'star prisoner' I was allowed to see them fortnightly; ordinary prisoners only had monthly visits. I tried to reassure George that I was all right, he was so tense and upset. He kept telling me that he was making every effort to have me returned to Holloway – my Member of Parliament wanted to see me, as did my solicitor and Junior Counsel. Then Miss B. shouted, 'Visits over,' and I held George close and kissed him, then dear Rob, and fought to hold back my tears. They waved from the doorway, then all the visitors were gone, and we were told to remain at our tables while the doors were locked. One by one we were called round behind the stage, up some steps and into small cubicles, where two officers stripped us down to bra and pants, which they thoroughly enjoyed, and searched each garment carefully. They looked in my mouth, and behind my ears. It was very cold, and the whole performance made quite sure that no one had any dignity left. Most of the screws doing the searching were what I later learnt to call 'butch' – big masculine women, uneducated and badly spoken. Having been searched, we were told to stack the heavy metal tables and the chairs at one end of the hall and then line up in rows.

Shivering and utterly wretched, I was taken back to Size, where we were all locked in until 8 a.m. Monday, except for those who went to church on Sunday.

On Sunday we were allowed an extra half hour in bed. We were called at 7, signed the book in the office, and then set about doing our week-end jobs. Breakfast was not until 9. The church service began at 9.30, so breakfast was a rush for me. I was the only woman going from Size. An officer called for me at 9.20 and we joined up with the prisoners from other houses, walked up to just inside the big double gate, and were put into rows, then carefully counted by the senior officer in charge. The AG I knew was there too. The gate was unlocked and we walked in twos across the road and into the church ground, then along and into the building, another screw counting us as we entered the church.

We were told where to sit, and I thought what a lovely little church this was, although fairly new. There were some beautiful stained glass windows behind the altar, and flowers and plants on the altar steps. A prisoner was playing the organ softly – she was Peggy, a lifer – and then in came the women who were in the choir, followed by the vicar. The service was bright and cheerful, but completely without any real meaning. The sermon was vague, such a *waste*. Here was a captive congregation, coming week after week, about forty souls, and the vicar could have brought each and every one to a very real knowledge of Jesus Christ had he tried. There was no talk about the forgiveness of sins – surely everyone here needed to hear that – no talk of the love of God for sinners, not even of the commandment 'love one another', which was badly needed here, in this hostile place. One of the worst things about Styal was that it was an offence to show any normal affection or kindness to another prisoner. I saw a woman sent to Bleak for punishment because she put comforting arms around a young girl who was crying, and later I found myself in serious trouble for helping an illiterate woman to write a letter. Yet the wrong kind of affection, lesbianism, was not only not punished, a lot of the officers were butch, and having affairs with the prisoners and each other.

The rest of Sunday dragged slowly by. We were all supposed to be taken out for half an hour's exercise in the grounds, but nothing happened. As it was a bright day I went to ask the officer on duty if we might go out, but was told, 'The majority don't want to go.' Yet in the prison rules Sunday exercise is mandatory, and to be strictly enforced.

On Monday the whole routine started all over again. I was still in the assessment party, but on Wednesday night I was told that the committee had met the day before, and I was to report to the workroom on Thursday at 8 a.m.

During Wednesday night there was an uproar in my dormitory. The women were pulling each other's beds to pieces, throwing water, and getting into beds elsewhere to spend the night with current girl friends. On Thursday morning Miss B., the AG, sent for me and demanded to know what had happened the night before. An officer from another house had reported the noise. I told her I knew nothing. The word 'grass' had already been explained to me, and it was not something to sit on! Miss B. glared at me.

'If you refuse to tell me, I can send you to Bleak. I have the power you know. You have until tomorrow night to give me the names of the offenders,' she said. Luckily for me the night patrol crept round the next night, and caught those women who were 'bed-hopping' as it was called, so I did not need to grass. The four women were removed to Bleak to await punishment, which was slight compared with that handed out for more serious offences such as walking on the grass or feeding the birds.

On Thursday I started in the workroom, a large long old building with a high glass roof, where we froze in winter and roasted in summer. There were about seventy women working there, some at sewing machines, some doing hand sewing. The whole project was the making of shirts for the nuclear station in Cumberland. I was put on to 'passing', which meant that I examined the finished shirts for faults, very monotonous, mindless work, at which I was to remain for five long months. We were allowed to talk, but not to leave our seats without permission, and the windows were all too high up to see anything but sky. I felt very confined, having to sit still for so long. But the worst thing was the terrible noise. The radio was on full blast and twenty sewing machines going all out – we had to shout to be heard. I very soon had a splitting headache, as I was to do for every working day for five months. Only towards the end of my time there was I told by a prisoner, who had been in Styal for five years *twice*, that women over sixty need only work half a day. I saw the Governor, who confirmed this. I only had to be in the hated noisy workroom from 8 a.m. to 12 p.m. each day. But although from then on I was able to be in the house in the afternoons, I was not allowed upstairs, not even to rest on my bed.

There were four civilian women in charge of the workroom. We worked from 8 a.m. to 4.30 p.m., Monday to Friday, and my first week's wage was 66p! There was a woman called Liz who did hand sewing. She was about forty-eight years old, had suffered an attack of polio at sixteen, and now wore calipers on both legs, and a special boot on one twisted foot. Liz could only walk with the aid of crutches, and as she was lodged in the hospital, dragged herself up and down the hill four times a day. She was in prison for two years, for forging a cheque for £89, her first and only offence. She complained bitterly about the medical treatment. She suffered a good deal of pain in her legs and foot. In fact a few days before she left on parole I saw the officials from a society for polio sufferers who had come to investigate her complaints.

On Friday morning Miss B. again sent for me and told me she was moving me to Howard House across the road. I had made friends in Size with a very pleasant German girl who was doing two years for smuggling, and I did not want to move at all. But Miss B. insisted. She told me that Howard was a very unruly house, and she wanted me there as a 'sobering influence'. So once more I gathered up my bundle, and moved across to Howard. There were also sixteen women there, mostly young; there was no one over thirty. I was given a bed in a dormitory for three. There were two young married girls in Howard, both having affairs with women for the first time in their lives, obviously another thing first offenders were exposed to here.

Each house had two permanent officers, one on duty from 6.45 a.m. to 2 p.m., the other from 2 p.m. to when she locked the house up at 10 p.m. Mrs P. went off duty at 2 p.m., and when we all came in from the workroom, I found the second officer Mrs L. in charge. She had me in the office, and told me in her gruff way that I could ask anything I wanted to know and she told me that we were all being encouraged to be too soft.

'If I had my way, this place would be run like the army, the men's army,' she said. I was very glad that she did not have her way, life here was already tough enough for a sixty-year-old grandmother, with not very good health.

I had tried several times since my arrival to get some treatment for my migraine – but to no avail. I just had to lie awake and suffered the pain that only fellow migraine sufferers will understand. One night a few weeks after my move to Howard, my head was especially bad, and when the night patrol came round at midnight, I sat up and asked one of the two officers if I might have a dose of Panadol, which was better than nothing.

'Certainly flower, I'll get it from the office,' she said and went downstairs. She came back a few minutes later, and told me that she could not give me any of the Panadol kept in the house and would not explain why. A few days later I was in the office getting the clothesline from Mrs L., when I saw the big bottle of liquid Panadol on top of her locker. On the table in large red letters it said, 'NOT TO BE GIVEN TO MCSHANE' and underneath was written, also in red, 'DON'T PHONE HOSPITAL THE ANSWER IS NO'.

When I moved into Howard, one of the beds in my small dormitory was occupied by a middle-aged Turkish woman from Cyprus, who spoke little English. A week later a young Greek Cypriot was put into the empty bed. The utter stupidity of putting a Turkish *and* a Greek Cypriot into one room could only happen in prison, where the powers-that-be seem to do all they can to *create* 'aggro' rather than to avoid it. So these two women, from two races that have been enemies for generations, were locked in Howard, in the same small bedroom, every night and of course bitter rows broke out. Maria, the Turkish prisoner, appealed to me to befriend her, and the young Greek girl did all she could to upset us both. But when I approached Mrs P. to move one of them, I was of course refused, and although I then asked Mrs L., I was still refused, and told that the running of the house was not my business.

Howard was indeed an unruly house, and my restraining influence given by Miss B., the AG, as her reason for sending me there did not seem to have any effect. The dining room was at the other end of the hall from the common room, and one evening I was sitting quietly in the dining room. All the other women were watching 'Porridge', usually a favourite of mine, but I had a bad headache. I went past the office where Mrs L. sat reading, to go to the lavatory, when I saw a young girl called Anne run from the back of the stairs into the common room. I thought nothing of this, I knew that she was emotionally disturbed anyway, but when I came out of the cloakroom, there was smoke pouring out from under the stairs. Anne had set alight some old letters pushed through the gaps between the stairs! I went to the office, called Mrs L. and helped her to throw two fire-buckets of water on to the small blaze. She then rang the fire bell in the hall and herded us all into the dining room. The other women were very excited by the arrival of the fire engine and shouted directions (and other things!) to the men. The AG, Miss B., arrived, and she and Mrs L. asked us all if we knew who had lit the fire. No one spoke. Then she asked us where we were just before the fire, and I told her quite truthfully that I had been sitting in the dining room; all the others had been in the common room. Mrs L. looked hard at me, she knew that I was no 'fire bug', but she had an idea that I knew something. Just before we all went to bed she took me aside, and said, 'It's a great pity you didn't see anyone, it would help towards my promotion if I could name the culprit.' I agreed that it was a pity, and we all retired to bed.

But the thought of a fire at night had troubled me ever since my arrival in Styal. With the windows heavily barred and the doors locked from the outside, our escape would depend on the door on the landing at the top of the fire escape, and this was fastened on the outside by a piece of wood nailed across the door, which in theory gave way when pushed hard enough. But would anyone be able to push that hard, I wondered, and my vivid imagination conjured up images of what would happen if no one *could* push and break the wood. Although the fire bell would alert both the Admin block and the fire brigade, when we later had a series of power cuts, due to industrial disputes, I knew that all alarm bells were off, including the fire bell. In fact all the lights were off too, and we had oil lamps!

While I was living in Howard, two girls in another house actually did escape one night, breaking out of the fire door, which is connected to the Admin block by an alarm bell when opened. They were quickly caught. Mrs P. came in rubbing her hands with glee, and told us that *she* had found them, and this was the tenth time she had foiled an escape! This did not endear her to anyone. We all hoped that someone would be fortunate enough to get away from Styal.

A new prisoner arrived in Howard. Her name was Dora and she bitterly resented my daily Bible reading, and attending church on Sundays. Just before her arrival, I had been moved into a dormitory with four beds, and now Dora occupied one of them, opposite to mine. She had been in Styal before, and she told me that she had never seen anyone read a Bible night and morning. One Saturday morning I left my Bible on my window ledge as usual, and on top my expensive reading glasses, which I had bought a year before my trial. I could not read anything without them. This particular day, I went off to do my week-end household jobs, and when I returned to the dormitory my glasses were gone. I told the other women and two of them helped me to search. Suddenly one of them called out, and I went to her, in the lavatory. Down beside the seat were my glasses. They had been smashed to pieces on the floor. I was very upset indeed, as were the other women – I got on well with them all, except Dora. I took the broken glasses to Mrs P., and for once she seemed really sorry, especially since I could not now do my daily work of passing shirts. She asked me who had done this, but I said I did not yet know. Later that day Dora told me triumphantly that she had broken my glasses so that I could not read my Bible.

After tea Mrs P. again asked me who had been responsible, and told me that if I made an official complaint the culprit would be sent to Bleak. I said I did not want to make any complaint – what good would it do to punish Dora? I preferred to try to win her friendship. But a week later she took my clean vest from the hot pipe by my bed where it was airing, and put it down the lavatory, so I gave up my efforts to talk to her.

The two cooks in Howard were lovers – they slept in a twin-bedded dormitory. Mary was the butch, and Jamie her girl friend, but they both wore their hair cut like men, which was unusual. Generally at least one partner looked like a woman. These two had become staunch friends of mine, especially Jamie, who had often comforted me when I was feeling very low. Once I broke down with a terrible migraine and Jamie had put gentle arms around me and wiped my tears. In spite of her relationship with Mary, she was a thoughtful girl, only nineteen years old, and I thought that there but for the grace of God is my Andy, or anyone else's precious daughter.

But Mary was a tough character, and when a good-looking girl from Brazil came to Howard there was trouble. Marion was aggressive, cared nothing for anyone's feelings or opinions, and every other word she used was the famous four letter one – she had a really foul mouth. One evening we were all watching television – Mrs L. had gone to visit a friend – and Marion and Jamie were sitting beside each other. I noticed Mary glaring at them. Suddenly, without any warning she sprang on Marion, bore her to the ground and they fought like tigers, scratching and biting and tearing at each other's hair. Marion's was long, so Mary had an advantage. I was terrified, they fought in dead silence except for the sound of heavy breathing, clothes ripping and nails scratching on flesh. The other women stood round in a circle, also silent. Mary managed to get her thick shoes off and began to bludgeon Marion's head and face with the heel, opening a long gash over her eye. I edged my way out of the room, and rushed into the lavatory where I was very sick. I was shaking all over with the sheer animal hatred between the two women. Then Mrs L. returned. A woman on look-out gave the alarm, and when I followed the screw into the common room, Mary had gone upstairs (cooks were exempt from the rule) and Marion was in the dining room. Everyone else was watching television with rapt attention.

It was now the end of March, and I had encouraging letters from George. He and Robin came every other Saturday, too. He told me that he was trying hard to get a re-trial, for several reasons, one of them being the misdirection of the jury by Judge Purchas. I longed and hoped to at least be out on bail pending another trial. Easter was approaching. I knew that our little church next to Lanlivery Manor would be full of spring flowers. Other years I had cut armfuls of daffodils from our garden and helped to decorate the church for Easter Sunday. So I wrote to my vicar, the Reverend H. Yorke, who was now the Rural Dean, and who had travelled from Cornwall to be a character witness at my trial. I asked him to pray very hard that God would allow me to be in our little church at Easter.

Chapter 12

There were three houses on the road between the hospital and the workroom at the bottom of the hill, each surrounded by its own area of grass, on which we were not allowed to walk. Next to the hospital was Wilson, Howard was the last house, and in between stood Wrighton, where about twelve women were shut up in individual cell-like rooms. No one knew the exact number of prisoners there, as several were never seen outside at all. They were all either mentally defective or inadequate. Their plastic chamber pots could be seen 'airing' inside the barred windows of their rooms, where they were kept locked up between 8 p.m. and 7 a.m. every day. Some who were not considered dangerous were allowed to sit in the common room, and in good weather a pathetic little group would straggle up the road for exercise, gazing aimlessly at the ground, one very disturbed woman hanging on to the arm of a screw who was having an affair with another officer. None of these women left their house to work, as they were all to a great or lesser degree mentally deranged. Some were serving up to two-year sentences, and for first offences. One of them was a very large woman called Daisy, and when I worked for the hairdresser much later in the year the screw sometimes brought Daisy to have her hair cut or washed. Poor thing, she told me that there was a very violent black girl in Wrighton, serving two years for assault, who kept threatening Daisy, and saying, 'If you don't let me kiss you I'll knife you.' Daisy was over fifty and had three children who never came to see her. She was what might be called 'simple'.

It became obvious that I was not going to be home for Easter, and I became more and more depressed and lonely. The worst thing in Styal for me was the total lack of anyone to talk to. I had yet to find a single woman interested in anything other than 'Top of the Pops', their sex life and the sex life of the screw in charge of us. I had tried to see the vicar and talk to him about Jesus, but I found that his belief was so different from mine that our talk was futile.

For the first time in my sixty years of life I had no one to love, no outlet for my intense caring for all living things. Even to feed the birds was a punishable offence, and yet I did feed them, and the several cats and their kittens who lived wild in the grounds, but these things were done secretly. I found it interesting how the other women began to notice the existence of birds and animals outside the bars. Several of them saved scraps of bread and food for me to throw out, a risky thing for them as well as me.

It was a terrible indictment on the whole prison system that *nothing* was being done to teach these women to care for their fellow creatures. If a prisoner like me could have an influence after so short a time, how much more could be done? So many women in need of guidance and assistance with their lives inside and their families outside had said with great bitterness that they themselves had no idea how to begin to cope with their own problems.

George and Robin were to visit me on Easter Saturday, but on the Wednesday I developed one of my septic throats to which I was prey and I went to see the doctor yet again. All he ordered was a twice daily dose of Panadol until Saturday, but would not allow me an antiseptic gargle. My throat became worse and worse, I could hardly swallow. On Friday night I could not sleep, the pain was so bad. I again asked the night patrol for something. A vain hope. I was told, 'No, we are told not to give you anything, sorry flower.' It was difficult to conceal from George and Rob how low in health and spirits I was, and George was very worried about the infection in my throat. Despite this we had our usual lovely visit – they had brought me a bunch of daffodils from our garden. When they left I held Rob tight and begged him to try to get me back to Holloway, where at least I could have proper medical care. Poor George was doing all *he* could I knew.

There was the usual strip search, it was bitterly cold. We had tea at 4.30 as we always did on Saturdays, and I asked Mrs P. if I could lie down, I felt so ill. But of course she could not allow me to, even had she wanted to say yes, no prisoner can go to bed or even lie down without permission from one of the doctors. Maybe some people need to be in prison, but does that mean that they have *no* rights as human beings, and must be treated like mindless, unfeeling cattle?

At 8 p.m. I was taken up to the hospital dispensary for my dose of Panadol. It was liquid, in a small 5 ml plastic container and I managed to hide it in my hand and get it safely back to Howard and into my locker. I could not face another night of so much pain and no sleep. But I did sleep, worn out by the distress of saying good-bye to my family yet again, so the tiny dose of Panadol remained on the front of the shelf in my locker.

Sunday morning, Easter Sunday, our lockers were inspected by Mrs P. When I opened mine there was the Panadol. She was furious, and although I tried to tell her why it was there she would not listen. I was not allowed to go to church, and Miss B., the AG, was sent for. She had me in her office, and I told her exactly what had happened. After a very stern lecture she said, 'That's all, now get out.' I was very, very relieved. The other women were afraid that she would take me down to Bleak, the one prospect in Styal that really terrified me, the thought of being locked in a small, bare cell for days. Some prisoners were even kept there for weeks, as I was to discover.

On Easter Monday I felt a little better, and went to the sports with the rest of Howard. There were games of volleyball, etc., held in the big hall, and I was even persuaded to play 'goalie' for my house! Dozens of screws stood round watching, including Miss B., the AG, who called out, 'Well done, Yolande,' to me.

Tuesday morning I went into the office at 6.50 to sign the book as required, and Mrs P. told me that she was taking me to Bleak after breakfast. I was terrified. Jamie and the others were very kind, they advised me to put on a lot of warm clothes, and two pairs of socks, as there was little or no heat in Bleak. I drank a cup of tea, then got my Bible and glasses and waited. The women said I would not be allowed to take the Bible, but I somehow felt sure that God would not allow it to be taken from me.

When we got to Bleak, Mrs P. unlocked the heavy door into the corridor and handed me over to another screw who was a well-known butch. She took me into a cell about 8 ft wide and 9 ft long, with an iron bed-spring with no mattress, and a plastic chamber pot in the corner. The window was not only heavily barred, it was also covered by wire mesh on the outside, but I was relieved to see that the top was open about three inches. The cell smelt horribly of stale urine. The screw then told me to strip, and she searched both me and my clothes thoroughly. Then she looked at my glasses and Bible on the wire bed-spring, hesitated (while I said a silent prayer) and told me to get dressed. She said that at 11.30 a.m. I would go before the Governor to be told my punishment, and then she slammed the heavy, solid metal door behind her and I was alone. It was 8.30 a.m.

I put on my overcoat, sat on the wire bed, and looked around the cell. I was not yet disturbed beyond control. It did not seem possible that at my age I would be kept in solitary confinement here. The walls were white-washed bricks, the floor a kind of lino-tile, and the high ceiling had a wire-covered electric globe. It all reminded me strongly of a cell in a mental hospital. I was lucky to have somewhere to sit. All the other fifteen inmates of Bleak sat on the bare floor I discovered later.

I looked at the solid grey metal door, with its tiny peephole, and then walked to the window. Across a fenced-in yard were some tall elms just coming into leaf, and there was a blackbird singing. How lovely God's world outside was, and how cruel and utterly evil the place in which I stood. I could hear other women shouting and screaming. One was banging incessantly. Someone knocked on the pipe running along between her cell and mine. It seemed to say, 'You are not alone.' I knocked back in answer. I sat down on my bed-spring again, and picked up my Bible. Surely I would be released from here in time for dinner. All the women in Howard had assured me that would be so because of my age and the trivial offence I had committed.

At 11.30 the heavy door swung open, and two screws told me to take off my shoes (in case I kicked the Governor!) and follow them. I was marched into a small room where an officer stood at each side of me. I was totally dismayed to see the Deputy Governor facing me across the desk, the real governor was away. Two weeks before this I had made a 'Governor's Application' to my house officer, which meant that my name and number were phoned through to the Admin block, for the Governor's list the next morning. When I was called into the office, I had discovered that the Governor was away, and the Deputy was doing all the applications. I had stated my name and number and then said, 'Good morning, sir, I wanted to apply again for an open prison.' He had looked at the chief standing by the window and then said, 'Application refused.'

Now in Bleak, the senior officer read out my 'crime', and I looked appealingly at Miss B., the AG, who sat behind the Deputy Governor.

'Have you anything to say?' he asked, and I told him about my bad throat.

'*Please*, sir, don't lock me in here. I get such bad claustrophobia,' I begged.

He turned to Miss B. and asked if she had anything to say on my behalf, but she shook her head, and he turned to me.

'Four days' loss of all privileges, prisoner dismissed,' he said. Thankfully I followed the two screws into the corridor. I was smiling with relief, when one of them said, 'You know that means loss of association with other prisoners, and *that* means being locked behind the door?'

I could not believe it, four days and nights in here.

'No, *no,* please let me see the Deputy again,' I cried, but they seized my arms and hurried me into my cell. The heavy door clanged shut and I became hysterical with fear. I beat on the door, sobbing wildly and shouting, 'Help, help,' but no one came, and at last I sank on to the wire bed-spring, huddled into my coat (it was bitterly cold) and fell into a stupor. There was still the unceasing sound of human misery all around. Some women had been here in solitary for many, many weeks, but I did not know that then.

At 12.30 the door opened, and to my great relief it was the doctor. I got to my feet, and began to cry helplessly again as I explained about my terrible fear of being locked in a small space, but to my horror he turned to the screw by the door.

'Passed fit for confinement,' he said, and the door swung to behind his back. He had just left when the door opened again, it was the dinner trolley, and a plate with a mess of stew was pushed into the cell, then a dish of watery custard and a mug of tea. There was no sugar, so I could not even drink the tea, it was so strong. The food was unthinkable. I sat on the wire spring again. My hands and feet were freezing cold. Time ceased to have any meaning, I just sat in a state of shock.

The most terrible part of being locked in a small cell in solitary confinement is the knowledge of being totally isolated, cut off from all human contact. Later in my time in Styal, I met women who had been kept in Bleak for as long as three to four months. *All* the prisoners there are held at the total and absolute discretion of the Governor. There is no other source of appeal. And yet as a senior officer at Holloway said to me much later, 'We are here *only* to contain you all, it is no part of our work to punish. But the officers in Styal seem to have forgotten that.' How right she was. Some women told me of being kicked and hit, and they had no redress – who would believe a convicted woman against an officer?

It was dark outside when the door was again opened. This time it was a senior officer, Miss H., whom I knew to be fair and just in her dealing with prisoners. Her parents had been in the Salvation Army. Now she came and sat beside me.

'Why Yolande, you haven't even taken off your coat, what's the matter?' she asked.

I began to cry silently again, and she held out some tissues – I had none. I told her that I *could* not stay locked in here, I would go mad, my migraine was already almost past bearing. She was kind and sympathetic and promised to see if she could talk to the Deputy for me, but she did not return that day. Tea-time came and went, this time there was some sugar, so I managed to drink the mug of tea, but my migraine made it impossible to eat.

At 6 p.m. the light in the ceiling was switched on from outside. I still sat huddled in my coat, holding my aching head in my hands, when the door was opened and one of the hospital sisters was there. I ran to her and begged her to get me released from this cell, but she said she had no authority – only the doctor could have me released now. When I told her about my migraine, she gave me a large dose of the liquid Panadol to ease the pain. After a while the Panadol had some effect, the pain grew a little more bearable, and I managed to stop crying, and to read my Bible. Surely God was near, even in this dreadful place, and He must have some purpose in my being here, or it could not have happened, I knew.

At last it was 8.30 p.m. The cell door was unlocked, and two young prisoners carried a small table and a chair into my cell.

'Miss H.'s orders,' the screw told me crossly. '*And* you can have your mattress early, go and get it,' she said, pointing down the corridor. I was again crying weakly, I did not seem to be able to stop, and I walked to a storage area where pillows and foam pallets were lying in heaps. As I heaved up one of the pallets ('mattress' they called it!) a huge cockroach scuttled across my foot, and I saw two more run along the base of the wall. I quickly grabbed a pillow; one of the young women took my foam pallet and carried it to my cell. The screw then told me to fetch a red plastic bowl of water from a tap, and to put it on the table in my cell – it was for washing myself. Then the young woman prisoner handed me a mug of cold water and my cell door clanged shut again. The screw shouted, 'Have the bowl ready to empty in ten minutes and your chamber pot too,' and then there was the awful silence once more. But now at least I had something to do, and set to work to wash my face and hands, and comb my hair. There was no mirror, of course. During the afternoon my toilet things had been brought to my cell, and my nightdress too. I lay on my bed and tried to doze, but the ceiling light was very bright, and the walls seemed to be closing in on me. How *could* I survive four days and nights here, in solitary confinement?

At about 10.15 I wanted to go to the lavatory. I began to hammer on the door with my shoe, the metal hurt my knuckles. After about five minutes the peephole cover was pulled aside, and to my surprise a male screw shouted, 'What the hell do *you* want?' I explained.

'Use your pot,' he said, shut the peephole and walked away. But I went on knocking, and shouting too. At last he returned.

'What the bloody hell are you doing?' he yelled. I told him coldly that I had no toilet paper. He opened the door and shouted in my face, 'Where the hell do you think you are, in the Hilton?' I had put on my coat over my nightie, and I stood my ground and again asked for toilet paper and to go along to the lavatory. He then thrust two squares of lavatory paper at me, pointed down the corridor and said, 'Get on with it then, I don't want to stand here all night.' He was a big and burly screw and after he had locked me in my cell again, I thought how very wrong it was for a male officer to be alone in charge of the sixteen women in Bleak.

After a fitful sleep, I got up and dressed at 7 a.m. and was again unlocked, and told to get a basin and wash, and then ten minutes later, to empty it and my chamber pot, which I had been forced to use in the night because of my weak bladder. Then breakfast came, but again I could only drink the tea, and as soon as that was over the heavy metal door shut out all human contact. I began to cry again and to beat on the door I am ashamed to say – I was in an absolute panic. I called and called, and cried and cried. No one came until 11 a.m. Then the door opened and the doctor stood there again. I fell to my knees and begged and begged him to help me, or at least to give me something to ease the pain in my head, and subdue the endless crying. He turned to the screw as before and said, 'Fit for confinement,' and the grey door clanged shut.

On the morning of the third day, I woke from my uneasy and fitful sleep, and lay looking at the wall by the window. A shaft of lovely April sunshine was golden on the whitewashed bricks, and suddenly a great peace filled my heart. I was totally spent from all the many, many hours of bitter crying, of beating on the door. The only sound of any other human life the woman in the next cell tapping on the water pipes, and the intermittent shouting and screaming of the other prisoners. I had reached the bottom of the great well of loneliness and misery of solitary confinement and of my claustrophobia. Now I gazed at the sunlit wall, and a tiny patch of blue sky outside my window, and I knew beyond all doubt that my torment was over, God was in my head and in my heart, and I *would* walk out of Bleak a stronger woman than when I walked in. I dressed, then read my Bible, the wonderful promise of the Psalms, and when the screw opened the heavy door I smiled and wished her 'Good morning'. She looked at me in stunned silence for a minute, then in her usual loud voice told me to get my washing water.

That morning I ate a piece of bread and margarine, the first food I'd had in here, and then began to work out a routine for the rest of my time in Bleak. So many paces from window to door, for half an hour, then sit on the chair and read my Bible (later that afternoon a new screw brought me a book about a missionary!), then stand on the chair and look out at the trees opposite and at the little squirrel who came for the bits of bread I had thrown out through the top of the window, and then begin the whole sequence again.

I slept properly that night, I no longer cried all the time or beat on the door. The system at Styal had *not* broken me. By the grace of God I had survived the worst they could ever do to me. When a person reaches the limit of human endurance, that person either breaks and is defeated and embittered for the rest of life, or emerges stronger than ever before.

During my last day in Bleak I prayed and prayed for all the poor creatures locked up there who did not know God as their Father as I did, and so had no help from anywhere. All day long I heard their pitiful cries, in spite of the screw, who kept coming along and shouting, 'Pack it up, *stop* that noise.' They seemed to have been reduced to poor, frightened, captive animals. We were all supposed even by Styal's laws to be taken out into the yard for half an hour's exercise every day, but that only happened once during my four days' stay, in spite of the lovely spring weather. One of the women told me later that the big male screw sometimes took them out singly, but on his own *again*, no female officer being available it seemed.

My last morning came, and just before dinner my house officer from Howard came for me. She opened the door, and looked me up and down quizzically, as though to say, 'And what have they done to *you*?' Then I gathered up my big bundle from the Bleak office, and staggered after her up the slight incline to Howard. Two women watched from Size, and later they whispered to me in the hospital queue for our medicines (we were not allowed to talk). They said that I had looked so terribly weak and ill that they thought I could not live much longer if I remained in Styal. My weight was now 9 st 4 lbs, I seemed to get thinner every day.

I was given such a welcome in Howard. Jamie carried my bundle up to my old bed, and they were all very angry because the screw had told them that on account of my age and health I was being kept in solitary in the hospital, and not in Bleak at all. One of the 'lifers' even tackled the Deputy Governor about it, and told him that in all her years in Styal, she had never seen anything so shameful and so unnecessary. I heard later that every single female prisoner in Styal was enraged by what was being done to me. I was the oldest woman ever to be shut up in Bleak.

Chapter 13

Before I went to Bleak I had made a friend who had been moved from another house to Howard. She was fifty-four years old and this was her second time in Styal. Sheila came from London, and told me that her solicitor was a real ball of fire, and would be very well able to get bail for me, and my appeal brought forward. I had managed to smuggle this solicitor's name and address to George on a visit. It was not allowed to put things like that in letters – all mail both in and out was strictly censored. I had wanted to write to Mr R. but the AG had refused to send the letter. So George had phoned Mr M., the new man so well recommended by Sheila, and he had agreed to take over. He told George that he was very confident of getting bail for me pending appeal, and would visit me in Styal. My husband and son were getting really frantic about my obvious ill health and lack of medical care.

A week after I was released from Bleak, Mr M. visited me.

'I will have you out of here in no time, either on bail or to Holloway,' he told me. He also said that he thought I looked very unwell. On his advice I petitioned the Home Secretary to be sent to Holloway so that I could confer with my new solicitor to prepare my appeal, and also with the new Junior Counsel Mr M. had urged me to allow him to brief.

'Mr Winstain's a real fighter. *He* will win your appeal,' he said.

I was only allowed a Junior Counsel on legal aid, although the prosecution were opposing my appeal with a Queen's Counsel, a Junior and a solicitor. Mr M., my new solicitor, had said in his letters to George that it was iniquitous that the prosecution had had four months to prepare their objection to the appeal, and that they had a leading Queen's Counsel and a Junior Counsel (who had been assisting Mr Frisby at my trial) and that this hardly seemed to be British justice for me to start under such a handicap.

Mr M. put my request for bail before Lord Justice Scarman at the beginning of May. The judge recommended that my appeal should be heard 'as soon as possible in view of the nature of the case' (by this I presumed he meant the unusual police involvement), but he refused the application for bail because he felt it would be very unkind to allow me to leave prison; if my appeal were to fail, I would then have to return and start my sentence all over again. The full Court of Appeal set a tentative date for the hearing during Jubilee week, on 6 June.

On Monday, 30 May, I was told to report to the Governor's office at 11.30 a.m. The Deputy Governor was once more in charge of the prison, and he showed me the reply to my petition to the Home Secretary which had arrived that day. It said, 'You are requested to transfer the prisoner to Holloway Prison at your earliest possible convenience, in view of the reasons given by the prisoner in her petition.' These reasons were to give me enough time for proper conferences with my new solicitor and Junior Counsel, whom I had not yet met. I asked the Deputy which day I would be leaving for Holloway, but he said he would let my house officer know. Nothing happened. Every day I asked Mrs P. for news and was told there was none. In desperation I booked to see the Deputy on Thursday. I stood before him and asked why I had not yet been transferred as requested by the Home Secretary. He replied that it was not possible yet.

I was frantic. On the Saturday when George and Robin arrived for their visit I told them all that was happening.

George said that he would take action. On 13 June, my Member of Parliament, Mr Robert Hicks, wrote the following letter to my husband:

Robert Hicks, MP
House of Commons

Dear Mr McShane, 13 June 1977

Following our telephone conversation on Saturday last, I write to confirm that I have this morning contacted the Private Office of Lord Harris of Greenwich, Minister of State at the Home Office and I am assured that his Department will immediately make an investigation into why the delay has occurred in transferring your wife to Holloway, following the instruction from the Home Office.

Should you feel I can be of any further assistant please do not hesitate to let me know.

Yours sincerely,

Robert Hicks

Day after day dragged by, and I became more and more depressed and ill. The Queen's Jubilee was no joyous celebration for me. Even the house officer remarked that I was going downhill very fast.

'You *must* make an effort to pull yourself up,' she said.

At last, on 16 June, Mrs L. called me after dinner and told me to get all my possessions together and go at once to reception as two officers had arrived from Holloway to take me back there. So at 2 p.m. Jamie helped me to carry my big bundle up to reception. Everyone in Howard wished me luck. Everyone, even the officers, thought that I would not be returning there. Mrs L. said, 'Even if you lose your appeal, you will probably go straight from Holloway to an open prison.'

Having been stripped and searched in reception, I dressed and got into the minibus for Holloway, with a middle-aged officer and a younger, very tall, blonde one. They were both so nice to me. They treated me like a human being, so different from the way Styal officers treat prisoners. We drove through the glorious June countryside. It was wonderful to see fields of hay being cut, and green corn ripening in the sun. I felt as though I had returned from the grave! The senior officer told the driver to stop at a wayside café for tea. I sat in the minibus with her, while the other officer brought tea and buttered scones out to us! We talked a lot about life in prison. She was an intelligent woman and the first educated officer I'd been able to talk to since February.

'The trouble is that a good officer goes to Styal, and in a few months either leaves, or becomes as bad as all the rest,' she said. She also made the remark about the officers' duty being to contain not punish. Oh, *how* I hoped to stay in Holloway if I lost my appeal and was not sent to an open prison.

I told this officer that in my opinion there was a totally wrong attitude to prisoners in general. So many had never had such a good life as in prison, even in Styal, with four meals a day, hot baths every night, and television in the evenings. That was why so many of the young ones kept coming back. It was a better standard of living than they enjoyed outside. But the great need was for some kind of guidance, some kind of teaching. No one was helping them to have a responsibility towards society in any way at all. Above all, *no* one cared deeply about each woman prisoner, no one loved them with a Christian love. Almost all came from broken homes, and they had never known any real, genuine love from anybody. The officer agreed with all this, even when I said that instead of more *prisons* we wanted more *care*, more teaching, more *love*, and more practical help.

We arrived at Holloway quite late, about 8.30 p.m., and I said a reluctant good-bye to my two friendly officers. I went through all the performance of the reception office again, and then to a very dirty cell for the night. The windows were all broken and it was very draughty, but I didn't care this time – I *could* be home soon!

The next morning I was moved to another wing, and given a large cell with only one bed. For the first time since February I was able to be alone. At Styal, I had lived with the other women twenty-four hours a day. It was never possible to be really alone, and now it seemed like heaven. There were some tall trees opposite, outside the prison wall, and I thanked God with all my heart that I could wait peacefully here until my appeal. I lay and slept all the afternoon.

I wrote to George that day. It was Friday, 17 June. As far as I knew now, my appeal was to be heard on 27 June. Saturday came and went. George and Rob could not visit me because I had not had time to tell them of my move. On Sunday I went to church, and had a brief talk with Sister Jennie. She was very busy but promised to see me in my cell the next day. I was resting in my cell on Monday after dinner, when I was told that my solicitor and new Junior Counsel had arrived to see me. I was taken down to the visiting room and put into a solicitor's cubicle. After about ten minutes Mr M. arrived, and introduced me to the Junior, Mr Kevin Winstain. We sat down to talk. He told me that he supported my appeal, but seemed totally out of sympathy with my approach. But he did agree that I *must* have a leading QC, as the prosecution had, and told me that he had agreed for the appeal to be postponed to 29 or 30 June to suit the prosecution QC who was not available on 27 June.

However, I was very alarmed by Mr Winstain's views, which he expressed so firmly. I felt that it would be better to try to find someone else, even at this late date, so I asked Mr M. to come and see me alone the next day, and he promised to do so. I went back to my cell feeling so depressed and worried. What could *I* do? I had no way of finding another barrister or of getting a QC and time was running out fast. Then Sister Jennie came to see me, and we talked and prayed together, and she told me that people all over the *world* were praying for me, which was a wonderful source of strength.

Tuesday passed in the routine of going to the workroom from 8 a.m. to 11.45, then dinner, and then I was alone in my cell. I was very glad to catch up on sleep in the afternoons – I got so little sleep in Styal. Wednesday came and went, and then on Thursday morning my MP, Robert Hicks, arrived. We spent over an hour talking together. He was very concerned about my not having a QC.

'It is *not* justice if you are not equally well represented at the appeal,' he said. He also told me that a member of the Howard League would be at the appeal watching closely, but I never found out who or what the Howard League was!

The Reverend Yorke, my vicar, was coming once more to speak for my character and also about our urgent home problems, i.e. George's bad heart, and our eviction from Lanlivery Manor on 1 August. We had at last come within sight of an agreement with CSA. They would release us from *all* our guarantees if George would sign documents agreeing to vacate our home on 1 August. That meant they would waive their charge on my grandmother's trust too. So we would have no money and no home in August. Mr Yorke was hoping that the appeal judges would see how much I was needed at home, in addition to the way my health was suffering in Styal.

In the afternoon I wrote to George, telling him about Mr Hicks's visit. In my letter I said, 'If things do go wrong at my appeal, *please* don't be afraid for me my love, God will be right with me, and I *will* hold on. But please God the three judges will know the *real* issues, and will see that it doesn't make sense to leave me in prison any longer. They are three intelligent men, and they must surely see something odd in all this big fight, just think what it's costing the taxpayers!'

On Friday, 24 June, I was moved to the wing I had been in in February, C4Y, and shared a double cell with a friendly young woman, married and an ex-nurse, aged thirty-six, called Pat. I had the top bunk again, and was glad of Pat's company as I now had a message that the appeal *was* to be on Monday, 27 June, after all. I had seen no more of Mr M. or Mr Winstain, and felt that their chances were pretty slim against a leading QC and the barrister from my trial.

Saturday and Sunday were days of so much tension and anxiety, but the doctors here were very good, and I was given valium at night. The officers too were so kind, so different from Styal, and of course I had Pat for company. She was a first offender like me, and missing her husband and eight-year-old son very much. Also she liked reading, and could hold an intelligent conversation – if only she had been with me in Styal, but for her sake I hoped she never would.

Monday morning came. I could only drink a cup of tea. I went to reception at 8 a.m. – all my possessions were to go with me to the Appeal Court. If I were freed, I would not return to Holloway. I was taken to the Court of Appeal in the Strand in a minibus. It was so strange to look out at all the people hurrying about on this lovely June morning. They were on their way to work. *How* I prayed that soon I too would be free to walk outside in the sunshine.

The officer in charge of me was a very nervous, rather irritable little woman and my obvious fears and tension upset her, I'm afraid. I was put into a cell. There was a bench to sit on. The door was left open so I did not feel shut in this time. At 10 we made our way up the long spiral iron staircase to the court room, then into a kind of gallery looking down at the well of the court. The judges' seats were to my left on the same level as the gallery so that they too looked down into the court. I was very surprised indeed to see the two Sussex policemen who had been the principals at my trial and even more to see Di Burgess from Yorkshire Television sitting beside them with her boss, John Willis.

The three judges came in. The chief one was Lord Justice Orr. The appeal went on all morning and after a break for lunch (I could not eat, only drink a cup of tea) continued in the afternoon. Lord Justice Orr told the legal men that they would be informed when a verdict had been reached and I was taken back to the cell below. My Junior Counsel's grounds of appeal were based on the fact that 'no suicide had taken place, so no crime committed'. His whole case was wholly concerned with 'points of law' as he called them. He had come to see me for a few minutes before the hearing and I handed him the sworn statement from Mother that it was all her fault and her idea, but he told me that it was of no use. I asked him if he thought the appeal stood any chance but he refused to answer. I felt very worried indeed.

Mr Yorke had spoken very well of my character in the Appeal Court, and he told the judges how much I was needed at home. Just before I left my cell I had been allowed to speak to him for a few minutes. We sat each side of a wire-mesh window, and I became very upset, and told him that rather than return to Styal, I would kill myself in spite of my strong Christian beliefs. He begged me not to take such terrible action, but *he* had not been in Styal and in Bleak, and could not really know that to return there would be worse than death to me. He was returning to Cornwall the next day, and would see George and Robin. I made him promise not to repeat to them what I had said. Then I and my belongings were taken back to Holloway.

The next few days dragged by. My wonderful husband wrote to me every day, loving cheerful letters. Without them I don't know how I could have waited so calmly for the judges' decision. Then on Friday morning, 1 July, I was told that I was to be in the Appeal Court after dinner. This time a very senior officer with several stripes took me and all my possessions back to the Court in the Strand.

We actually went up the winding staircase at 4 p.m., and I felt ill with the suspense. My legs seemed about to give way under me. I sat down, the officer beside me, and there once more were the CID men from Sussex, plus Di Burgess and John Willis. The senior officer remarked afterwards that it was unheard of for senior CID officers to travel so far just to listen to an appeal, but of course she did not know what nameless power in very high places was behind all this farce.

Lord Justice Orr called upon the court to rise. Then he told Mr Winstain that the decision of the court was that the sentence was to stand, because no one would ever know whether Mrs Mott would have taken any of the pills or not. He had already said a lot more about different points of law, but his concluding sentence was all that mattered to me – I was to remain a prisoner. We had been in court just half an hour.

My appeal was over. It seemed just then that there was no hope left anywhere in the world. I could not understand why God seemed to have said 'No' to all the many, many prayers for my release.

The officer supported me back down the stairs to the open

cell, sat me down and went to get some water. I was on the point of collapse. The officer sat with me, I was crying hopelessly again, and then the minibus came, and I and all my things were returned to Holloway. The officer was so good to me, and so concerned that she arranged for me to see the doctor for a sedative at once. Having been given some valium, I returned to my cell, and Pat's understanding and comfort. How glad I was to have her there, and if she ever reads this I hope she will know how much her kindness meant.

The next day was Saturday. George and Rob were to visit me, and in the morning Sister Jennie came and we talked and prayed. I told her that I *knew* this must be happening with the permission of God, in some way it was necessary for all this to happen to me, but that did not lessen the responsibility of the corruption that was making it happen.

George and Robin brought me a big bunch of roses from our garden, the garden that I would never see again now, as they would leave our home long before I left prison. I tried so hard to be cheerful, but could not keep back the tears. I was still physically so weak from my time in Styal. But I was able to tell them of the kindness and concern of so many people in Holloway – even the Roman Catholic priest told me that he was praying hard for me and had been very sympathetic. Now the vital thing was to either remain in Holloway, or to go to an open prison, to try at all costs not to be returned to Styal. George told me that he was seeing Mr Hicks, our MP, and also the Reverend Yorke was asking the Bishop of Truro to intervene on my behalf. I told George and Robin that I felt sure I *could* survive the rest of my sentence in prison, but only if I were left here and not returned to Styal. In Holloway the staff were so humane and kind, and most vital of all I received the medical help I had had for years, and still needed badly. So they left, filled with determination to do all they could, to prevent my immediate return to Styal, which was what I feared – once there neither Mr Hicks nor the Bishop could get to see me.

The next day I wrote to George, a letter to reassure him, and to tell him of my gratitude and love. In it I said, 'Wouldn't it be wonderful if Mother somehow managed to get her own lawyer, and give him a signed *true* statement? I would be free at once! Well, no harm in dreaming, Pam and the nuns would never let her get in touch with him, that's for sure. Poor Mother, she is a worse prisoner than I am, *she* can't even write or receive letters.' Some weeks earlier Susan, a close friend of mine, had written to Mother asking for news of her health, so that I could be reassured. Susan had even posted the letter in Exeter, so that the postmark would not be recognized. Two weeks later, she had received a letter from my sister's solicitors saying that her letter had been opened, and that if she wrote again legal action would be taken against her! Susan's husband Peter had also written to Pam before my appeal, asking her to have some mercy, but there was no reply.

On Monday I was told that I was being sent back to Styal on Thursday. I booked a private interview with the Governor of Holloway, who was a qualified doctor. I saw her in the evening and told her all my fears, and my anxiety to remain in Holloway, at least until I had recovered my strength a little. She was very kind. She told me that the Home Secretary could allow me to remain if he wished and gave me a form to petition him. She even said that as time was so short she would phone the contents of my petition to the Home Office and post it the next day. So I wrote it at once, in my cell, and in it I put all about my bad health, lack of medical care, and also that my family were finding it difficult to travel the round trip of 700 miles to visit me in Styal. I said too that my MP and my Bishop were anxious to be able to talk to me about the possibility of a new appeal, and that my MP was a friend of Lord Harris at the Home Office. I gave the completed petition to my officer, and went to bed, thankful once more for the valium and the pills for my migraine which had been prescribed here.

The next day, Tuesday, we were all walking back to dinner from the workroom when I had a blackout. I found myself lying on the path with a cut knee and an anxious officer bending over me. She sent me to the doctor with another officer, while she took the other women back to C4Y. The doctor examined me. I told him I had never done anything like that before, and he said that in view of my age he would keep me under observation for a few days. I told him that I was being returned to Styal in forty-eight hours, and he said, 'We will see.'

I lay awake that night, and made up my mind that even if I *did* have to *kill* myself against all my beliefs, I was *not* going back to Styal. The next morning on the way to the workroom, I dawdled behind the others, and picked up a piece of glass from beside the path – there was plenty about from the broken windows. I hid it in a tissue up the sleeve of my cardigan, so when we had a 'rub down' before going into the workroom, it was not found. After an hour I asked permission to go upstairs to the lavatory – only one woman at a time was permitted to go, so I was alone. I did my best to sharpen the piece of glass on the window ledge, then I sawed and sawed at the back of my head, to try to make a deep cut. I succeeded – blood was on the glass. I threw it far out of the window, and then lying on the concrete floor, I bashed and bashed my head until there was blood on the concrete and I felt very sick. Then I lay still, eyes closed. Soon a woman prisoner arrived, sent to look for me. There was a great fuss, the screw came, and then two nurses, who carried me on a stretcher to the doctor's surgery where I lay on the couch. The doctor was a youngish woman (there were four or five doctors taking it in turns to be on duty) who was very concerned. She examined the deep cut on my head, put a dressing on it, and ordered bed rest for twenty-four hours. She promised to see me tomorrow, which was Thursday. Mrs C. now appeared to take me back to C4Y. The doctor told her I might have concussion and to let her know if I did any vomiting. I had been given an anti-tetanus shot, and some pain killers, and I lay on my side on my bunk (the back of my head was very sore) thinking that now I would be here for at least another week. I knew that there were three other women going to Styal the following Thursday, so if I went at all, it would certainly be then, not tomorrow I felt sure.

But at 9 p.m., when she was saying good-night, Mrs C. said, I'll say good-bye.' I could not believe it. I told Pat that *no way* was I going to Styal. Very reluctantly she agreed to my plan, which was to further injure my head, be unconscious on the floor, and Pat would ring the bell for the night screw. But Pat was a nurse, and she was desperately worried in case I seriously injured myself at my age, or even killed myself. I was past caring, I could *not* go back to Styal.

Lights out is at 10 p.m. in Holloway. Pat and I lay in our bunks talking until nearly midnight, then I got off my bunk, put on the dim light in our little lavatory, and then tried to find somewhere I could bang my head really hard. The back was too sore even for me, so I tried bashing my forehead on the taps at the wash basin, but it wasn't going to work. Then I saw the metal door-stop which prevented the door hitting the wall when it was opened. I lay down on the floor, and banged and banged my forehead and eyebrow on that. Pat became more and more frantic – she was sure I was injuring myself very badly – and after about thirty minutes she insisted on ringing the bell. I was almost unconscious by now. The night screw came, Pat told her that I had fallen again, and so another screw was called, and they heaved me on to the bottom bunk, and told Pat to get into my top one. They gave me a glass of water, looked at my head, and then left, talking in whispers. I felt very ill indeed by now, and vomited into a bowl we had for washing the floor. Pat again rang the bell, the screw came and looked at me and the bowl, then went away.

I could not sleep. I had a blinding pain all over my head, and poor Pat was afraid that I was seriously ill. At 6 a.m. two big screws unlocked the door, and said to me, 'Get dressed, you're leaving for Styal in half an hour!' I could not believe it, and demanded to see a doctor. I told them that the woman doctor had said *yesterday* that I was to stay in bed, and since then I had injured the front of my head. I was told. 'No doctor,' and one of them packed all my things, while the other helped me to dress. I was hardly able to stand. Pat was awake and stared in silent horror – there was nothing she could do, of course, so we said good-bye and I was walked out between the two screws, one carrying my belongings.

When we reached reception I again asked to be seen by a doctor, or at least a nurse, but the answer was still the same. A well-spoken officer of about forty-five now appeared. She looked anxiously at me – I had a huge lump on my eyebrow and a fast blackening eye. We got into the usual minibus. There was no other woman going, and yet in a week three other prisoners were moving to Styal. What a waste of public money, apart from all else.

I sat in the back seat, only half-conscious, and the officer sat near by. When we reached Birmingham she told the driver to go to the men's prison near there, and when we arrived she told the officer in charge that she wanted me examined by a doctor. The prison doctor came – he was an Indian, and seemed very surprised when told that no doctor had seen me at Holloway before we left. He examined me, and wrote a letter for the doctor at Styal. I do not know what was in it. The officer with me insisted that I should drink some tea, and eat a sandwich, but I could not eat, I felt too sick. There was a little kitten playing about, and I took it on to my lap – the first animal I had been allowed to touch since I left home six months ago. I missed my own dogs and cats very much indeed.

We arrived at Styal during the afternoon, and once more I went into reception to be stripped and searched. I said a regretful good-bye to the kindly screw from Holloway, who gave the Indian doctor's letter to Miss P., and then left for the officer's mess. As soon as I was dressed, I was told to go over to the hospital and take the sealed letter to the sister in charge. Sister J. looked at the wound on the back of my head, and the lump and black bruise on the front, and told me I would see the doctor in the morning. Back I went to reception to collect my things, the ones I was allowed here. There was a very tough elderly officer waiting for me – she was Mrs J., from Fox House, across the road from the hospital.

The morning after my return I saw the doctor and told him how ill I felt, and asked him not to send me back to the workroom. He read the Indian doctor's note and said, 'You can rest until Monday, then return to the workroom.' Now when he opened my medical notes I saw a newspaper cutting about my case in the front of the file. How I longed for the reassuring face of Dr Hanan, my doctor in Mevagissy.

On Saturday morning I fainted on my way for my dose of

Thyroxine. One of the sisters put me in a wheelchair and took me into the dispensary, where she took my pulse. After I had rested she sent me back to Fox, in the care of another prisoner from my house. There was no doctor at week-ends except for emergencies, and apparently this was not in that category.

On Sunday we were all taken out for our half hour walk before dinner. It was very hot and I blacked out again. Sister once more wheeled me to the hospital, but this time I was put to rest on a bed until tea time, then sent back to Fox. On Monday I was so ill that the civilian woman in charge of the workroom refused to have me there. The screw from Fox took me back to the house. After that, my new AG, Mrs K., gave me the job of scrubbing all the passages and the cloakroom downstairs. I was only too happy to do so, I was alone in my work, and above all it was quiet.

Miss K. was sympathetic and somehow I struggled through the days, till the following Saturday, when George and Robin again did their marathon journey to visit me.

Miss K. had seen George in the big hall and warned him about my appearance, and how ill I looked. I now had a *very* black eye! We had a lovely, long visit, in spite of my ailments, and George told me that the Bishop of Truro, Dr Graham Leonard, had made a very strong appeal in a Sunday paper for me to be shown some mercy and sent to an open prison.

George was to sign all the documents giving up our home on 1 August and from that date we would be free of *all* guarantees and charges. CSA had also said that George and Robin could remain in the house until it was actually sold. But I was *still* so worried about poor Mother, and the fact that nobody could get a letter to her or see her. I wondered if she knew that my appeal had failed, or indeed if she knew anything about me now. After all our years of such love and closeness, were we never to be together again?

Chapter 14

Fox, the house I was now living in, was much larger than Howard. There were twenty women there, several of them pregnant. I had a bed in a dormitory with three other women. I got on well with all the women in Fox, as I had done in Howard, but we had two of the toughest screws in Styal. 'The old school' they called themselves. They seemed to dislike me on sight. Both had strong Lancashire accents and my way of speaking irritated them very much, as did the fact that I did not lose my temper or use the word 'fuck' with every other sentence.

There were two 'mother and baby' houses in Styal. The pregnant prisoners actually had their babies in Wilmslow Hospital nearby and then returned to Styal, where they could keep the babies up to the age of one year, when they were either taken by relatives or fostered. The mothers and their offspring lived quite separately from the rest of us in the two houses, Melanbe and Hooker. It seemed so strange to see the prams outside the houses in this closed prison. But even mothers with tiny babies were not safe from the threat of Bleak, which hung over all our heads. While I lived in Fox, one girl of eighteen left to have her baby, moved back to Malanbe when her child was a week old, and then got involved in an argument with an officer. The officer hit the girl, who complained to her AG, and was promptly taken down to Bleak. She was told the next day that she would remain there, while the screws cared for the baby (under the eye of the nurse) until she had cancelled her complaint. She was out in a week, and who can blame her for backing down. As she said to me, 'My baby comes first.'

In Fox there was one young girl who was seventeen. She was pregnant for the second time – she had had an abortion at fifteen. Poor Lorraine, her parents were divorced when she was seven and she lived with her father. When she was eleven he raped her, and continued to abuse her for two years until a relative found out. She had then gone to her mother, who had since married again. With such a background, how could I blame Lorraine for her rudeness to me, and her filthy talk? One day I spoke to her, and she shouted, 'You're not worth the steam off my shit.' Yet that very night in the dormitory which she shared with me and two others, she had cried bitterly in my arms, and begged me to forgive her and take no notice. Like so many, many young prisoners here, Lorraine had never in her whole life known love or security. Is it any wonder that she, and others like her, are in and out of prison like yo-yos? The police chiefs urge stiffer and longer sentences for 'young offenders'. They would think very, very differently if they could be a prisoner in Styal for even one week and see the appalling human misery of these 'offenders'.

Another woman in Fox was a negress from Birmingham. She was in for prostitution. She was always joking and laughing, and told us a very amusing story. One day she and a friend who was also on 'the game' decided to go to London for the evening and see what they could make. They strolled round the Piccadilly and Soho areas, and the friend went up to an elderly man, and said, 'Do you want business?' He said yes, he did, and asked how much.

'Five pounds inside, and ten for something special,' the black girl told him, 'Which do you want?'

'Oh I'll have the special,' her client replied, whereupon she opened her large handbag, took out a brick and knocked him unconscious. That was the something special! Then they went through his pockets and walked off. She laughed and laughed when she was telling the story, and said that she and her friend had made £200 a night by this method. They knew the 'mark' had at least £10 in his wallet for the 'special' and of course they did not have to actually work for the money.

On one of their visits George and Robin brought another bunch of flowers from our garden, including a lot of lavender, which smelt so lovely. I put it all in a big vase in the common room – we were not allowed any flowers in our dormitories. On Saturday evening I went into the dining room and found four women *smoking* my lavender! They were always desperate for anything they could smoke in a roll up. The day before we were paid each week they hunted everywhere for old dog ends, even lifting the edges of the lino in the dormitories. But the lavender made two of them very sick, and the other two stoned, so I hid it under my mattress to dry. Later I secretly made little lavender bags with some muslin I stole from the kitchen.

There was a big traffic in tobacco in Styal, everyone bought Old Holborn and packets of papers on pay day. The tobacco was 43p for half an ounce. So a woman would buy an extra half ounce for 43p and by Monday (we were paid Wednesdays) she could sell it for 80p, and was paid when we got our actual cash. So several prisoners became 'Tobacco Barons', and were making quite a lot of money out of their fellow inmates' desperate need for smokes. But it was dangerous as it was forbidden. One girl was caught and spent many weeks in Bleak. I saw Lynne in the hospital queue one day – she had just come from Bleak and looked dreadful. She had been transferred to another house.

The senior house officer in Fox was Mrs Egerton – an exceptionally fine officer. She was intelligent, well educated and compassionate, and was well aware of the abuses taking place in Styal Prison, where one young girl has made a complaint of lesbian rape. When she spoke at a meeting of prison officers in 1978, her speech was reported in the *Daily Telegraph.* She was complaining about the degree of lesbianism amongst the officers in the prison service. Of course, the Home Office has swept this under the carpet once more. This cannot go on much longer; there is so much that is glossed over, including the way in which I was treated. If enough people supported a fine and experienced officer like Mrs Egerton, something might be done to expose what is really going on in Styal. Even the Home Secretary cannot ignore public opinion for ever.

It was August – a week-end. I was suddenly filled with anxiety about Mother. I *knew* something was very wrong. I had always feared that because of her terrible pain and poor health she would not live until I could see her again. Now I felt her presence close to me. We were a strange family, bound together by our very differences from other people. Mother and I were especially bound by our unusually strong love for each other, still undimmed at our ages of eighty-eight and sixty-one.

At 5 p.m. on Monday, 14 August, tough old Mrs J. came into the dining room where I was having tea. She told me to go with her to the Deputy Governor's office. As we walked along in the hot sunshine, I felt a black depression – something very bad had happened, I felt sure. The Deputy called me into his office alone.

'Your mother died early this morning. I am told it was peaceful,' he said.

I covered my face with my hands.

'No, no, not Mummy, not Mummy,' I began to cry desperately.

I tried to be calm – but all I could see was Mother dying in that horrible, hostile place. Now I would never see her again.

When I was calmer I asked the Deputy when the funeral was to be held. I assumed that I would be going – I had seen many women in Styal taken to the funeral of relatives. 'You will not be going to your mother's funeral. Your sister's solicitors phoned to tell me of the death and your sister does not want you there,' he said.

I protested strongly. I was legally Mother's next of kin, her elder daughter. But it was useless. Then I asked if I could let George know, so that he and Robin could attend, or at least send flowers. I was told to return to my house.

Outside the door I found my AG, Miss K., waiting for me.

My senior house officer, Mrs Egerton, was there too and she put her arm round me. I was sobbing uncontrollably. Mrs Egerton took me across to the hospital and asked one of the nurses to give me a sedative.

'She has just heard her mother has died,' Mrs Egerton said quietly.

'Stop those crocodile tears. We all know it's what you wanted. Now you've got your wish,' the nurse shouted at me. This cruel and untrue remark distressed me even more. On or way back to Fox, Mrs Egerton reported the nurse to Miss K., who marched off to reprimand her.

Miss Egerton let me go straight to bed – unheard of in Styal – and I lay, crying, crying the bitter tears that are shed when it is too late, too late to see and talk to Mother ever again. It seemed as though the objective had been to have me locked up until Mother died (she *was* very old) so that we would never again be together.

The next day the new vicar came to see me. I pleaded with him to phone Mr Yorke, my vicar, who lived near to home, and ask him to break the news of Mother's death to George and Robin. They, at least, could try to be at her funeral. He refused – he could not interfere in prison affairs. I argued – this was not a prison affair; surely one vicar could phone another on a spiritual matter? He left saying he would think about it.

Two days later the AG sent for me. I was to be lodged in the hospital for a few days, 'for your own protection,' she said. Apparently the newspapers were full of articles about my attempted 'crime' against Mother; the *Daily Mirror* even stressed my 'depravity'. The officers were not sure how my fellow prisoners would take all this, especially as I was reported to have inherited £40,000 on Mother's death. I took a few necessities and, still numb with grief at Mother's death, I went to live in a single room in the hospital. My heartache was selfish I realized – at least my beloved mother was free now and beyond any more hurt.

Lying on my bed that night, I thought about my sister. I remembered that when she had left art college (she was nearly eighteen), she had been offered a very good job in London with a firm called Heaton Tabb to design materials and wallpapers. Pam was quite talented in that field and Father knew the managing director of the firm. But to take the job would have meant that Pam would have to leave home and live in London. She refused to go. She could not break the extraordinary bond that bound us to Mother, a bond that neither of us really broke until Mother's death. Our ancestors had been held in the strange way too. No one had ever broken out of the magic circle. We were all one in some dark and secret unity.

I found out on Friday that George had learnt of Mother's death on the Wednesday night. A reporter from the *Daily Mail* had phoned up at 10.30 p.m. and asked if he was going to her funeral. Apparently she was cremated on the Thursday, but I still do not know where.

Later that evening I was reading in bed when Mrs Egerton came to see me. All twenty women in Fox had held a house meeting and demanded my return at once. Mrs Egerton was very pleased.

'You must feel very gratified that they feel so strongly after your short time in Fox House,' she remarked. It was comforting, especially as I now had not only Mother's death on my mind, but was also in turmoil about a totally unforeseen event about which I had only learnt that afternoon.

Earlier that day I had again been summoned to the Deputy Governor's office. To my great relief I saw Miss F., the senior AG. She was the only other person I knew to be a practising Christian. There were several newspapers spread out on the desk. I now learned that Yorkshire Television were going to show an hour-long documentary about me. The programme was to be called 'The Case of Yolande McShane'. In it they were going to use part of the secret police video-tape taken in Mother's bedroom. The police were actually allowing the television company to show their video-tape, the very evidence they had used for my conviction, to the general public. It was an unheard of action for them to take.

I was outraged. No one had the right to allow millions of viewers to see Mother getting on and off her commode, to listen and to watch our last private talk together in what we thought was the privacy of Mother's bedroom. I knew that Mother would never have agreed to this television spectacle; as Mother's next of kin, I would never agree to it either.

In view of the gravity of the situation, Miss F. allowed me to phone George. He was already making frantic efforts to stop the film being shown on 24 August. He appealed to Lady Plowden, the head of the Independent Broadcasting Authority, to show the film to the Bishop of Truro and Robert Hicks, my MP, before any final decision was taken to broadcast it. But we seemed absolutely powerless to prevent it. The decision that it should be shown was already taken.

It was reported in one newspaper, the *People*, that in July, while I was in Holloway, Pam had refused permission for the tape to be shown, though other newspapers subsequently reported that this was not the case. While Mother was alive, her permission would also have been needed. Had I won the appeal, there would have been no question of it being shown.

The television company went so far as to claim that I had been approached and given my permission for the video-tape to be used in a documentary. They even said that I had been paid a fee for appearing in this documentary myself. This story was reported in the newspapers *before* the film was shown, and it must have totally misled the public. I had been paid a fee and agreed to appear in a documentary before my trial, when the television people had spent two days filming at Lanlivery Manor. The suggestion that they might use the video-tape was not raised then, nor at any other time. John Willis from Yorkshire Television eventually admitted, *after* the film had been shown, that I had not been approached for my permission to use the tape. What he actually said was: 'Mrs McShane is not an innocent person and in the circumstances we do not think her permission was needed.'

I was utterly powerless to prevent it. There was nothing I could do – shut away in prison. The documentary was shown the following Wednesday night, 24 August, on all ITV channels in spite of all efforts to have it stopped. It was shown when we prisoners were all in bed, at 10.30 p.m., I believe. The next day there were reports in all the newspapers, mostly condemning what one called a 'Second Trial by Television'. Another asked, 'Surely the woman has been tried and sentenced once, was it necessary a second time?' Apparently telegrams and phone calls had poured in from all over the world in protest, especially from America where the question was asked: '*How* could this happen in England?'

Although no prisoner saw the programme, I learnt later that *all* the officers had watched. One prisoner subsequently told me that the morning after it had been shown, she had heard the officers discussing it. The general opinion was summed up in a remark made by a senior officer: 'Well, if that's the case against McShane, she should not be in prison.' Almost all the officers felt sympathy for me. I certainly noticed a much kinder attitude from most of the screws.

Back in Fox I returned to my bed in the corner and into my protective shell without which I could not bear to go on living. I was becoming more and more withdrawn, but did not yet realize this fully. There was a little window on the landing, out of sight from the stairs. I spent all the time I could standing there, looking out through the bars. I could see a field of cows in the distance, outside the wire fence across a busy road. Those cows became a symbol of normal life to which I clung desperately. I would stand there and pray, talk to my Father in Heaven and to Jesus, my friend, and tell them of my wretched loneliness, of my anxiety about George's health, about George and Robin having nowhere to go from the house we had lost. Sometimes there were lapwings on the grass inside the fence. I listened to their plaintive cries, then watched them rise and fly away. My heart went with them, up and away into the freedom of fields and woods.

George and Robin still visited me every two weeks. When they arrived after Mother's death they had found fifteen to twenty cars of press and camera men waiting for them outside. Miss K., the AG, had met them and conducted them straight into the big hall, but even so there had been a delay and we, who were waiting inside, had wondered why. On the day before their following visit, yet another disaster had befallen me.

It was Friday and I had just finished washing the cloakroom floor when the stores for the kitchen were delivered. The two women from the stores put the big open box just inside the back door. I saw with surprise that there were strawberries in the box – 'For your teas,' the women said as they left. I wondered that the fruit should be ripe at this late date in summer. I stooped down, picked one up and was examining it when the screw rushed in the door and grabbed my wrist.

'You're stealing food,' she shouted. I looked at her in astonishment. I explained that I could not eat strawberries, they made me ill, always had. Each time they had been served for tea here I had given mine away.

'Ask any of the other women. They will tell you,' I said. But she marched me into the office, put the one strawberry on her desk and told me I was on report. The next day, Saturday, I was marched down to Bleak, put into a cell totally empty except for the chamber pot, the screw gave me a wooden chair and locked the heavy metal door. I was once more in solitary.

Dinner time came. I could eat nothing. George and Robin were due at 1.30 and there was no sign of my release. At 1 p.m. the screw unlocked my door, and handed me a clean dress and a comb. One of the other women had been allowed to bring them from Fox, ready for my visit. I sat on my chair waiting in the suffocating heat of the cell. The window was nailed shut and the smell sickening. The screw did not come for me until just before 2 p.m., almost half an hour of our precious visit had gone. When we got to the big hall, I was taken up behind the stage and found George and Rob sitting in one of the 'stripping' cubicles. The screw said this was called a 'closed visit' and was because of my being in Bleak. She sat herself in the doorway so that she could 'hear all and see all'. I began to explain what had happened to my bewildered family and to reassure them as much as I was able. I still did not know what was to be my punishment for picking up one strawberry! When the visit was over, I was marched back to Bleak. The flowers

George had brought were taken to Fox – there was no place for flowers in solitary.

I sat down on the hard chair again and waited. I had sat there from 8.15 a.m. and my seat (which is very thin) was quite numb. At last the door opened again. It was 4.45. I was taken before the Deputy Governor once more, having removed my shoes, of course.

'You are charged that on this day, Friday, — August' – I forget the exact date – 'you did steal one strawberry. Have you anything to say, guilty or not guilty?' It sounded so like Alice in Wonderland that I could have laughed, but for Bleak hanging over my head.

'Not guilty,' I said. He told me that he did not believe me.

'You are a common thief, you have descended to the lowest level in this prison, stealing food from your fellow prisoners.'

I began to shake inside. Was I to be locked up *again*? But the Deputy now concluded, 'I am going to punish you severely,' – I held my breath – 'you will loose three days' remission,' he said. I smiled and said, '*Thank* you, sir.' If only he knew how relieved I felt! I was taken back to my cell, where I sat until 5.30, when the screw from Fox came to get me. When I told the other women of my punishment they simply could not believe it – to lose three days for picking up one strawberry! But I only felt great relief that I was not in Bleak that night.

A week later I was sitting reading in Fox. It was pouring with rain, and I and the other two house cleaners were taking our fifteen-minute afternoon break ('tea break' it was called, but there was no tea). A young screw appeared and told me to pack my things. I was being moved! My heart leaped at a wild hope of open prison, but I was in fact going to Block 3.

Block 3 was on the other side of the prison from Fox. It was a house that had been decorated and furnished ready for new officers' quarters, but there were not enough officers to occupy the dwelling, and now a select group of women prisoners lived there. They all held responsible jobs in the prison, and to live in Block 3 was considered a great privilege. On arrival I found my old friend Sheila there in charge of the house cleaning, and she took me up to a dormitory for four, with a vacant bed. What a vast difference in this house. There were pretty curtains at the windows, new lino on the floor, even curtains to pull to screen each bed for undressing. Sheila hurried me proudly from room to room, to show me how lucky I was to be here. But I did not really know just how fortunate I was until I met Mrs Mac, our senior house officer, later that day. She was a stout, motherly figure, and full of kindness to those prisoners who behaved properly – woe betide those who did not! She never, never sent a woman to Bleak, but kept control by force of personality alone.

A few nights after my arrival in Block 3, I had a particularly bad migraine. Mrs Mac had taken me across to the hospital to insist that the sister should give me something. While I waited in the queue there was a sudden panic, the phone rang, and the sister grabbed the first aid box and hurried down to Bleak in her usual bedroom slippers. We learnt later that a young girl had managed to break the light globe and had tried to cut her throat. I was extra glad that Mrs Mac did not send her women to Bleak.

Mrs Mac had been in the prison service for over twenty years (she retired in September 1978) and much preferred the years when she had been a Borstal officer. We had many long talks, and during one of them she said, 'You can *do* something with the young Borstal girls, by the time they get here it's too late.'

It was very difficult to get used to being in Block 3, there was such a totally different atmosphere from the other houses. (I have always been sensitive to atmospheres. I could walk into a house and receive strong feelings of good or bad, and of the people who had lived there. This kind of thing, like 'second sight' and putting curses on people, ran in my family. We took it all at a matter of course.) Of the thirteen women who were to be my fellow inmates in Block 3, all, except the two cooks and Sheila and me, worked outside the prison gate, in the mess or in the officers' quarters. One of them, a woman called Denny who worked in the mess, had the corner bed opposite mine. In our dormitory there was also a tall, reserved woman serving her first sentence for shop-lifting. In the fourth bed was the little Turkish Cypriot, Maria, whom I had befriended in Howard.

I had a new job as well as a new house. I was made the education orderly and my money went up to 86p a week! The house next to Block 3 had been converted into classrooms for evening classes and the top floor (where I worked) was used for training the Borstal girls in Styal. There were about twenty of them. Two very pleasant women from Wilmslow ran the home economics course, which included cookery. There was a truly magnificent kitchen. It was huge, with cookers all along both sides, interspersed with stainless-steel sink units. There were about ten electric stoves and about eight run on gas so that the girls could learn to cook on both. Then there was the sewing room, with ten super modern electric sewing machines, and three large classrooms, containing desk and chairs. Everything was brand new. My job was to clean it all and also to run errands for the two teachers, Miss Whitfield and Mrs Gelber, both of whom treated me very kindly indeed. On Mondays I took a metal supermarket-type trolley down to the main stores near Bleak (I used to shudder and listen for the cries, but I could hear nothing) and collect the food for the girls to cook during the coming week. But there was really very little work to do and I was always finished by dinner time. After dinner I had to go back there. I used to take a book and just sit at a desk and read.

The classroom at the end of the corridor became my favourite spot, far enough away to remain undisturbed. I got so attached to that room that I used to walk in at 8.15 a.m. and say, 'Hello room,' and when I left at 4 p.m., I often said, 'Good-night room, *one* day I'll have such good news for you.' I meant open prison, of course. I spent many, many hours in that room, gazing out across the wire fence to the trees and houses beyond, and once I actually saw a dog, a spotty Dalmatian, stroll by. That was a real event. As I now had so much time alone, to think, I began to realize what was really wrong, why my clothes hung on my thin body, and why my son told me that my eyes had sunk back into their sockets, and that my face was drawn and pale.

'You look as though you are slowly dying, Mother,' he had said anxiously on a visit while George had gone to fetch our three cups of tea.

Now in my special room I knew that Robin was right (he too has 'the sight'). I *was* slowly dying, deep down where I had hidden my real feelings, my real self. I had taken the pain, the suffering and the anguish of every woman in Styal into myself, every poor creature in Wrighton and even Bleak was *me*, and I carried a weight of misery that was destroying me. The atmosphere in Styal was so utterly evil and cruel that it seemed to soak into my skin, be part of the air I breathed, so that I could hardly eat or sleep any more. There was plenty of food available had I been able to eat, but I got thinner and thinner. Even Mrs Mac was worried and told me that she was praying that I would soon go to open prison.

'I can almost see the flesh falling off you every day,' the kind soul said. But how could I explain to her that I seemed to carry the whole weight of Styal inside me, as the Ancient Mariner had carried his burden on his back, or to tell her that my loneliness was so great that a *room* was my friend and I talked to it as though it were a person? I did not want to find myself in Wrighton, so I kept silent, and retreated further and further from things outside.

But it was impossible to shut out everything – particularly the filthy talk in the dormitory at night. We now had a new cook and she and another girl, Joan, became close friends with Denny. Every night after lights out, when Mrs Mac had said 'God bless' and walked away across the grass, they came and sat on Denny's bed across from mine. They smoked their roll-ups, and often made tea or coffee with hot water from the wash basins. The cook smuggled milk in from the kitchen. She was in for attempted kidnapping and disliked me intensely. I was not surprised, she had a very evil feel to her. These women did not talk to me at night. They sat on Denny's bed and discussed their sex life outside (there were no lesbians in Block 3, Mrs Mac would not have them). Joan sat there one night and recounted the various ways she used to 'turn on' her husband, who was a long distance lorry driver.

'I put my hands round the ice in the fridge, then I hold his balls. *That* gets him up quick,' she said, while I tried to hold my pillow over my head, but their voices were so loud. Then the cook would say, 'Well, I never actually let him come *in* my mouth, I mean it's kind of messy,' and Denny, 'Oh I do, I don't mind the taste.'

The other two women went to sleep as soon as Mrs Mac left, but I could not, and the sex talk got worse and worse. Then I had a reprieve, Denny had a cold, and for a few nights there was peace in the dormitory. But it did not last long, and I was forced to listen to absolute filth night after night. I could no more escape than if I were nailed to the wall. One night I had an argument with Denny about opening or not opening a window in our dormitory.

'Shut up you fucking shit stirrer,' she yelled. This was mild compared with some remarks.

Autumn came, October with all the trees turned to molten gold, and I shuffled through the deepening piles of fallen leaves, pretending I was a little girl again. Then one wonderful day, very early in the morning, I saw two little black and white kittens, popping in and out of a disused heating pipe, half under the Education Block next door. My early morning job was to clean all the brass inside and outside Block 3 (we all had work to do before breakfast) and Mrs Mac knew how much I loved to be outdoors. So I polished the outside doorknobs until they shone and breathed the lovely crisp morning air – the central heating in the dormitory was much too hot for me.

This particular day I had done my brass, and was standing quite still when I saw the kittens, and then the coal black mother poked her head out cautiously. All the screws and gardeners were determined to get rid of the cats, and so the poor creatures went in fear of their lives. I moved slightly, and with a flash of whiskers and little white paws they were gone into the pipe, but from then on my life became a crusade to feed 'my kittens', without discovery, as to feed either birds or cats meant loss of remission. Not even Mrs Mac could alter that.

While I lived in Fox House, there had been a tiny black kitten with no tail living in the bushes, and I had of course adopted it, and called it 'Stumpy'. As there was no other source of food, I had stopped eating meat or fish, and smuggled it out to Stumpy in my 'dolly bag', a cloth drawstring bag given to all prisoners in reception, for carrying tobacco and matches, etc. So I had become a vegetarian, and when I left Fox I found that I could not face eating meat again, it revolted me. Now my kitten near Block 3 had all the meat and fish from my plate, and all that I could steal from the other women's plates that went out to the washing-up room. I was afraid to let anyone see what I was doing, but soon found another couple of animal lovers, who would pass me sticky little parcels, and whisper, 'for the kittens'.

Besides becoming a vegetarian (I still am) I had found that my terror of spiders had vanished. In fact I seemed to regard all living creatures with deep respect, even reverence. Life was such a precious thing, somehow it seemed very important to hold on to that feeling in this evil and destructive place. I used to look round at the place where I worked, the kitchen for the Borstal girls, the sewing machines – the equipment must have cost many thousands of pounds, but *nothing* was being done in the far more important area of their future lives, *apart* from cooking and sewing. No one tried to talk to them, to erase any of the deep bitterness so many felt, the hatred of society, and the people who had put them in Styal. Yet if I could reach them, talk to them, and understand them, after only nine months in Styal, then why in the name of God, can't someone else help them to learn, or in many case to unlearn?

Just before I moved to Block 3, a truly wonderful woman started to visit me. Mrs D. was a real child of God. She had been an official prison visitor for over thirty years. My old friend Peggy had talked to the vicar in the little town where she now lives, and he had approached Mrs D. and put her in touch with me. How wonderfully God cares for his children, even in Styal, and even such a rebellious and self-willed child as I. Mrs D.'s weekly visits and our short prayers together, the very knowledge that she too really knew and loved the

Lord, these, plus Peggy's Christian support, and the books she sent me, were my real lifeline in Styal. And of course the love and devotion of George and Robin who never once failed to arrive for their fortnightly visits, all through the frost and fog, and the teeming rain of winter, and the heat of the summer sun beating on the roof of my little car, a journey of 340 miles each way.

But much as they enjoyed seeing me, there was a lot to distress them in Styal, apart from my sufferings. They told me of the fathers bringing small children to see their mothers week after week. Some of the children were quite small and had come very long distances. They were herded into the small, airless waiting room, and George felt for the harassed fathers, trying to quiet two or three tired and fretful little ones. Then when visits were over, the children clung to their mothers in the big hall. They had to be removed by force, and were led or carried away by the husbands, sobbing bitterly, while their mothers sat with tears pouring down their cheeks, waiting to be strip searched yet again.

Some of these women were in Styal for ten years or more, and it is a terrible thought that their children now aged four or five would visit this dreadful place every two weeks for the most formative years of their totally innocent lives, every other week up to fourteen, fifteen or even sixteen years of age. Yet *they* had done nothing to deserve this brutal punishment.

November was a cold and foggy month as it always is in the north of England. By now I had given up the hope of being sent to open prison. The thought of spending Christmas in this dreadful place hung over me like a black cloud. It would be bad enough to be away from George and Robin at what we had always made a very special 'family occasion', but how could the celebration of the birth of Jesus be anything but a mockery in Styal?

I had begun my parole interviews in October. The first had been an hour long discussion with Miss B., the AG, who, like everyone else now, was treating me in a much more gentle fashion. She had asked me a lot of questions, mostly about my family, and where we would be able to live (they were still in Lanlivery Manor as it was unsold). I would *not* be granted parole unless I could join George at an approved address. But we had also talked about my time in Styal.

'Prison isn't going to make a scrap of difference to you. You are *not* going to change are you?' she had said in exasperation. 'No, Miss B., I do not intend to allow Styal to change me,' I had replied. So she said that her recommendation would be that prison for me was useless and I should be released as early as possible.

Then in early November I had my interview with the Deputy Governor, as once more the Governor was away. (She always was when I needed to see her.) He asked me what I thought of Styal. Carefully I replied that the grounds were beautiful – after all I wanted my parole in February very much indeed. But I did risk saying a few things about the prison system in general, like the fact that it was a total failure as proved by the constant return of women to Styal.

Finally the vital talk was with the official from the parole board. He was a very pleasant man and told me that as my behaviour and work reports were excellent, he hoped that I *would* be able to join my family on parole. I had also to write a paper giving the reasons why I thought I should be paroled (how did those women manage who were illiterate?). I had said, amongst other things such as my family's need of me, that I felt that my remaining in prison was a waste of time and I would be a much more useful citizen outside.

George and Robin had been making frantic efforts to find somewhere else to live, even a large caravan, as I *had* to have an address for parole, but with two dogs and five cats it was extremely difficult. Robin was only on a student grant and George was living on social security, so rent was also a big problem. But at the end of November our friend Susan Miln and her husband Peter managed to find a small unfurnished house in a nearby village. The owner was abroad for about a year and Peter was able to arrange for it to be made available for us and the Department of Social Security (bless them) agreed to pay the rent. So now our worse worry was over, I did have an approved address. Now all we had to do was wait for my case to come before the parole board in January or early February. My earliest possible release date was 11 February, one year and one day after my conviction. But in spite of this wonderful answer to prayer, I became more and more tired and depressed. My whole body seemed to have taken as much shock and unhappiness as it could bear.

Then on 8 December, at 8 p.m., a relief officer from Wilmslow was on duty in Block 3. Calling me into the office, she said, 'Yolande, you are going to open prison tomorrow after dinner!' I gave a yell of joy, and flung my arms round 'Polly' as all the women called her affectionately (she was one of the *very* few good officers in Styal). I was beside myself with excitement and rushed into the common room with my good news. It was greeted there with almost as much excitement as mine. Next morning I packed and took all my things to reception, left them there to be searched, and returned to Block 3 to wait to be fetched. One of the girls promised to feed the kittens. I rushed next door to tell Miss Whitfield, it was Mrs Gelber's day off. Then I flung open the door of 'my room'.

'There, I *told* you we would get good news one day – good-bye dear room,' I said then. I closed the door gently and returned to wait in my house.

Polly had not been allowed to tell me where I was going and Miss M. in reception had also refused to say. But I met the vicar on my way back to Block 3.

'Congratulations, I hear you are going to Moor Court,' he said.

'Yes, so I believe, good-bye,' I replied calmly.

At 11.30 a.m., earlier than expected, a taxi arrived with an officer from Moor Court. I said a hasty farewell to the women in Block 3. Sadly it was Mrs Mac's day off, but I had left a note thanking her for making my life at least bearable during my last months in Styal. I went up to reception. Miss M. strip searched me for the very last time, and then I got into the taxi beside the well-spoken officer, whose name was Mrs Kent. We drove out through the hated big gate.

By the grace of God, and that alone, I had survived, and was leaving Styal alive with my spirit unbroken. I thought sadly of Mother. I knew that she would have quoted, 'My head is bloody but unbowed,' and so it was. I was leaving Styal for ever.

Chapter 15

The drive to Moor Court Open Prison took about one and a half hours. Although it was 9 December and pouring with rain, it was wonderful to look out at fields of cows and sheep, and I found Mrs Kent a pleasant and informative companion. At the end of our journey we turned off the road into big gates (standing open!) past a small lodge, and up a long tree-lined drive with a white farm fence each side. I saw two horses grazing. Then we were at the big grey stone house, with a circular driveway and an island of grass with a tall old pine tree in front of the house. Mrs Kent told the driver to take us around to a side entrance, and he helped me to carry my suitcase and boxes in through a door by a very large kitchen. Having paid the driver, Mrs Kent took me down the shallow steps into a corridor. Then she unlocked a door on the right and we put all my possessions inside.

As it was dinner time I was to be locked in until the reception officer was ready for me. Imagining Bleak I was very scared. But there was no need. I was put into the little passage outside the three cells, where there was a table and chair. Someone would bring my dinner. Another grey-haired officer, Miss L., locked the outside door and I was alone. I examined the three cells. They were the same size as those in Bleak, but with larger windows, and at the end of the passage in which I sat was a modern bathroom and lavatory. I learned later that although anyone on report *was* put into a cell, the Governor saw her at 10 a.m., and having been told her punishment, i.e. loss of pay, extra duties, etc., she was released at once. No woman was ever kept locked up at Moor Court.

After my dinner, which a prisoner brought on a tray, the reception officer arrived and took me into her office. What a totally different procedure here! Mrs B. asked me to take off my jersey and slacks.

'No need to search you further, they do it so very thoroughly at Styal,' she said, with a friendly smile. I sat down while we went through my things, listed them, and I took out the three sets of clothing I was allowed to keep in my room. Mrs B. told me that if I wanted to change any items at any time, I had only to ask her. She sent for two cups of tea, and then I signed for my goods in her storeroom.

At 4 p.m. she sent for another prisoner and told her to take me up to Dorm 6.

'Come any time if you need anything,' she said before I left. 'It's no trouble at all.'

I went along the passage, through a large common room and into the front hall. My dormitory was at the top of the front stairs. The girl showed me the empty bed in the corner facing the window. There were six beds in all, three on each side of the room.

'Come downstairs when you've finished making your bed,' she said and closed the door behind her.

I went and sat on the wide window ledge and looked out. Moor Court was the private residence of the Bolton family until ten years ago. It is a lovely old house, with magnificent views from the windows out over lawns and a formal garden with clipped yew trees to fields and woods beyond. There is a low stone wall along one side of the garden dividing it from the neighbouring field. The most wonderful thing of all – *no* bars at the big windows. As I sat looking out, I felt stunned. So *much* freedom, such a totally different atmosphere from Styal.

My head ached very badly so I went to look for an officer.

I found one at the bottom of the stairs.

'I'll ask sister to give you a headache dose,' and she took me back upstairs and along to the dispensary. I saw a friendly sister who wore glasses. She was the senior of three nursing sisters who took it in turns to be on duty from 8 a.m. to 5 p.m. Sister gave me a dose of Panadol and told me to come to see her in the morning if my headache was still bad. This was Friday, the doctor only came on Wednesdays, but the sister promised to read my medical notes and give me any medicines I needed.

Tea was at 5 p.m. here as in Styal, but there were a hundred women in Moor Court, and one big dining room where all ate together. I collected my plate from the big serving hatch from the kitchen and was astonished to see a choice of three main dishes, plus bread and margarine and a slice of cake. There was a chef supervising the four kitchen workers and an officer helping them to serve at the hatch. I was told that all the tables were called after the days of the week. They were in rows, four women to a table, and I was told to sit in Thursday row. There was a teapot for each table, with milk already in the pot. We each had the usual half egg-cup of sugar, but at every meal here, instead of twice a day as at Styal. We were all allowed to go up for second helpings. The food was very well cooked, compared with the amateur efforts of the conscripted cooks I had been used to, but I was too tired to enjoy my meal. I had been living and eating with sixteen to twenty women for so long that the noise of the hundred prisoners in the dining room was overpowering.

We could leave as soon as we finished eating, and go upstairs until 6.30, when a bell rang and everyone went downstairs, to sit in one of the two common rooms – one had BBC, the other ITV – or listen to the player in the record room. Young prisoners were actually allowed to dance, a punishable offence in Styal. I asked a senior officer if I might go to bed as my head was aching so much. To my amazement she said, 'Yes, of course. One of the girls will bring your tea and bun up.'

The officers here were all kind, friendly, and mostly well-educated women, an even better type of officer than at Holloway. Next morning I discovered just how good the Governor was here. I was told to report to the small workroom at 8.15 a.m., but I had a very bad migraine, and when I went into the noisy room, with its bright lights, I sat down and cried uncontrollably. It seemed to me like Styal's workroom all over again. An officer took me out, and sat me on a chair in one of the cloakrooms. I was crying bitterly, when someone knelt down and asked in a familiar voice, 'What *is* the matter, Yolande?' It was Miss K., the AG from Fox House, and now Deputy Governor here. She took me along to the Governor's office and sat me down in the hall outside, while she had a talk with the Governor. Then I was called in and while Miss K. sat in a chair nearby I stood in front of the governor, Miss L., and she asked what the trouble was. The Governor's office was like a large drawing room – there were flowers on her desk. She listened attentively to my tale of misery in Styal's workroom and my very bad migraine. She told me to wait outside, and after about half an hour I was told that I could take the morning off and see her again on Monday. Everyone here worked until 11.30 a.m. on Saturdays.

The officer sent me to see sister again, who gave me a sedative *and* a headache dose, and told me to lie down for a hour. I just could not take in such kindness, I felt utterly lost and disorientated!

The women in my dormitory were all very kind to me. There were two older ones, both doing two years, and both had been sent straight here as they were first offenders – so I had *not* needed to suffer as I had in a closed prison for ten months.

On my first Sunday (and indeed all the following Sundays here) I went in the coach to the parish church of Cheadale, the nearest small town. We had only two officers in plain clothes with us. We sat amongst the normal congregation. On several Sundays we were invited to join them in the adjoining church hall for coffee after the service. Then back to Sunday dinner, and visits for some, TV for others, and on fine days those who wished to go were taken on a long country walk by one of the officers out of uniform. The sister would not allow me to join the walkers, but I was told I could stroll in the grounds alone or with anyone who wished to join me.

The senior sister seemed very concerned about my loss of weight in Styal, and indeed my general health which was very poor by now. I think that perhaps I was moved to Moor Court because the Home Office realized that I could not take much more physical distress. Had I died there I would have been an even greater embarrassment to them than I already was. My MP and my bishop, and of course my husband and son, had made a great deal of fuss about my remaining in Styal for so long, and I was very grateful that they had. At least in Moor Court I was given the medical help I needed.

On Monday morning I again saw the Governor, this time alone. She told me to sit in a comfortable chair while we talked. Miss L. is a very fine woman, a woman of compassion and understanding. She asked me if I would like to work outside, to be a 'garden girl'. I was delighted to accept, but she stressed that I must only go out if I felt well enough, and because of my arthritis must keep warm and dry. She also said that I need only work until 12 a.m., then I could read or rest on my bed.

So off I went to collect my garden clothes from the officer in the laundry. They were dungarees, a thick sweater, duffle coat and wellington boots, and I felt like a land girl again. The garden officer was Mrs A., one of the most charming and friendly officers in Moor Court, and she took me up to the big greenhouse to work. The next day we were to start making holly wreaths for Christmas. There were four other gardeners making decorations. Our wreaths were to be sold for £1 each to officers and even to us prisoners to hand out on visits. They were meant to be hung on the front door for Christmas.

Mrs A. had owned a florist's shop before becoming an officer, and she was an expert. She bought the round wire frames, then covered them with moss, and then pushed holly and evergreens through the moss. The final touches were wired pine cones painted silver or white, and sprinkled with glitter, and a big red ribbon bow on a long wire twisted in the wreath. Our job was to take sacks and secateurs, and collect the holly and evergreen from the grounds, and a very pleasant task is was, walking in the crisp air, and on the dewy grass. The bushes were hung with spiders' webs sparkling with diamonds of dew in the pale winter sunshine. I stood and looked out over the low wall at the fields and woods across to a low line of hills on the horizon, and I thanked God for rescuing me and sending me to this lovely place.

There was a private farm up the small hill from the house, and six girls worked there. The jobs on the farm and in the garden were much coveted, and I was very grateful to have joined them. Sister warned me that the doctor might not allow me to continue working outside, so I did not look forward to his visit on Wednesday. But my fears were groundless. He was a pleasant Indian (the women called him 'Dr Curry') and he just asked me if I felt fit. I, of course, said, 'Yes', and that was all! The medical side of Moor Court depended on the sisters anyway, so I hurried happily back to wreathmaking in the big hall.

This was where we had visits on Saturdays and Sundays. The only thing it had in common with Styal was a small raised stage at one end, where we sat making our Christmas wreaths. There were evening classes here, as in Styal, and the English teacher was putting on a play, to which all the old people in the village were invited. They were also given a Christmas dinner the week before 25 December. The proceeds from our wreaths went towards the cost of this, and everyone in Moor Court looked forward to feeding and entertaining the old people.

George and Robin visited me on the Saturday. It was about thirty miles nearer than Styal, so cut about sixty miles off their round trip from Cornwall. Visits were on Saturdays and Sundays, from 1.30 to 3.30, and on arrival they drove in through the big front gates and right up to the front door, where they could park, handing in their visiting orders (sent from the prisoners) to the officer at the front door. I was watching eagerly from the front dormitory window, and when they arrived I ran down to a side door, and told them to ring the front doorbell. It was very relaxed and informal. An officer took them across to the big hall, where there were small tables set out, with comfortable chairs, two each side. I could actually sit next to George and hold his hand! Several couples were hugging and kissing, and the children visiting here could run about. The whole place had an atmosphere that was friendly and calm, with only two officers sitting at a table by the door. George and Rob were very impressed by the incredible difference between this and the many, many visits to Styal, and they left feeling much happier about my health.

During my last two months at Styal I had worked for the hairdresser on her two days a week in the prison. She had a small salon, and cut and washed and permed the women's hair. They paid out of 'private spends' – money held by the office, which could only be spent on hairdressing or buying tights. The hairdresser was Pat, a married woman from Wilmslow, and I had thoroughly enjoyed my days with her. She was friendly and kind, and we had many long talks about happenings in Styal. It was here that Daisy had told us so much about Wrighton. My job had been to assist Pat (we used to joke about the oldest apprentice in the business) make endless cups of tea, for which Pat generously provided all the 'makings', and sweep and clean the salon. Each day I would empty the waste basket, and quietly remove Pat's dogends (she smoked 'straights', of course) into my overall pocket, to be given to the tall, serious woman in my dorm in Block 3, who never had enough smokes. My days with Pat were a real pleasure, and once a week she washed and set my hair, for which I paid like everyone else.

Now in Moor Court I wondered how to get my hair clean. No curlers could be worn downstairs, and yet with my arthritis in my neck, I could not go to bed with wet hair as the other women did. Then I was told about Jeannette, a young first offender also doing two years, who washed and set hair, and who had the use of a hair drier. So every week Jeannette did my hair after tea, and told me about her little girl of five, whom I had seen crying on visits. She was missing her mother very badly, and I only hope and pray that Jeannette gets her parole soon. There is no possible reason to keep her in Moor Court while her child frets at home.

I met so many sad cases at Moor Court. There was a woman called Molly who was in prison for the first time for shoplifting.

She had four children aged between fifteen and eight years. Her husband was an alcoholic and Molly herself was about forty years old. She was very upset when she arrived and I did my best to comfort her. She told me she found it impossible to keep her family on the social security provided (her husband was a lorry driver and could not work since becoming an alcoholic). It seems absurd and wrong that to keep her in prison (all of us in fact) cost the government £90 a week, yet the state will not give her enough to live on and keep out of prison. What a crazy world we're living in.

(Molly also told me that she had watched the TV programme, 'The Case of Yolande McShane', in her home. She had cried and cried. 'The love between you and your mother was so obvious and I felt so very sorry for you both,' she said. This seemed to echo the feelings of all the people I have spoken to who saw the documentary.)

One of the women took me under her wing. She had spent ten years in Styal as a 'lifer' and was in Moor Court hoping to be granted parole in the spring. It was her third time before the parole board. She was a normal, kindly woman, but had been sentenced to life for being an 'accessory to murder'. When a baby can be battered almost to death and the father or mother given a suspended sentence, how can our laws make any sense? A child can be ruined for life, but the person responsible is not shut up like an animal for life, so why must this sane and normal woman receive such a sentence?

While I was in Moor Court a young girl arrived from Styal. Her twenty-first birthday was a week later. She had been in a closed prison since she was *twelve years old* for what she said was the accidental death of a child. Even if the child's death had not been accidental (as the judge probably believed), could it make sense, could it be morally right to keep her in prison all those years? Remember, she had not had any rehabilitation, no treatment or guidance of any kind – just exposure to thieves, prostitutes and lesbian officers. Now she told me that the thought of the outside world terrified her, much as she longed to be free to join her parents.

'Rehabilitate' comes from the Latin – 'to invest again with

dignity'. Here in Moor Court, for the first time since I was sentenced, I saw a Governor who understood the full meaning of the word. We were all given *back* our dignity, treated as human beings and actually encouraged to help one another. In Styal I saw a woman go to Bleak for making a little gift and giving it to a woman for her birthday. Is that to 'invest with dignity'? And when a woman is locked in Bleak for months, at the mercy of tough screws, both male and female, is that to 'invest with dignity'? Yet the Home Secretary would have us believe that the chief purpose is to rehabilitate the convicted prisoner. Perhaps he should buy a Latin dictionary.

The senior officer from Holloway told me 'Our task is to contain prisoners, not to punish.' If Holloway is to contain and Moor Court is to rehabilitate, what is the purpose of Styal? Just to be some kind of concentration camp, which is seems to resemble so closely? Having lived in all these prisons, I can see no reason why women cannot be imprisoned for their whole time in a place like Moor Court, unless their crime is thought to make them a danger to the public. Even then the only need is for a higher fence and closed gates. After twelve months in prison, living with women convicted of every kind of crime, I know that most of them are ordinary people, no different from you or me. Life has just handed them a rougher deal, that's all. The exception is, of course, those women in prison for crimes against children or crimes of extreme violence. But these are the people who desperately need some kind of help and guidance. Even here in Moor Court the women did not have any teaching about their responsibilities towards society, excellent though the Governor was.

The three young women in my dormitory suddenly decided to have their ears pierced. This was against the rules; to come in with pierced ears was all right, but not to have them done inside. However, a friend of theirs borrowed a large needle and some cotton – 'For sewing, Miss' – and on three nights in a row the piercing took place in the dormitory, while I and the two older women watched in horrified fascination. The woman doing the job just took hold of an earlobe and *forced* the needle threaded with cotton through the thick flesh. Leaving a loop of cotton in the hole, she removed the needle and tied the ends of cotton to form a small ring through the raw and bleeding earlobe. Strangely enough it did not seem to hurt very much. But as all the new holes became sore and inflamed, and the cotton rings had to be turned to keep the holes open (as sleepers are turned), the three victims were in a lot of pain, especially when they lay down to sleep on their sides. They had great difficulty in moving the cotton round in the mornings, it was stuck fast with pus, and I told them to dip the ear lobe and cotton into a mug of warm water. I was told I was a 'silly old fool, who knew nothing,' but I noticed that they adopted my suggestion, although of course nothing was said to me.

I asked one of them why they were suffering like this in here, when they could so easily have done the job properly outside.

'Well, I'm due for release in a few weeks' time, and I want to be able to walk into a good jewellers, put a pair of diamond earrings in my holes, and walk out of the shop. It's easy, my sister did it several times,' she explained. She was in for shoplifting and could hardly wait to get back to work!

Just before Christmas I received the final statement from Grandmother's trustees. It seemed I should receive about £1,000 when it was all settled. The actual trust had been sold for £27,000, Pam had had £2,000, I owed £24,000, which included the £15,000 of my personal saving which I had put into the property company, interest, death duties and legal fees. So the large sum which I was supposed to have obtained through persuading Mother to commit suicide, and on which motive I had been convicted, was (hopefully) to be £1,000. Mother had left all her personol money to Pam and Rodney (about £3,000) – I had known this since she made her will years ago – so my sister was better off after Mother's death than I was, in terms of money. Yet I was in prison for this 'financial gain', what the newspapers had called 'Greed, and a rare kind of depravity'.

The day before Christmas Eve I went to bed with flu. There were about fifteen cases in the prison, and our little hospital room had only three beds, so we had to remain in our own dormitories, and the other women brought our food up. I felt very ill, but sister was wonderful and gave me all the medical help possible. Once more God was taking care of me, imagine my having flu in Styal.

One of the girls who brought my tea one day was wearing a polo neck sweater, and I was reminded of one of the more amusing times in Block 3 at Styal. A woman had come in from work with a big love bite on her neck, whether from an officer or another prisoner I did not know. Denny had lent her a roll-neck sweater which came high enough to cover the tell-tale mark. It meant Bleak for a love bite to actually be seen by a screw.

The house was gaily decorated for Christmas Day, and at dinner there was turkey and all the trimmings, Christmas pudding, mince pies, and the officers waited on the women! I managed to stagger down for tea, the Governor herself persuaded me to make the effort, and there was a magnificent spread, with trifles and cake, etc., and crackers to pull. We all wore paper hats, the officers too. The Governor gave each woman a small gift, cigarettes for some, and sweets for the non-smokers, which she bought out of her own pocket.

After Christmas I went to work in the big long greenhouse, which ran along a high wall, and had a lovely old camelia tree in one corner. I worked alone, taking and potting geranium cuttings. There were several panes of glass missing above the camelia and six or eight blue tits came in and out for crumbs I put for them. The weather was very cold, snow fell several times, and all the birds were very hungry. One day I saw a little field mouse pop up by the base of the tree, and from then on she came every day for food. I called her Mrs Tittlemouse from Beatrix Potter's book. She was quite tame.

One day when I returned after our morning tea break (fifteen minutes *and* there was tea), I opened the door of the greenhouse to find a large male blackbird had got in and was making frantic efforts to escape. He could not find the hole in the roof again. I tried and tried to catch him to set him free, and at last had him cornered. I made a grab and his *entire* tail came away in my hands! I was truly horrified. What *had* I done? The bird fluttered under some shelves near the ground and I went on with my work. Presently to my great relief he actually *flew* to the tree, and sat looking up at the roof. He was the strangest sight, with a completely bare rear-end. After a while he flew up and out and away, and I wondered if he *could* survive without his big fan-tail, which is such a feature of an adult bird, needed for balance and flight. Next morning I waited anxiously to see if he would come for the bread I put down outside the greenhouse each day. There were many sparrows, several finches, lots of tits, about a dozen blackbirds, and one lone thrush. Suddenly there he was, sitting on the fence with no sign of a tail. He came down and fed, and it looked as though he could survive after all.

The task of getting enough bread for my increasing family of birds was really a problem. I took more and more bread from the serving hatch to conceal in my dolly bag, and I knew that the officers must wonder how I ate such a large amount and remained so very thin! One of the girls at my table did not eat bread, but she took three or four slices each meal and gave them to me. I used to leave the dining room with my bag stuffed full – to be found taking any food from meals means loss of remission, and had I been found out I would probably be there still from the amounts I took every day.

One day when the snow was thick on the ground, a pair of blue jays came to feed, and a pair of ravens were regular visitors to the banquet I put down each morning. I left work at 11.30 on Saturdays like everyone else, and in theory should not have returned to the greenhouse until Monday morning. But what about my birds? So on Sunday mornings I would put on my own green windcheater, take my bursting dolly bag and slip out of the side door. I would hurry up to the greenhouse, which since my arrival was always left unlocked, go inside and put food for Mrs Tittlemouse and the blue tits, then scatter bread thickly outside for the other birds. Then I would go quietly back inside. No one ever saw me, or if they did (and I suspect they did) nothing was said. Most of these officers loved birds too.

My tailless friend continued to thrive. Week by week his new tail grew until at last I could no longer pick him out, he looked exactly like his fellow blackbirds. I had been so afraid that he would not have a tail when the nesting season arrived. What lady blackbird would want a tailless mate?

As my parole date drew nearer and nearer, I became more and more anxious and tense. Dear sister helped with sleeping pills and headache doses, but the suspense was terrible. I was not the only one waiting – several women had earlier dates than mine and were waiting eagerly to be called by the Governor for the big news.

One afternoon I was called and rushed along to see Miss K. (it was the Governor's day off). But when I went into her office and sat down, she told me very regretfully that my sister had issued a summons against me for £1,000 and that it was her unpleasant task to serve it on me. I could scarcely believe my ears. Wasn't it *enough* that I was still in prison? How much more did Pam want? It was the £1,000 that twenty years before I had agreed to pay when Mother died because Gran had changed her will. But, as I now wrote and explained to Pam's solicitors, I did not yet have *any* money at all. Miss K. suggested that I should ask for the court hearing to be delayed, in the hope of my parole being granted for 10 February. Otherwise I would have to be taken from prison to Haywards Heath Court in Sussex on 2 February. So I wrote to the Court, and they very kindly adjourned the hearing to 23 February.

February came, and still no news. How thankful I was at this anxious time to spend each morning with my plants and birds, and how thankful too for the kindness and understanding of the Governor, the sisters and all the officers – I could not call *these* women 'screws!'

On 8 February, Mrs A. came up to the greenhouse at 9.45 a.m.

'The Governor wants you, now don't run, keep calm,' she said, but I was already on my way. This *must* be my parole news! I waited outside the Governor's office. Several officers passed and wished me good luck. Then I was called in, and Miss L. told me that my parole had been granted for 20 February. For some obscure reason I did not get it for my due date, the 10th. But I didn't care, only ten days.

I rushed outside and one of the officers, Mrs Sandover, flung her arms round me and gave me a big hug. Then I ran along to the dining room where all the women were drinking their 10 a.m. tea.

'I've got my parole,' I shouted. It was a very emotional moment. Several women started crying and a great cheer went up – I had not realized how much I was liked here!

After break I went to the welfare office to let George know. The welfare officer had not yet arrived, but her assistant let me phone a neighbour, who would go along to the new little house and tell George and Robin the glad news.

So my time in prison was nearly over, but several other women were still waiting for news. Some had even gone *past* their release dates and heard nothing. I often wondered about this 'parole board' in London. Who were the nameless, faceless men and women who made the decision to release a prisoner, or not? How did they reach a decision as to the date of release? Several women were forced to remain in prison for two or three *months* after their parole was due – why was this, what purpose could it possibly serve? I made a lot of inquiries, both then and after my return home, but all I learnt was that the members of the parole board were unknown except by the Home Office. I wonder what makes them so qualified to reach decisions with such far-reaching effects on people's lives, decisions that are always *final* and not open to question in any way, and which *they* make and then communicate to the Home Secretary? It seems very like a secret society, with powers above even the Home Office. Why cannot the public know about these God-like creatures?

George and Robin were to fetch me by car on 20 February – 'the journey of a lifetime,' as George said – but on 17 February it began to snow heavily. Soon it was several feet deep round Moor Court. Two days before my release we heard on the television that the west country was cut off with the worst snow for over twenty years. Miss L. came to my dormitory on my last night (it was 6 p.m. – I was always allowed to go to bed after tea) and told me that if my family could not get through, I was very welcome to remain for a few days as a guest! At 7.30 Robin phoned. I was called to the office to speak to him. The whole of Devon and Cornwall was under thick snow, up to twenty feet deep, all roads blocked and it was impossible to get farther than Plymouth. We arranged that I would get a train from Stoke to Plymouth direct, a journey of some seven hours, and they would meet my train at Plymouth. Miss L. had already looked up the time of the train from Stoke station.

It is the rule in Moor Court that on the night before their release all women going out are locked in a cell after supper. It is purely for their own protection on their last night, as otherwise their friends would carry out terrible practical jokes such as throwing them fully clothed into a bath of cold water. The day before my last night I was walking away after tea when a young girl came rushing up.

'Is the Guv puttin' you in the cells?' she asked in a very cockney accent. ' 'Cos if she does I'll bash her face in,' she said fiercely – I had only spoken to her once or twice before. But I assured her that I was not to be put in a cell. Miss L. had thought that my age and poor health made it unnecessary.

I spent my last night in my dormitory. Needless to say, I could not sleep. I lay looking at the moon shining on the snow-covered hills and thinking with pity of all the poor women still in Styal, *and* of those yet to come. The women in Moor Court had committed crimes no different from those of the women in Styal. Why then were some incarcerated in that cruel and evil closed prison while others were treated like human beings in Moor Court?

On 20 February I got up at 6.30, folded up my bedding (all my possessions were already packed and waiting in reception), said good-bye to my room-mates, and went to be locked in the little passage outside the cells, where I had waited on arrival from Styal in December. A fellow prisoner brought my breakfast. I could have anything I ordered on my last morning here, but chose only tea and cornflakes. Then it was time to go through reception for the last time. Mrs B. was on duty again and I was glad. She had seen me 'in' and now she saw me 'out' in such a kind and friendly fashion. Even the inevitable search was nothing. Then the officer said that my taxi had arrived. I took out my suitcases and several women ran up and kissed me good-bye – Molly, my little Chinese friend Choy, and Jeannette. There were tears in their eyes, and in mine too – although I was going home. The Home Office rule that no former prisoner can write to a woman still inside meant that I could not write to them at all, although they would have been glad to have heard from me.

Then into the taxi, driving carefully along the cleared roads, with snow banked high each side. In half an hour we were at the station. Mrs S. helped me to put my luggage near the booking office where I would exchange my travel warrant for a ticket. Then she shook my hand and wished me luck, and was gone.

The train came in, I put my suitcase aboard, sat down in a window seat and as we sped through the snow-covered countryside I thought of Mother, whom I would never see again, and of my only sister. I made up my mind to write to Pam and ask if we could forget the past. I did write later, but there was no reply.

I put my head back and closed my eyes. Soon I would be with George and Robin and all my friends at home, animal as well as human. My ordeal was over, and God had sent me safely on my way.

THE END

(And a New Beginning)

Epilogue

At Easter 1977, I was locked 'behind the door' in Styal Prison in the punishment block known as Bleak House. I was in solitary confinement. My crime? Taking a dose of Panadol from the hospital and concealing it in my locker in case I needed it in the night. But I was lucky – I was only there for four days and one of the screws took pity on me and allowed me to keep the bare frame of the bed to sit on. But there were others in Bleak much worse off than I, women who had been locked in their cells, their bare, solitary cells, for many, many weeks, and who beat on the doors and knocked on the heating pipes and screamed out their desperate need for human contact in the long weary hours alone. They had nothing to do, no books were allowed, nothing to see; only their misery for company. One was so wretched that she tried to cut her throat.

This Easter Day, 1978, I spent at home on parole, and my family and I watched the film *Joan of Arc* on television. As the Maid of Orleans was burnt at the stake, I thought that the cruelty and inhumanity of the State cannot have changed at all since they burnt Joan up to 1978 when it turns a blind eye to what really goes on in our women's prisons. Did Joan die in vain? Mother, in her extremity, cried out, 'God forgive them, they know not what they do,' the same cry that came from the Cross, and from Joan of Arc. But who is listening? Does anybody care?